DAVID PICKELL

AZER.

il

Caspian
Sea

Rasht

Qezel Ozean

Qazvin

R.-ye Rud

Babol

Gorgan

Nebit-Dag

TURKMENISTAN

Ashkhabad

Mary   Bajram-Ali

Tédzhen

Neyshabur

Sabzevar

Mashhad

Meymaneh

Hamadan

Teheran

Qom

Arak

Daryacheh-ye
Namak

D a s h t - e   K a v i r

Harirud

Herat

AFGHANISTAN

khorramabad

I   R   A   N

Najafabad

Esfahan

Yazd

D a s h t - e   L u t

Farah Rud

Farah

Girishk

ye Zagros

Zaranj

Darya-ye Helmand

khorramshahr

Abadan

Kerman

Bam

PAKISTAN

UBITAN

wait

madi

Kazerun

Shiraz

D.-ye Tashk

D.-ye Bakhtegan

Hamun-e
Jaz Murian

L a r e s t a n

Bandar Abbas

Dasht

Dhahran

BAHRAIN

Al Manamah

P
e
r
s
i
a
n

Gulf

QATAR

Doha

QESHM

Strait of Hormuz

Dubai

OMAN

Gwadar

uf

Abu Dhabi

Gulf of Oman

UNITED ARAB EMIRATES

O   M   A   N

Masqat
(Muscat)

DEADLY BUSINESS

LEGAL DEALS AND OUTLAW WEAPONS

The Arming of Iran and Iraq,
1975 to the Present

DEADLY BUSINESS

LEGAL DEALS AND OUTLAW WEAPONS

The Arming of Iran and Iraq,
1975 to the Present

BY HERBERT KROSNEY

FOUR WALLS EIGHT WINDOWS

NEW YORK LONDON

Published in the United States by:
Four Walls Eight Windows

39 West 14th Street, #503
New York, N.Y., 10011

U.K. offices
Four Walls Eight Windows/Turnaround
27 Horsell Road, London, N51 XL England

First printing January 1994.

Library of Congress Cataloging-in-Publication Data:
Krosney, Herbert.
Deadly Business: Legal Deals and Outlaw Weapons:
The Arming of Iran and Iraq, 1975 to the Present / by Herbert Krosney
p. cm.
(cloth) ISBN: 1-56858-002-9
(paper) ISBN: 1-56858-006-1
1. Iraq–Military relations. 2. Iran–Military relations. 3. Arms transfers–Iran.
4. Arms transfers–Iraq. 5. Iraq–Armed Forces–Weapon systems.
6. Iran–Armed Forces–Weapon systems. I. Title.
UA853.I75K76 1993
327.1'72'07–dc20   93-11637
                                                  CIP

Text design by Marcy Kass

Illustrations by Edgar Blakeney

Printed in the United States

TABLE OF CONTENTS

Acknowledgements

Deadly Business stems from my research for "The Secrets of Samarra," the first TV exposé of Iraq's secret chemical weapons program, and a series of television documentaries that followed. A number were co-produced with BBC Television's "Panorama" program. I also worked with the national German television network ZDF on a program on German arms exports, Britain's Channel Four, American programs on PBS and elsewhere, wrote occasional articles, and pursued research independently. The films included "The Condor Conspiracy," "Saddam's Secret Arms Rings," "The Arms Boomerang," "The Swiss Connection" and "Arming for Islam." This book incorporates much of the research and makes it coherent in a different media and a single work. My knowledge about arms control subjects partially derives from an earlier book I co-authored with Steve Weissman, *The Islamic Bomb: The Nuclear Threat to Israel and the Middle East* (Times Books, 1982), which was also initially based on a BBC "Panorama" documentary on which we had both worked about Pakistan's nuclear program. That book expanded from a focus on Pakistan to look at nuclear proliferation generally in the Middle East, including Iraq, Libya, India and Israel and, more tangentially, Egypt and Syria.

I owe a debt of gratitude to the many journalists with whom I worked or who offered occasional help or advice. Among them: in England, above all, television colleagues, especially the energetic and extraordinarily capable Jane Corbin of BBC "Panorama," and also Brian Barr, Owen Boycott, Charles Furneaux, Ed Harriman, Robert Harris, Guy Smith and Paul Woolwich. A print journalist, Alan George, played a pioneering role in many of the areas upon which I touch, and I owe him a special debt of thanks as well. The work of Alan Friedman in the *Financial Times* was also important.

In Germany, I thank Hilda Buder, Horst Kalbus, Ernst Martin, and Udo Philipp, and also Mark Hibbs and Harald Muller. In France, I particularly thank Gilles du Jonchay and Michel Zlotowski, as well as several people, who must remain anonymous, in French governmental service.

In Switzerland the following, among others, were helpful: Frank Garbely, Andre Marti and Marcus Rohmer.

In the United States those who were helpful included my partner Robert Ross in particular, and Joe Bermudez, Claudio Gatti and Robert Windrem, all of whom provided valuable advice, information or leads, and numerous others.

In Israel, Al Ellenberg, Clinton Bailey, Gerald Steinberg and Hirsh Goodman offered insights, advice and coaching.

In addition to journalists, a number of academic and government officials located in four or five different countries played an especially important role in this work. Sometimes it wasn't easy to get appointments with all those I would have wanted to see, and some of those who did see me preferred not only to remain anonymous, but made this anonymity a condition for meeting. Concerning exports in general and the kind of expertise and experience that is priceless to a generalist, both Dr. Stephen Bryen, once of the Pentagon and now an independent business executive, and Seth Carus, once an academician with the Washington Institute for Near East Policy and now of the Pentagon, helped in special ways. Both men discussed matters in depth with me only when not in governmental service.

My research into chemical warfare owes a mammoth debt to Julian Perry Robinson of the University of Sussex in England, and I also benefitted by talks with Matthew Meselson of Harvard University and Elisa Harris of the Brookings Institution. Regarding missiles, I had lengthy conversations and benefitted from the writings of Joe Bermudez, Seth Carus, Tim McCarthy, Janne C. Nolan and Richard Speier, all of whom made particularly important contributions to my own understanding of the subject.

Concerning Iraq, Israeli expert Amatzia Baram's insights aided enormously. I also enjoyed conversations with Nick Peck, Norb Garrett and Jules Kroll of Kroll Associates, who provided me with a unique perspective on Iraq's financial affairs. On nuclear matters, four Washington-based experts were generous with their time and resources, including David Albright, Paul Leventhal, Gary Milhollin, and Leonard Specter. George Amsel in France was always helpful. Also, I thank Marvin Miller of M.I.T.'s Department of Nuclear Engineering, who provided specific technical advice at a crucial time.

My agents, Julian Friedmann and Al Zuckerman, proved untiring. Janet and John Rodgers were crafty title inventors. Editor John Oakes performed yeoman service that helped shape and polish the book in crucial ways.

Mary Stewart Krosney provided inexhaustible patience, motivation and love, and was an incredible help at all times, including but not restricted to certain clerical duties which were often repetitive. She gets a special vote.

PREFACE

In Friedrich Dürrenmatt's play, "The Physicists," the protagonist invents a machine capable of causing mankind's destruction. He considers eliminating the machine by blocking its future production, then he surmises the job is impossible because "what was once thought can never be unthought." The battle lines of the next decade are now being drawn. A central issue is how to halt the diffusion of lethal technology into "unsafe" and "irresponsible" hands. The perception of who is "unsafe" and who "irresponsible" is necessarily subjective, though I admit a bias against petty dictators in unstable countries who seek to rule and dominate —and who resort to terrorism. It is not always necessary for the ambitious megalomaniac to first transform his own society from have-not to have, from primitive to industrial, from impoverished to prosperous in order to get his hands on the tools of mass destruction. It is only necessary that he has the resources to buy the weaponry and, even better, the resources to produce it. Then he must find his willing accomplices among the techno-mercenaries.

In our global village it will be excruciatingly difficult to impede the proliferation of technology or halt the apparently irresistable spread of knowledge. The axioms seem irrefutable in the force of their logic: as man's technology has advanced, so has man's capacity to destroy himself. The more sophisticated the technology, the greater its destructive potential. The greater the number of those who have the technologies, the greater the odds they will be used. So long as the technologies exist, vainglorious men will seek to master them, improve them and use them. Others will engage, perhaps unknowingly, in that deadly business of selling them. Sadly, scientific and technological know-how, often derived from advances in weapons systems, has proven to be a two-edged sword. Many of us may hope that the benefits of science and technology will be used for peace and that the good will supercede the potential harm, that the madness of the acquisition and accumulation of more and ever bigger arms will cease, that the kind of peace will come that will enable men everywhere to live more securely. Logically, however, the odds are against it. The future history of mankind could be determined by the way we respond to the proliferation of weapons of mass destruction to a new generation of countries.

This book required an active search for witnesses and evidence. Any investigation of a country's most sensitive military programs is reliant upon reluctant or unwilling sources. Countries buying materials never want to reveal what they have acquired, or intend to get, and companies selling the goods are equally reticent. But individuals working with these governments and companies may have their own interests. These individuals may tell you what they know, or think they know, or want you to know, but their stories are rarely augmented by convincing documentation.

Whenever I have felt it incumbent to shield a source, or have promised I would, I have done so. Those who tried to take a conversation off the record after it had taken place are out of luck. Hopefully, no one has been decieved. I've made every effort to see to it that all conversations were recorded accurately, though regrettably some will not like the consequences of their own words.

Occasionally, no one but I thought a particular story or lead important. Sometimes I had to push colleagues to get a story, other times I was the one who had to be pushed. Still, only I bear responsibility for the way the information in this book has been pieced together. To be sure, there are gaps and others will fill in where I have failed. Regretfully, while the writing of this book is finished, the story I write about continues....

Herbert Krosney

September 1993

CHAPTER ONE

A Nest of Vipers

"Our firm deals with precision technology, but at my level I don't know how to be precise in identifying it.... only Mr. Schrotz would be able to bring you more complete information."

Monika Braun, executive assistant to
Ekkehard Schrotz, businessman

EKKEHARD SCHROTZ was on the road to riches. His personal cash register had already rung up hundreds of thousands, maybe millions of dollars, and it didn't particularly matter whether the cash flowed in Deutschmarks, American green, Egyptian pounds or Argentinian pesetos. He was fit, smart and persistent. A business colleague called him "cold" but the type of fellow who knew his way around.

He was also cautious. He had his own villa in Sparacedes, a small village just outside Monaco in a rustic mountainous area above the Riviera that the French call *les Alpes Maritimes*. The exclusive residence, surrounded by a six foot high wall, had video cameras mounted in strategic crannies and an electronic alarm and surveillance system wired in the gate. The word among the high-tech missile set was that Schrotz played a fair game of tennis and enjoyed the good life when he had time for it, which wasn't often.

1

Early on the morning of May 27th, 1988, a carefully-placed "plastique" exploded in Ekkehard Schrotz' assistant's car, a red 205 Peugeot parked in the village square in Speracedes.[1] It was still dark. No one was hurt. An obscure, hitherto-unknown group, "the Guardians of Islam," claimed credit. One of the members of the group telephoned the Reuters press agency as light was breaking over the Côte d'Azur claiming to have killed Schrotz in nearby Grasse. Reuters called Schrotz' office at the S.A.M. Consen company in Monaco to verify the story. His assistant, Frau Monika Braun, picked up the phone, heard Reuters' questions and got afraid.

She immediately telephoned her boss at the Sparacedes villa. Schrotz answered the phone. Frau Braun, relieved that her boss was still very much alive, told him about the attack and that he and his family had been threatened. "I thought it was a joke," Schrotz remarked later.

Within moments, Gerard Baussy, Schrotz' assistant and driver—who lived in town with his girlfriend Patricia—called Schrotz. He reported the dramatic news directly: that his car had been blown up during the early morning hours in the middle of Speracedes village square.

Schrotz hung up, alarmed at the realization that his life was in danger. His wife, Gertrud, and their two sons, Christian, 13, and Martin, aged 6, lived with him and he feared for them, too. If not murder, a possible scenario could involve kidnapping one of his children. Schrotz notified French police.

Ekkehard Schrotz, born during World War II in Heidelberg on the 19th of September, 1944, the son of Kurt and Karasek Erike, had passed beyond the fascination with ideology and politics that had charactized the Nazi demagogues of a previous generation. He lived in the here and now, like many of his generation growing up in Germany. More pragmatic gods had replaced the old discredited ones. Pragmatic, in his case, meant an appreciation of money, lots of it. Schrotz was a missile expert, an examplar of a professional tradition begun in the Weimar Republic, developed in Hitler's Germany and then pursued in the United States and the Soviet Union for four decades. He was of a new breed: a "techno-mercenary", selling his services to a range of countries in South America and the Middle East. "Public discretion for private profit," could have been his motto.

In addition to his hillside villa, Schrotz had an apartment in the elegant Columbia Palace on Princess Grace Avenue in the Principality of Monaco, not far from the sparkling blue Mediterranean.

Around one o'clock that afternoon, the telephone rang. An anonymous stranger on the line spoke French with an accent the police thought might stem from either Arabic or Farsi, the language of modern Iran. The tone was unfriendly. He claimed allegiance to the "guardians of Islam." The caller's message became more ominous with each sentence. He accused Schrotz of having sold armaments to Baghdad "causing the death of thousands in Teheran... The error just now was a technical one," the caller declared, meaning the failure to kill Schrotz. "But if you do not stop dealing with the Iraqi president, you and your family will be executed."

Schrotz tried to entice the stranger into conversation. The longer he could keep him talking, the better to identify him. Schrotz later claimed his caller was wrong on two counts: both as to the nature of the business and the destination of the goods. "I tried to tell this man that I had never sold arms to Iraq or elsewhere," Schrotz told French police, "and as I had never started, I couldn't stop. He didn't want to listen to reason and he hung up."

During interrogations conducted over the next weeks by both Monaco and French police, Schrotz expressed surprise and even shock that terrorists would attempt to waylay him.[2] "I have never been the object of threats. I was totally ignorant where it came from." He categorically denied that he had had any business dealings with Iraq.

The shadowy "Islamic Guardians" notified local news agencies that they would strike again if Schrotz didn't desist from selling death-dealing weapons to Iraq. To make sure there were no misunderstandings about the extent of their knowledge of Schrotz' affairs, they called Friedrich Winklhofer, an engineer working for Schrotz' company, and threatened him, too. In the days after the attentat, Schrotz hired two security guards to protect him around the clock. He more frequently retired to the relative safety of his Sparacedes villa. Surrounded by its high walls and electronically controlled gates, he became a recluse. He watched his every step. He told police that, as soon as French investigators agreed, he wanted to slip off to visit

Munich, West Germany, his old hometown and hangout where he had both friends and business.

Baussy, who as Schrotz' driver was fortunate not to have been in the car when the bomb went off, wanted to make it absolutely clear to anyone who asked that he had nothing to do with Consen business and should not himself have been the target of an attack. "I'm just the man's chauffeur," he mumbled when a BBC Television producer sought him out. "Listen, when you see your car burning in the middle of the night, it has an effect on you... I've got nothing to do with it. I don't want it to happen again."

As both the French and Monaco police pursued their investigation, they discovered the outlines of a vast operation in Monaco and elsewhere that belied Schrotz' assurances that he had no idea why he had been attacked. What they found out, without yet understanding all the implications, was that the tiny principality, known for its blue sea, night life, and casinos, was home to a community with high-level connections to missile-hungry Middle East and South American nations.

•   •   •

S.A.M. Consen Consulting Engineers, the company Schrotz headed in Monaco, had been founded in 1982. Schrotz took over as director in 1983. Located at 84 Boulevard d'Italie two terraces up from the seashore, the office building had a commanding view of the Mediterranean. Consen was a daughter company of the Swiss-based firm of the same name, Consen S.A. based in Zug, near Zürich. Consen Monaco numbered less than 20 persons—including seven engineers and some ten secretaries and drivers. Schrotz told police that he was not an arms merchant. Nor, he insisted, was he fuelling the Persian Gulf war between Iran and Iraq, and neither country was his client. Consen had no business with any country in the Middle East except Egypt, where the company had a factory near Cairo. Consen did not sell armaments per se. Consen's purpose was to provide technical advice and supervision in the construction of factories.

Technically, Schrotz was correct. But he was only telling part of the truth, what he thought would cause no direct or peripheral harm to him or his operation or lead to further inquiry. He hid what police would not automatically discover.

For example: Schrotz kept to himself the knowledge that his firm, and the company in Egypt, was linked to Consen by a devious web of ownership that had its branches in places as diverse as Austria, Switzerland, Luxembourg, and South America and its roots in Essen, Germany. Its patrimony traced back to the Nazi war machine and before. Nor did he tell police that Consen, more generally, provided technology and expertise for the fabrication of missiles, especially medium range ballistics. Nor that he had a close working relationship with a major German company where he had once worked, the giant German aero-space and armaments firm, Messerschmitt-Boelkow-Bloehm, or MBB.

Still, the Monaco investigation, though limited and far from complete, opened up a window on Consen's operations and personnel. Other members of the company opened it a crack further by offering additional details. Wilhelm Vullride, a 53-year-old mechanical and chemical engineer, denied that Consen worked with Iraq, but related that a principle client was a firm called "I.N.T.E.A." based at Cordoba in Argentina. He indicated that the relationship wound indirectly through a Consen "sister company" based in Zug, Switzerland. He added: "The Consen company works as well for a similar company in Egypt..." He didn't want to mention that company's name to police. He referred the matter back to Schrotz.

Vullride's statements opened up a Pandora's box of secret deals and hitherto ill-documented relationships between his company and various governments. "I know that ties exist between the Argentinian and Egyptian companies but I don't know which ones," he said. He denied that any points of serious contention existed between Consen and its clients. He declined to elaborate further.

Monika Braun, Schrotz' long-time assistant, claimed to police that to her knowledge the Consen company had no market whatsoever with Iraq. "The only countries we have business with are Egypt and Argentina," she stated. "Our firm deals with precision technology. But at my level I don't know how to be precise in identifying it."

Like Vullride, she referred police back to Schrotz for more information on Consen's technology secrets. He "would be able to provide you more complete information," she said.

Over the next few weeks, the French intelligence services and Monaco police cooperated in pursuing the inquiry. As nothing was previously known about Consen, every piece of information added to the puzzle. French agents suspected that Consen might be selling arms to Iran as well as other Middle Eastern countries, and wanted to identify the precise nature of the secret deals. Monaco police had a more practical interest: they wanted to stop the tiny principality from becoming a terrorist battleground between clandestine groups. The threats against Schrotz provided an opportunity to examine Consen Monaco's records and get a glimpse of Consen's labyrinth of connections with firms in Argentina, Luxembourg, Austria, Switzerland, Egypt and elsewhere.

Monaco police only scratched the surface of company links. But detectives did turn up fragmentary information on company guests that could provide significant clues. Among those visiting Consen:

Edgardo Stahl. He had visited Monaco on at least six occasions staying at the Beach Plaza Hotel, Monaco's most luxurious, situated literally 100 meters below Consen offices on Boulevard de l'Italie and smack on the Monaco shore. On the first five of these visits Stahl travelled as an Argentinian citizen, but on his last trip he travelled on a German passport issued by that country's consulate in Cordoba, Argentina. Stahl, notwithstanding his non-Hispanic name and his German descent, turned out to be a general in the Argentinian Air Force.

Keith Gilbert Smith. An Englishman born on September 7th, 1937, Monaco records listed him as being both a scientist and an independent company owner based in Milton Keynes. Smith's name turned up a few months later in U.S. court records in a case that involved smuggling high technology out of the United States to Egypt. His presence in Monaco provided U.S. security agents with a handy cross-reference. A year later, journalists from BBC's "Panorama" program caught up with him to ask him questions about his role in Consen. He refused to elaborate and threatened a correspondent with court action if his name were slandered or mentioned wrongly.

Mohamed Mohamed Diaa El-Din. Variations on his name included such as El-Din Mohamed, or Mohamed Diaa Eldin Soliman, or Diaa Mohamed, or El Din Diaa, or Diaa El-Din, and the police noted that El Din, a former Egyptian army officer and aeronautical engineer, was both a director of sales for Consen and a purchasing consultant to the Egyptian Army. He was married with two children. He earned a monthly salary of about $10,000, about ten times what he could earn in Egypt. His presence indicated an Egyptian hand in Consen.

A second Egyptian mentioned in the inquiry, Youssef Ahmed, turned out to be a high-level employee of the Egyptian Defense Ministry. His real name was Yousef Ahmed Khairat. He was based in Salzburg, Austria.

The investigation turned up links to Germany, too, and, more specifically, to a firm in Essen called Bohlen Industries. The police noted the name but did not vigorously pursue this aspect of the investigation. The company was a little-known part of the legacy of Germany's most powerful industrial enterprise, Krupp. The Bohlen brothers who ran it were direct descendants of the von Bohlen und Hahlbach Krupp family and beneficiaries of one of Europe's most incredible industrial empires. Police reports noted that Consen owners had used a German citizen, Jürgen Spaethe, as a proxy to set up the Monaco subsidiary. Spaethe first came to Monaco in 1981 as a temporary resident to set up and become managing director of Von Bohlen Investment and Management Services, part of the wide-flung network of Bohlen companies. In 1983 and '84 he helped set up the fledgling S.A.M. Consen.

Other names discovered by Monaco police included Helmut Raiser, a German technocrat. Raiser had previously been general manager of Bohlen Industries. He split from Bohlen in 1982 and became president of the Swiss Consen company. The inquiry revealed his address in Zug was the same as that of the company. Another German, Karl Hermann Schmidt, was both resident in Monaco and a director of Consen. He had been officially employed in Monaco since October 1982 by Von

Bohlen Investment and Management Services, part of the Bohlen Industries web. He had worked in Egypt in the late 1960s. Then, after a five year period in France, he moved to Salzburg, Austria, to work for "Induplan," a firm owned by Bohlen Industries.

Finally, there was an Austrian called Robert Trummer, who made frequent visits to Monaco. He hailed from a small village just above the Yugoslav border and below the Austrian city of Graz. Police noted that he got his Austrian passport in Buenos Aires, Argentina, on the 12th of March, 1983. Trummer, it later turned out, was Consen's project head on a number of major projects: first in Argentina, then both in Egypt and on a separate missile facility in Saddam Hussein's Iraq. Trummer's presence, as much as anyone's, would show that Schrotz' answers to the police about Consen activities were purposeful deceptions, designed only to close the window that had been opened on Consen and stymie further inquiry.

•   •   •

Who did it? Who would threaten Ekkehard Schrotz?

The bombers left few clues and none that could identify them. In the world of high-tech espionage, that was in itself a hint. The outward signs revealed too much professionalism to be an amateur show but not enough precision to demonstrate competence. That was precisely the impression that might have been intended: a display of expertise might lead police investigators to conclude that the band of bombers were high-tech experts themselves.

The bombers' identity would most likely remain a secret for decades. Among the suspects: secret groups from either Iran or Israel. Both countries had an interest in stopping sales of dangerous technologies to Iraq and were suspect. Iranians in the hundreds and thousands were dying in the Gulf War and, like many other Middle Eastern countries, Iran had a tradition of a cruel and ruthless secret police. Nonetheless, French investigators dismissed suggestions that the bombers were genuine "guardians of Islam." These criminals were far too skillful to be Iranians, this semi-official analysis went. One police official remarked they were "people like us," meaning Western security personnel. French insiders believed the perpetrators hailed from one of the big

"I's." Not from Italy, Ireland, Iraq or Iran. Rather, from Israel. Not from the Mukhbarat or Mujahadeen, not from Mecca or Medina or Meshad, but from the Mossad, from Jerusalem.

If the bombers did come from the Israeli secret service, the Mossad, it was hardly surprising that they hadn't acted in their own name. They never had before. Even when the Mossad was brilliantly successful, it was reticent about taking proper credit. As in an earlier campaign, which could have been either Islamic or Israeli, which threatened French and Italian nuclear specialists working for Iraq in 1980 and 1981, there was no conclusive evidence— in fact, there was no evidence at all—as to who had really "plastiqued" Schrotz. The assumption that only Israelis could act with precision and efficiency seemed to reflect a certain French and, more generally, Western racism about Arab and Iranian capabilities. They were seen as "primitive" Moslems and, therefore, as hopeless blunderers. The Jewish Israelis, on the other hand, were looked on as endowed with native intelligence, intuitive chutzpah and extraordinary commando skill.

The attempt on Schrotz' life sent shock waves through the cushy world of high-tech missile specialists. "No one knows exactly who was behind it," Udo Philipp, spokesman for the German company for which Schrotz had once worked, MBB (or Messerschmitt-Boelkow-Blohm), also based in Munich, candidly speculated. "Some say the Mujahadeen (Iranians). Some say it was the Mossad (Israel)."

While the "who" could not be proved, the "why" was "as plain as a wart on your nose," in the phrase of another observer. The attack on his assistant's car was a carefully planned warning designed to frighten the arms dealer but not to kill him. It was an attempt to raise the stakes in Monte Carlo and elsewhere to a point where the techno-mercenaries might lose the wager and pay a bill far higher than expected.

Terror bombs, even those that are precisely designed, can accidentally explode at the wrong time. Once the Consen group and its engineers became the target for unknown bombers, who could be sure where violence would end or whether anybody's life was really safe? In the amorphous dawn light of the Côte d'Azur, the inflated salaries and perk-filled work conditions offered to Consen personnel suddenly seemed less attractive.

•   •   •

Monaco police stopped their inquiries after a few weeks. Though they did not find much evidence about the bombing of the Schrotz car, investigators discovered a wealth of information and leads concerning Consen. The bombers, whoever they were, had done their work well. They had called attention to Consen's activities both inside Monte Carlo and out. The police found enough to show that Consen was up to no good.

Police recommended that Monaco close the company's local office. Monaco could be a legitimate base for gamblers who placed their bets on Monte Carlo's gaming tables. It could not be home for gamblers who wagered their own futures in lethal high-tech missile weaponry.

After the incident at Speracedes, those who worked for Consen knew the stakes had risen. They could no longer enjoy sumptuous expense account lunches at outdoor bistros near the beach. When and if they dined at public restaurants they had to sit literally with their backs to the wall facing front, grabbing a glimpse, perhaps, of the sea but surveying each passer-by as a potential threat, a possible bomber ready to kill first and ask questions later. For those who could afford it, like Ekkehard Schrotz, a bodyguard stood by on alert.

With one blast, symbolic or not, employees of Consen were made to feel that lives—their own lives—were at stake.

CHAPTER TWO

1975: Nuclear Dawn

"A number of the buyers we dealt with really wanted a tool that could provide Iraqi scientists with the training to enter the nuclear world. They knew it was a long-term process—that is, the people we were dealing with."

Yves Girard, French nuclear executive

"I cornered Chirac that day and said we had to finish the agreement. Before he went, he said okay."

Dr. Akbar Etamad, president, The Iranian Atomic Energy Organization, 1974-79

TERRORISM was one way to fight the weapons spread. A minor threat, supported by a not-too-subtle suggestion that more serious action would be forthcoming, could do as much as dozens of pages of regulations to halt the proliferation of the kinds of arms that threatened the survival of individual states, and even entire regions of the planet.

•   •   •

1975 was a deceptive year for the Middle East. Oil prices rose and billions of petrodollars flowed eastwards from the oil markets in London, Frankfurt and New York, largely into the hands of semi-worldly sheikhs

11

and desert princes. This was a result of the Arabs' economic boycott of the West, which had the effect of doubling and tripling oil prices to record levels. Money had never flowed with such abandon. Those Middle Eastern countries blessed by oil became dramatically richer than they had ever been before.

Yet the region, with its gerrymandered states and uncertain borders, was pregnant with instability. Two of the region's richest countries, the Iran of Shah Reza Pahlevi and the Iraq of Ba'athist leader Saddam Hussein, signed a secret agreement in 1975 in Algiers to stabilize the Persian Gulf area. Through that often-fought-over barrier of water between the two countries traversed the oil tankers that were the economic lifeline, not only of each country, but of what is euphemistically called "the Western world": generally, the countries of Western Europe, North America, and Japan and Australia, and those countries having a white population and a Judeo-Christian background. The Algiers agreement was a compromise, brilliantly and deceptively stage-managed by the crafty Iraqi politician, Saddam Hussein, that enabled each country to control its side of the Gulf and abandon claims to the other. Additionally, the Shah promised the Iraqi leader that he would halt his financial and logistical support of Iraq's Kurdish minority, which was fighting against the central government for greater autonomy. (There was also a large Kurdish population within Iran.) The Shah thus effectively double-crossed the Kurds, much as many other leaders had betrayed them before.

The entire Algiers agreement was Middle Eastern "realpolitik" at its most extreme, most effective and also most cynical, and showed that the new wealth only papered over the region's long-term problems. The secret deal demonstrated the transitory nature of a peace on paper, and the difficulties of achieving real peace on the ground where deep-rooted religious beliefs, ideologies, and stubbornly egoistic views of the world resisted abandonment or compromise. Beneath its wording another strata of secret activities was churning, one that more accurately reflected the true ambitions of the signatories. This was the domain of nuclear science. 1975 was a year of nuclear reveries in which both the Iraqi and Iranian leaderships, unknown to the other, nurtured ambitious dreams of nuclear capability that would supposedly enable each to become more independent, and eventually dominant.

Each side wanted, at least, the capability to make a bomb. A nuclear program was an indispensable sign of prestige, status and future power. Unlike Pakistan, which in the early 1970s embarked on its own clandestine nuclear bomb program, both Iran and Iraq were signatories to the Non- Proliferation Treaty. Both Iran and Iraq used their status as Non-Proliferation treaty members to gain the kind of nuclear capability that could underpin an atomic bomb program, and both countries used their ample oil monies to purchase the essential technology and equipment.

The leadership of both countries had similar characteristics. The Shah and Hussein, each in his own way, saw the technological development of his country as the key to future power and prestige. Both leaders were, by Middle Eastern standards, moderately secular, and in each country there was enormous respect for science and industry. Traditional foes, both Iran and Iraq were haughty about their own histories and suspicious of the other's. Iranian and Iraqi rivalries centered on strategic concerns and cultural differences that went back centuries. Both were Moslem countries, but those who ruled Iraq were Sunnis (though they were a minority in their own country) while Shi'ism was dominant among the Persians of Iran. Each country spoke a different language with fundamentally separate linguistic roots. The Iranians claimed to be descended from the glory of Cyrus, the Iraqis from the practical wisdom of Hammurabi. Monarchial Teheran was cautious about the fervent egalitarianism of the socialist Ba'athists who ran Iraq, while the Iranians were taught never to trust an Arab.

If either country had a major military threat to its existence, it was the other.

•   •   •

Iraq's leader, Saddam Hussein, lived at the heart of what an Israeli scholar, Amatziya Baram, described as an expanding ring of concentric circles. "What is good for Saddam is good for Takrit, his home town, and what is good for Saddam and Takrit is good for Iraq. What is good for Iraq in turn benefits the Arabs. What is good for the Arabs is for the general benefit of mankind."

Saddam Hussein lacked a defining sense that precisely delineated the borders of these concentric circles. In 1975 still formally the number two man in Iraq, but actually the real power behind the Iraqi president, Hasan al-Bakr Al Bakr, Hussein's vision welded his country and himself into one entity. Though anti-religious and determinedly secular, he exhibited no compunction about invoking the heritage of Islam when he deemed it necessary, either to support himself personally or Ba'athist political doctrine. Iraqi artists depicted Saddam riding tall and straight on a prancing Arabian steed against the pastel background of sturdy Islamic castles, looking remarkably like Crusader fortresses, from an earlier age of Moslem glory. Outwardly conservative and even plodding in the way he made decisions, he had a tendancy to be led and deceived by his own enormous ego, to overplay his hand and suddenly make a bold move that would turn into an outrageous blunder. This is what happened in his nuclear thrust during the 1970s, also when he invaded Iran in 1980, and a decade later when he ordered his troops into Kuwait. Though Hussein had a tendancy to self-aggrandizement and even megalomania, he had the street instincts of an outlaw and the tenacity to see his goals through.

Iraq, like Iran, was blessed by oil in huge amounts beneath its surface. Petroleum experts judged the country's crude reserves to be the second largest in the world, after Saudi Arabia, amounting to over 100 billion barrels. The supply seemed plentiful until the second half of the 21st century. Iraqi wells churned out literally millions of dollars daily in the form of high-quality crude, massing hundreds of millions if not billions of petro-dollars in Arab and European banks. That oil treasure thrust Iraq into a category of nation that never need want for its basic requirements, and made Iraq potentially one of the world's wealthiest countries.

Hussein wanted his political power to match his oil wealth. The path to that goal led—in Hussein's eyes—through nuclear power. The Iraqi leader wanted not just a single atom bomb, but a full-blown program that would make the country self-sufficient with the capability of producing its own fissionable materials. This would provide him an atomic arsenal, and also the military clout and independence to carry out his political goals.

•   •   •

Saddam Hussein's quest for the bomb—even in those early days in 1975—had to be tempered by the realities and vagaries of the international nuclear market and also by the restrictions imposed by the international community on nuclear sales. Hussein and his cohorts studied history's nuclear lessons and how they might apply to an ambitious Third World country.

No one in the Iraqi inner circle seems to have disagreed on the goal. The problem was the means. For a bomb, Iraq needed kilograms of either plutonium or highly enriched uranium. Hussein had the choice of either attempting to buy the bomb furtively, step by step, as the Pakistanis were then doing, or commit himself to international rules and regulations that would enable him to get the technology but not very easily enable him to use it for military purposes.

The first path—furtive purchases—was fraught with risk. At the lower levels of technology smaller items and materials could be bought for either nuclear or non-nuclear installations. Capitalist firms in the West were eager to sell whatever they legally could. At the higher levels, many nuclear goods could be bought from Western companies without Western governments even knowing about it. Iraq would attain "nuclear weapons capability" before anyone woke up and realized what had happened.

But the chances of getting caught were also great. A number of "choke points" existed in the nuclear industry, areas of technological sensitivity where a sophisticated item manufactured by only a few firms could easily be subjected to strict governmental controls. The major choke point loomed directly in front, a giant barrier almost impossible to pass without the approval of nuclear-capable industrial giants like the United States, the Soviet Union, or France. That was the reactor. Simply put, it wasn't realistic to clandestinely buy a reactor on the international black market. Of the countries that sold reactors, neither the medium-size countries such as France or Canada, nor the two Superpowers would sell the installations without international agreement and safeguards.

Hussein and his aides appreciated the nuclear game and played it. Iraq would abide by the regulations, as defined by the international community through the Non-Proliferation Treaty and the International Atomic Energy Agency. N.P.T. membership paradoxically permits countries to buy sensitive nuclear equipment and develop their own programs, though under "safeguards." Generally, nuclear equipment, when and if sold, would be visited regularly by I.A.E.A. inspectors to certify that weapons-grade plutonium or enriched uranium had not been diverted for military use. The international controls enabled the transfer of nuclear technology to take place—if not safely, then at least with legitimacy and an illusion of safety.

Iraq had a tiny two-megawatt research reactor provided by the Soviets in the late sixties—the kind that was genuinely appropriate for research and little else. Saddam asked the Soviets to upgrade this reactor from two to five megawatts, which they willingly did, a job that was complete by 1978.

Beginning in the mid-1970s, the Iraqi leader sought to buy a larger reactor, one that could produce bomb-grade quantities of plutonium. The Iraqis headed for Paris. There, the Iraqis found the prospects for purchasing a nuclear reactor not nearly so difficult as they had feared. Not only was Paris a pleasant place to visit, but the French of the 1970s were the Western world's most enterprising and ambitious nuclear salesmen. The Iraqi envoys got along famously with the French representatives of C.E.A., the Commissariat de l'Energie Atomique, and state-owned companies to which they were introduced, such as Technicatome, Framatome, and Electricité de France.

The Iraqis' first choice for a reactor was a giant: a powerful gas-graphite workhorse that spewed out plutonium like waste water and could double to manufacture electric power. As repository of giant stores of crude oil, Iraq had adequate energy resources to provide cheap electrical and other power for at least a century. Still, the Iraqis justified their desire for a plutonium-producing reactor by pointing out to their French friends that the supply of oil was finite by nature. At some future point the pools of oil beneath Iraqi soil would run out or dry up. The Iraqis corralled Prime Minister Jacques Chirac into promising them an atomic reactor to reduce that danger.

The gas-graphite reactor, with its enormous capacity for plutonium production, was both too obvious and too dangerous a choice. At Iraq's stage of industrial development, the purchase of a gas-graphite reactor could only be for one purpose—atomic bombs. French technocrats, though known for their free-swinging nuclear sales policy, were aware of long- range Iraqi intentions and became reluctant to authorize such a sale. They foresaw that such a nuclear installation could set alarm bells ringing among the world's statesmen and intelligence officers. Paris wisely backed off before the deal was concluded.

Instead, the French steered the Iraqis in the direction of a smaller reactor, one that also had some plutonium production capacity, but which fit within a "research" category. Nicknamed by the French after an Egyptian god, Osiris—the king of the lower world and judge of the dead—a prototype was on display at Saclay, the French nuclear research center located to the south of Paris. The Osiris was a full-blown, ready-to-assemble, 25 megawatt French reactor. As the French-Iraqi talks progressed, the reactor got dubbed with the nickname "Osirak." Similar in size to the Israeli reactor at Dimona, it had adequate power to produce plutonium. It could, with proper technical supervision, throw off enough waste fuel to make one or two bombs a year, depending on the size of the bomb and the operating efficiency of the reactor. If not perfect, it was at least suitable for Saddam's military dream.

•   •   •

Yves Girard, a French nuclear official, offered me some insight into the selling of Osirak.[1] While an adviser on nuclear affairs to the French Department of Energy, he accompanied Prime Minister Jacques Chirac in 1975 to Baghdad. "It was a time of great confusion," he recalled. "Everything that there was to be sold could be sold," he explained. "And we wanted to do the selling. We were determined to keep an inside track on the contracts."

Operating beyond the platitudes of the diplomats, the businessmen in charge of nuclear sales were pragmatic. In order to make the sale, French officials—just like their Western competitors—had to highlight the benefits of the reactor. Girard asserted that the research reactor's plutonium-producing capability was a key point in the French sales campaign, just as it was for France's competitors from Canada, Germany and the United States. That was the way business was done in the nuclear industry. If anything, governments and the nuclear industry used a country's commitments to the Non-Proliferation Treaty, and the existence of future safeguards, as a kind of formal permission to sell their products—and avoid responsibility for policing the sale.

Girard was particularly sarcastic concerning the role of the hard-driving, competitive Canadians—like the Americans, a moralistic folk— who first boasted to the Iraqis of the plutonium-producing capacity of their own Candu reactor as equal to or better than Osirak's, and then later, hypocritically, castigated the French sale of the similar Osirak reactor as a nuclear proliferation danger. Every nuclear salesman knew what the Iraqis' secret motives were, and that to make the Iraqi sale they had to have a first-rate plutonium producer, a reactor that could spew out adequate quantities of waste fuel for a bomb. Otherwise, the Iraqis would ignore them. Girard didn't appreciate what he regarded as Canadian moral posturing, especially later when they acted shocked at the idea that Iraq would consider buying the Candu or any other reactor for its plutonium-producing capability.

Girard related that a similar process applied on the Iraqi side. Iraqi scientists had limited autonomy. Whatever their motives, they couldn't get the budget to buy a reactor unless Iraqi Army generals approved. The sine qua non of that approval was plutonium production capability. "A number of the buyers we dealt with really wanted a tool that could provide Iraqi scientists with the training to enter the nuclear world," he explained. "They knew it was a long-term process—that is, the people we were dealing with."

The French and Iraqis agreed on the sale. Though secret, the deal fell within internationally accepted norms. No alarm bells rang. Firms in France began to make the parts that would be assembled into the reactor. The sensitive reactor core took form at C.N.I.M. (Constructions Navelles Industrielles Maritimes) in La Seyne sur Mer, on the Côte d'Azur, in shouting distance of the French Riviera beaches where other kinds of usually cloaked forms were deliberately revealed without the slightest attempt at secrecy. French firms constructed the shell at the French nuclear research center at Tuwaitah near Baghdad. In a little-noticed action, the French supplied the Iraqis additionally with three metric tons of heavy water.

Shortly, Israeli, Iranian and American diplomats woke up and began to protest. Officials of the Arms Control and Disarmament Agency within the State Department tried to raise an early warning. The military-type secrecy surrounding the deal, upon which the Iraqis insisted, buttressed intelligence evaluations that the Iraqis and French were up to no good. The capable U.S. scientific attaché in Paris, Abraham Friedman, conveyed many of the American concerns to the French.

Neither French firms nor the Paris government took the diplomatic protests seriously. French nuclear executives told the Foreign Office that the Osirak was not a very good plutonium producer, if it were one at all. The contract specified that the reactor be "safeguarded." The French nuclear industry, like other national nuclear entities, had backed the N.P.T. and the imposition of safeguards on international sales. Why have international treaties, safeguards and inspections if nuclear sales still could not be made? Otherwise, the protests against Osirak were simply an attempt to deny technology to one of France's best clients, a country that paid its bills, and an example of the West wanting to keep the developing world down. Since French nuclear officials and diplomats were secure in the knowledge that France would not choose such a reactor for its own atom bomb program, how and why would others? The French assumed that their own Cartesian sense of logic would govern Iraqi thinking.

Saddam Hussein officially assumed the presidency of Iraq in July, 1979, by which time the nuclear program was well under way. The French continued to work according to schedule. Their salesmen argued that, if the French couldn't go ahead and fulfill the Iraqi sale with all the safety provisions that were contractually included in the deal, no nuclear sales to Third World countries could or would ever be made. Nuclear exports would become a dead issue. Either French firms could finance domestic French nuclear development with exports or they couldn't. If they couldn't, the future of the French nuclear industry itself might be in jeopardy. In short, it was now or never for the C.E.A. and France's bright hopes for a nuclear export business.

•   •   •

Even as Saddam Hussein indulged in dreams of nuclear power and masteries of the fuel cycle that could give his country a bomb, a select few in Iran sought to use atomic power as a wedge to modernize the country, to gain industrial self-sufficiency and assure their country's own long-term impregnability. Iran, too, felt it was a major world player, and should have the option of having an atomic bomb at its disposal.

The Iranian who first sought the advantages of nuclear technology and science, if not the atomic bomb, was the Shah himself—Muhammad Reza Pahlavi. The Shah was a leader with an enormous ego. He had ruled Iran with an iron hand for decades and intended to bring the country willingly or unwillingly into the latter part of the Twentieth Century. He called himself or had others call him "the King of Kings," the "heir of 2,500 years of Persian history and culture," and the "Light of the Aryans."

Like the Iraqis, Iranian interest in nuclear matters got serious by 1975. The Iranians had at least as good chances as the Iraqis to gain atomic expertise. Their top scientists were educated in the West's best institutions and they had more Ph.D.'s in nuclear physics and engineering. With over forty million persons, they were far more populous. They had as much or more money. Allied with the West and particularly the United States, they had friends, supporters, and partners among the more sophisticated players in Western political circles. They also had an intricate understanding of financial markets, international monetary and investment vehicles, and how to make deals.

The Iranians' nuclear fathers were the Americans. In 1968, the Iranians received a small "Triga" research reactor of five megawatts from the American Machine and Foundry Company, which later became General Atomics. Little appreciated at the time, the sale—which was approved and registered by the Board of Governors of the International Atomic Energy Agency in 1967—included a supply of several kilos of highly enriched uranium at 93 percent, which is bomb-grade. The Iranians also showed interest in developing the tools and plant facilities to master the reprocessing of the spent fuel into plutonium.

The Iranians also received from the Americans two small "hot cells" capable of separating out spent nuclear fuel and producing tiny amounts of bomb-grade plutonium. These were nuclear items of laboratory-scale that were reported to, and safeguarded by, the International

Atomic Energy Agency. Like most U.S.-supplied equipment in the nuclear field, the hot cells actually worked. When operational, the Iranians could turn their spent fuel product into bomb-grade materials—far short of the quantities required to make an atomic bomb, but as part of a process that would provide Iranian scientists with the expertise in plutonium production eventually useful for bomb production. In the view of Dr. Akbar Etamad,[2] the head of the Iranian Atomic Energy Commission from 1974 to 1979, with whom I met several times, such hot cells had a minor capacity for producing plutonium. But, depending on the fuel and reactor, they could produce only tens of grams of fissionable fuel in a year. Etamad confirmed buying this equipment for Iran and having his scientists work with it in laboratory-scale experiments that could produce plutonium.

In the mid-1970s, the Iranians went out on their own nuclear shopping expedition. The venture was legal, above-board, relatively in the open, and incredibly expensive. Iran's outward stance was that the country was interested in converting a fraction of its oil wealth—and some twenty percent of its electrical power generation—into the production of clean, nuclear-based energy. In the crazily competitive nuclear marketplace of the mid-1970s, there was hot pursuit for the Iranian business. Since Iran was, like Iraq, a signatory of N.P.T., it would have been a clear breach to re-configure or re-design a reactor designed to generate electrical power in order to extract reactor plutonium from spent fuel, a technically difficult practice. Yet the plant could provide Iran with a base of nuclear equipment, and enable Iranian scientists and engineers to gain knowledge and experience in nuclear matters. This could enable them to proceed towards weapons capability should the Shah and his aides eventually decide to go that route.

While the Americans wanted to supply Iran with conventional arms and tie Iran into U.S. policies, the Shah was, more generally, straining at the leash of American tutelage. The then-Secretary of State, Henry Kissinger, looked askance at Iranian nuclear ambitions and suspected a military intent. Gary Sick, a former National Security Council aide to President Jimmy Carter, in his book *All Fall Down*, and others have detailed how the Shah pushed the United States from the early 1970s to acquire the most advanced American weaponry and how these demands were often rejected. The nuclear program was the most sensitive program of all. Officials in the U.S. intelligence community concluded early on that the sale of the reactor, plus the reprocessing facilities sought by the Iranians, would provide Iran with a base that could lead to the installation of more significant infrastructure that, in turn, could lead to the development of an atomic bomb project.

Westinghouse, the major American nuclear power reactor company, was a chief bidder for the the Iranian reactor projects, but American proliferation concerns quickly got in the way. No one in Washington wanted to provide Iran with independent nuclear capability. The officials expressed strong objections. Yet disagreement existed within Washington on precisely what could and should be sold. In particular, American officials tried to impose contractual restrictions on the use of plutonium waste from the power reactors. Both internally and with the Iranians, the process of working out the precise nature of these restrictions took time. In 1978, according to Sick, the American nuclear authorities finally arrived at formulae that would enable the major U.S. producers to sell reactors and nuclear components to Iran, and still retain adequate safeguards to prevent the spent fuel from being diverted into a weapons program.

However, the decision-making process took too much time. All the U.S. officials managed to do was to put restrictions on American manufacturers and lose the Iranian business. In the meanwhile, the Iranians negotiated a massive deal for power reactors with the German nuclear power plant firm, Kraftwerk Union,[3] or K.W.U., for two 1000-megawatt reactors to be built in the south of the country on the Persian Gulf at a small but picturesque coastal site called Bushehr. The German-Iranian contract, concluded by the Iranians under Etamad's direction, was potentially worth some $6 billion to K.W.U., today the power reactor division of the giant Siemens Company. The deal was a major coup for the German nuclear industry, which faced stiff French as well as American competition for the work. It included plant construction, the sale of reactor components, fuel supply and related services. Each K.W.U. reactor used 230 kilograms of reactor plutonium. This kind of fuel is not very easily convertible to military fuel, though in optimal circumstances the reactors could be used to breed large quantities of crude plutonium which could then be transferred to reprocessing units.

The Iranians didn't stop there, but invested heavily in one of Europe's two main projects for producing enriched uranium. This was the French-inspired and controlled "Eurodif." Seen by Paris as a competitor to the Dutch-German-British consortium "Urenco," the Eurodif consortium, consisting of five countries, intended to build a major plant for enrichment using the gaseous diffusion method. Urenco used the competing ultra-centrifuge system. Eurodif's factory was to be built at Tricastin, nearby the existing military enrichment plant at Pierrelatte.

The French, ambitious planners eager to use nuclear power as the basis of their domestic electricity supply, needed a more economical military fuel for their own atomic bomb program, the force de frappe. The small enrichment plant at Pierrelatte produced bomb-grade fuel for the French army, but was known for its inefficient and expensive production. With the Eurodif facility working, the French could take the low- enriched uranium produced at the Eurodif facility, perform further enrichment at the military plant or elsewhere, and extract significant quantities of bomb-grade fuel at a reasonable price.

France turned to Iran as the country with the kind of assets that could make the Eurodif project actually happen. With oil money flowing into the Shah's coffers, the Shah literally had spare billions—in dollars, not francs—looking for an investment home. Iran jumped at the chance to gain a stake in one of Europe's two prime uranium enrichment projects. The Iranians offered France millions as their capital investment, and additionally agreed to loan Eurodif a whopping $1 billion as working capital to get the new system operational.

It took time and effort to work out the details. In 1975, Prime Minister Jacques Chirac of France, already committed to French nuclear export both for its own sake and to finance French domestic nuclear power, came to visit Teheran to negotiate a number of agreements, most of them having to do with the sale of French goods to the oil-rich Gulf. He had embarked on a similar aggressive export policy with Iraq. On his agenda, among other projects: the Iranian role in Eurodif. He was supposed to leave in the afternoon of the last day of his visit.

Etamad remembers it this way: "I cornered Chirac that day and said we had to finish the agreement. Before he went, he said okay."

Chirac changed his departure plans. "He stayed 'till midnight. By midnight we had it roughed out," Etamad recalls.

That $1 billion loan was in 1975 dollars—an enormous amount. "That was the money that France then built Eurodif on—it was Iranian money," notes Etamad, not without a hint of pride at his achievement having Iran become a partner in one of Europe's most sensitive nuclear processes and two prime uranium enrichment projects.

But with that billion hanging in the wind and France eager to lay its hands on it, the big problem was what to do about nuclear proliferation. The arguments spun back and forth as to what rights Iran would have for the low enriched uranium product and whether the Iranians would have autonomy in determining its use. If a country wants to make highly enriched uranium for bombs, it is far easier to make it from a low enriched uranium base of three or five percent than no base at all. France, already under pressure from Western anti-proliferation forces and a member of the Big Five, said the deal would have to be proliferation-free, meaning Iran could have preferential dibs on the product but would be forbidden from using the uranium for military purposes.

Iran—in the person of Etamad—surprised the French by turning the demand upside down. The Iranians asked for equal rights and privileges themselves. The Iranians said they simply wanted the same rights as other major partners in Eurodif, France in particular. What the demand meant was that the French shouldn't use the Eurodif facility to do even preliminary enrichment of uranium to three or four percent, for later enrichment to military bomb levels. This conflicted with French aims, which were to use Eurodif's civilian product as a basis for their military program, too. "France was in a trap, they walked into it," remembers Etamad, "because they had this very expensive military uranium enrichment process at Pierrelatte and the new facility was bound to be cheaper, to provide enriched uranium on a commercial basis or at a reasonable price. And our argument was, well, if we can't do it [use the uranium for military purposes] you shouldn't do it, either."

By making the demand, the Iranians not only showed diplomatic skill but tipped their hand about their own ambitions to be equal players with one of the world's recognized atomic bomb states in nuclear matters. The upshot was that promises were made that no one wants to be very specific about. My understanding is that in the formal deal

Eurodif became military-use-free. Neither Etamad nor the French are very clear about the ultimate arrangement. Would the French then use Eurodif product for their own atomic bomb program? Only the French, not the Iranians, know the answers. The French are not very forthcoming about such questions.

Nevertheless, the overall nature of the trade-off was clear enough. France got its billion-plus of 1975 dollars and began building the Eurodif facility with Iranian cash. The Iranians secured a proprietary stake through Eurodif to one of the world's most advanced nuclear energy processes, and future preferential access to both its nuclear product and technology.

•   •   •

Under Etamad's capable leadership, the Iranians invested in a number of technologies. They bought a set of lasers and an experimental laser system potentially capable of uranium separation and of making nuclear fuel. The source was a Los Angeles based firm, Lischem, short for "Laser Isotope Separation and Chemistry," headed by a Dutch-born American scientist and inventor, Jeff Eerkens. Though many Americans looked on Eerkens as a "kook"—he had been singularly unconvincing in several demonstrations of his theories when presenting them to U.S. officials and never received formal backing—Eerkens pursued his dream, and his particular approach to what he hoped would be commercial development of laser enrichment technology.

Two Iranian scientists sought Eerkens out. They were Dr. Mojtaba Taherzadeh, then-head of Teheran's nuclear research center and himself a 1964 graduate from U.C.L.A. with a Ph.D. in physics, and Dr. Ehsanollah Ziai, also of the Teheran center. They offered Eerkens the prospect of Iranian financing and research help and flew him to Iran in 1976. The parties came to an agreement that included complicated financing arrangements for Eerkens' research. The deal consisted of Eerkens providing Iran with four gas lasers which could produce an infrared light at different wavelengths, plus the same number of chemical reaction chambers where, if all worked according to theory, separation and then enrichment of uranium would take place.

Eerkens pursued the proper routes for formal permission to export from the U.S. Department of Energy and Department of Commerce.

Fortunately for him at the time, U.S. officials were skeptical about his program and did not take him seriously. "I don't want to be dogmatic about anyone's proposal, but I'm pretty skeptical about it," a Los Alamos scientist told *The Los Angeles Times* in a 1979 interview.[4] Another said: "He's got his physics on totally crooked." The chief of D.O.E.'s nuclear export branch, James Kratz, claimed that "We are reasonably confident that it is not a viable process for uranium.... We checked with our technical experts and they had no problem with it." On the other hand, Dr. C. Bradley Moore, a professor of chemistry at the University of California, Berkeley, said, "I don't consider Eerkens a crank. His (process) is probably more speculative than others and it needs more work to prove its scientific feasibility....[But] I think it's worth investigating."

The United States government approved the sale. Eerkens patented his process in April, 1978. "It should have been classified," he admitted. But since it wasn't, he affirmed, "I'm going to take advantage of it."

He added that he would only sell his invention to pro-Western countries that had signed the Non-Proliferation Treaty. Iran fit that bill. As he told me later when I visited him at his office in Los Angeles, the country was not only pro-Western. Shah Pahlevi was one of America's closest allies.

To cement their relationship with Dr. Eerkens, the Iranians were willing to put up risk capital. "It's ridiculous that we had to go to a foreign government," Eerkens said, but U.S. investors would call the people at Los Alamos, hear derogatory information about him or his process, and immediately get turned off. Still, Eerkens contended, "I wouldn't have gone this far if it didn't work. I'm no fool."

Generally, the Iranians under the Shah, through Etamad's leadership, were pursuing mastery over every possible nuclear technology and element of the fuel cycle. This included lasers, magnetic conversion, fusion, reprocessing, electro-magnetic isotope separation, as well as anything else one could think of.

Years later, there was still some debate within the American anti-proliferation community over Iranian intentions during the time of the Shah. Etamad provided me with some insight. He told me he spent long hours talking with the Shah, who spoke of his dreams and plans for nuclear energy. What he and the Shah wanted was simply to gain "mastery of the fuel cycle" so that, if necessary, Iran would become an independent and self-reliant nuclear power. Both men resented American intrusions into domains they considered to be Iranian areas of decision-making. Neither man had to be concerned at such an early stage of the program whether the goals were exclusively for nuclear-generated electrical power or possibly also for atomic bomb capability. The hard political choices about what to do with that atomic independence could be made at a later time. Etamad refused to go into more detail than that. He firmly denied to me that the intentions of those working under him at the Iran Atomic Energy Organization during the time of the Shah were military.

But one Iranian, Dr. Fenyati Fesheraki, was quoted in *The Washington Post* as stating that the Shah had embarked on a secret military program that even the top people in the Atomic Energy Agency didn't know about. When contacted by my colleague, Robert Ross, for a TV show we were doing together, Fesheraki denied he had ever made the statement.

•　　　•　　　•

William Shawcross described the Ayatollah Sayyed Ruhollah Mousavi Khomeini's rising place in the demonology of the Western world in *The Shah's Last Ride*: "He had been its implacable scourge, its unbending critic, preaching and practicing austerity and revenge. To many in the West he had seemed an utterly ruthless and even deranged enemy, a terrifying symbol of an anger and hatred that we had not expected, could not understand and had no hope of controlling. At the very least he had made the subject of Islam one of widespread fascination in the West."

The Ayatollah flew into Iran on February 1, 1979. Mobs greeted him and danced with joy in the streets. He and his entourage took control of the country. Shortly, his bearded face adorned thousands of posters during a march in Teheran. Iran was on its way to becoming a virulent force for Islamic fundamentalism and a proselytizer for the cause of religious revolution.

After the takeover, Iran descended into a state of almost total chaos. The newly formed "pasdaran," the Revolutionary Guards, gained control over many duties and functions from the country's military, assumed by the clerics to be riddled with royalist sympathizers. As if to emphasize their detachment from the Shah's grandiose goals, the new Iranian rulers disdained the Shah's nuclear purchases and determinedly ignored them with the purpose of letting them rust. This was particularly true for the major nuclear installation at Bushehr, which was 70 to 80 percent complete and on which literally billions of 1970s dollars—at least four billion dollars, at any rate—had been spent. The revolutionary leaders even let Jeff Eerkens' lasers languish in port. The Iranians attempted to return them to Lischem and refused to pay the bill. (A few years later, after Eerkens and his lawyers had taken the Iranians to an international tribunal at the Hague in Holland, the scientist finally got paid.)

One of the Ayatollah's first declarations was to decry the use of atomic energy as the "work of the devil" and inappropriate for a country soulfully obedient to the laws of Islam (as Iranian fundamentalists interpreted these laws).[5] The Islamic Revolution caused many of Iran's top nuclear scientists to flee the country. Among them was Akbar Etamad. Numerous others who decried the purge of modernity urged by the Ayatollah also departed Iran.

Iran descended into turmoil. The Iranians forbade the Germans from working further on Bushehr, or even delivering what was already paid for. Cargo ships, their holds bulging with containers holding literally tons of nuclear goods, sailed in circles in the Gulf, then threw anchor in the calm Gulf waters and finally headed back to Europe with their precious cargo. Some of it was offloaded in Genoa, other portions returned to Germany.

•   •   •

In 1981, about two years after the Islamic revolutionaries seized power in Teheran, I met and spoke in detail with Akbar Etamad. The discussion, which took place in a Paris café, was cited in my earlier book, *The Islamic Bomb*. Etamad, as the Shah's former nuclear chief, was one of the possible targets for the Ayatollah's God-focussed gunmen and at the time was cautious about his personal well-being. He glanced around him occasionally to check who was there. He told me he thought there was only a remote possibility that the Ayatollah would try to fabricate an atomic bomb. Many of the top rung of Iranian scientists, their best and brightest, had already escaped Westward. Etamad argued that Iran's atomic options were limited. Even if Iran had the motivation and ideology, he doubted that the still-shaky Iranian infrastructure would permit it.

Our talk at that 1981 meeting focussed mainly on Iraq. "The French reactor for Iraq made us nervous," Etamad, a favorite official of the Shah, told me then. "In our time we didn't like the fact that the Iraqis were scheduled to receive highly enriched uranium. It's relatively easy to divert this from the fuel cycle, and we expressed our concerns to the French."

Etamad lamented that the Ayatollah Khomeini had expressed his determination to expunge all traces of modernity and science from the Iranian consciousness en route to the creation of his Islamic republic of medieval faith. The aging Ayatollah had disparaged the nuclear program along with other aspects of modernity in Iran, referring to atomic science as "the work of the devil."

Etamad pointed to one of his former staff as possibly having military ambitions for Iran's post-Islamic nuclear program. This was Dr. Ali Sekhavat, head of the "Nuclear Applications" division of the Iranian Atomic Energy Organization. (My later checking revealed that Sekhavat had a reputation as "being brilliant," but having his head in the clouds.) Etamad suspected that Sekhavat, his former employee, might attempt to persuade the Iranian government to go after the bomb, but only if the Iraqis continued full-scale ahead with their nuclear program. Within a matter of months after that first talk with Etamad, the Israelis bombed Osirak, thus making Iranian fears of an Iraqi atomic bomb extraneous, and any Iranian plan to make their own bomb that much more remote.

Etamad had additional insights on some of his country's early relationships with world nuclear powers. He had fond memories of Chinese nuclear officials, who wanted to use Iran in the 1970s as a vehicle to obtain the West's nuclear technology. "How naive the Chinese were," he commented. "They asked us if they could read all our nuclear contracts."

"What happened then?"

"They would read whatever we gave them. They'd study it."

Then there were the Pakistanis. During Etamad's time there were no real working relationships with Pakistan though he and Munir Khan, the head of the Pakistani Atomic Energy Commission, were personally on good terms. Etamad emphasized that he didn't have any inside knowledge of Pakistan's bomb program and he and Munir Khan never discussed it. That was not the kind of thing that heads of national nuclear programs discuss, in any case. He thought that Pakistan, like many other countries, was energy-poor and needed the electrical power that a nuclear program could produce.

In general, Etamad emphasized, Iran was interested in mastery of the fuel cycle. He thought it was Iran's right to get it. "This is what we really wanted. We wanted to gain and master the technologies...

"You know," he added, "That's what the Iranians still want to do today."

Etamad remains a believer in nuclear power. He contends that Iran is energy-poor. The country has no domestic refining facilities. Oil is a finite product that can only be pumped till the supply is exhausted. His view is that Iran will require nuclear power for at least twenty percent of its energy needs by the early part of the 21st century.

Etamad denied that the Shah's regime, or he personally, had any direct military intention at the time. But, once the technology was mastered, he admitted, "it would become a political decision" as to what to do with man's most powerful invention.

Ultimately, if the capability were there, it would become an Iranian choice—not anyone else's—whether to attempt to manufacture of an atomic bomb.

CHAPTER THREE

Crisis!

"On Sunday, June 7th, the Israeli Air Force launched a raid on the atomic reactor Osirak near Baghdad. Our pilots carried out their mission fully. The reactor was destroyed. All our aircraft returned safely to base."

Israel Government announcement after bombing Osirak, June, 1981.

IN A SURPRISE ATTACK, Iraqi armed forces invaded Iran on September 21, 1980. Blatantly violating the terms of the Algiers Agreement of 1975, the Iraqis wanted to re-establish ancient territorial claims that would give them control of the Persian, or Arab, Gulf. The offensive against the Iranians was realpolitik at its most calculating. The Iraqi Army caught the Iranians off-guard and swiftly made dramatic advances into the Iranian heartland.

Iran mobilized. The secluded Ayatollah Khomeini had no doubt that Iran with its resurgent faith and new vitality could conquer Iraq and the man he saw as the devil incarnate, Saddam Hussein—a Ba'athist wedded to his own concepts of Arab socialism and secularism. Iranian military men preferred to rely on superior numbers and weaponry, not just religious belief, to do the job. The Iranian Army still had stores of

U.S.-supplied military equipment, much of it already lying unused and untended less than one year after the Revolution. Inside the Army remained a core of American-trained military men who had managed to save not only their lives but their jobs when the Ayatollah came to power. Though they were dedicated Iranian nationalists, some of them nurtured loyalties to the Shah and hidden feelings of friendship or respect towards the Americans. They were not trusted by the Ayatollah Khomeini's most fervent supporters, the pasdaran or revolutionary guards, the group that had invaded the American Embassy in Teheran in November, 1979. The pasdaran owed allegiance entirely to the new order.

A huge procurement effort came into being almost overnight. The pasdaran, not the Army, led the effort to firm up Iran's military strength after the outbreak of war. They were even ready to turn to the country's old allies and newly sworn enemies—the twin satanic powers of America and Israel—for weapons and other war material.

From the war's earliest stage, Iran's military chiefs felt obliged to take the Iraqi nuclear option into account. Iranian intelligence officials under the Shah had already cast a wary eye on the Iraqi nuclear effort. On September 30, 1980, the ninth day of the Gulf War, the nuclear issue heated up. Two of Iran's American-made Phantom jets hit Tammuz One, the Iraqi reactor located at Tuwaitah, just outside Baghdad. The damage was minimal, but enough to set back the Iraqi program by days if not months. It was possible that Tammuz One, or Osirak, was only a target of opportunity for the Iranian fighter-planes after a raid on an electrical power plant near Baghdad. At the time, the Iraqis suspected that the Israelis and not the Iranians were behind the attack.

Between that September and the next June, as Iran and Iraq waged war fiercely and without hint of mercy for the other's civilian population, a series of events stirred the nuclear cauldron. Many of them involved neither Iran nor Iraq but a third country not a direct party to the Gulf conflict.

•   •   •

Israel felt threatened. With the Shah deposed and a fundamentalist Moslem regime in place, Iran was no longer a strategic ally to keep the

Arabs, and particularly the Iraqis, on their toes. Israel had the enormous breadth of the Arab heartland to its east, and was more exposed. The Israelis could see, with the help of some very able intelligence, the potential mushrooming of Iraq's atomic cloud.

The Jewish state stood outside the framework of Iraqi- French relations. Governmental leaders in Jerusalem, as in Teheran, had nervously watched Iraq's progress towards nuclear capability. The Israelis' efforts to halt the growth of Iraqi atomic capability initially focussed, not on the Iraqi consumers, but the French suppliers. Israeli leaders decided that French motives were firmly rooted in commercial reality and legal obligation, based not necessarily on France's desire to provide the Iraqis with an atom bomb, but to sell reactors to finance France's own nuclear development. Israel's analysis that Hussein secretly had a plan to develop an atomic weapon raised one issue: whether Iraqi scientists and engineers could obtain and master the technology and manufacturing processes that would lead to the bomb. The Israelis correctly assessed that, protests notwithstanding, the French nuclear chiefs would continue to fulfill the lucrative contracts signed by their government to which they were morally and legally committed.

"It's clear that any country that really wants a bomb can get one," an Israeli official told me at the time, concluding that money and a purchase plan would conquer any diplomatic obstacle. While the process could be slowed down, it could not be fully stopped. Pressure through diplomatic channels failed to work.

Israel's leaders felt they had to act. Perhaps not all the actions that followed were Israeli—some may have been committed by Iranian or revolutionary groups—but some definitely were. A series of terrorist-type attacks (variously attributed to the Iranians, Shi'ite Iraqi underground cells, or the Israelis), on Iraq's nuclear personnel and suppliers—ranging from the murder of a top Arab scientist working for the Iraqis to the blowing up of a reactor core at a small factory, C.N.I.M., at La-Seyne-Sur-Mer on the French Riviera, to warning letters to French scientists—slowed Iraqi progress towards a nuclear bomb. But it wasn't, it appeared, stopped—at least not without far more decisive military-type action. When the French delivered 12.5 kilos, over 27 pounds, of highly enriched uranium to Iraq in mid-1980, the dye was cast. The

Israelis concluded that military preemptive action, as a last resort, could become a necessity.

On May 10, 1981, a presidential election took place in France. François Mitterrand, a long-time friend of Israel, won decisively. Though Mitterrand had gained the Presidency with an anti-Osirak and anti-nuclear proliferation plank in his platform, Israeli leaders were skeptical about a change in French trade policy on an existing deal. The reactor would shortly go "hot" or critical. A military strike after that could create serious environmental dangers. The Israelis, more sensitive to ecological dangers in Iraq than political sensitivities in France, felt they had to strike before it got too late.

In the afternoon hours of June 7th, 1981—a Jewish holiday in Israel—Israeli war planes took off from air bases near Eilat and elsewhere, traversed the skies of Jordan and Iraq, and looped in from the west, diving towards earth and onto the Iraqi nuclear site at Tuwaitah near Baghdad. Their sleek outlines were obscured by the bright rays of the afternoon desert sun. Using precision techniques and smart bombs guided by complex electronics, they bombed Osirak into extinction at five o'clock p.m. The attack was stunningly successful. "It's gone like a Swiss watch. Better than a Swiss watch," said one Israeli official reporting to Israeli Prime Minister Menahem Begin, although an undetermined number of Iraqis on duty and one French technician were killed.

The official announcement from the Prime Minister's office was succinct. "On Sunday, June 7th, the Israeli Air Force launched a raid on the atomic reactor Osirak near Baghdad. Our pilots carried out their mission fully. The reactor was destroyed. All our aircraft returned safely to base."

The Israeli bombing of Osirak was a seminal event in nuclear matters. Although the State Department condemned the raid and the prospect of additional violence in the Middle East, particularly at a time when the Egyptian-Israeli peace agreement was just taking root, many in Washington in fact admired the Israeli action. This was both because these Americans agreed with the Israeli conviction that if left unimpeded, the Iraqis could genuinely become a nuclear threat, and because the decisiveness of the Israeli action underlined what many Republicans and other U.S. hawks saw as America's "Vietnam complex"—the

Superpower's supposed vacillation and inability to act in the wake of the defeat in Vietnam.

●   ●   ●

In July, 1981, six weeks after the Israeli action, U.S. President Ronald Reagan delineated America's continuing commitment to nuclear non-proliferation in a statement released by the White House. "The need to prevent the spread of nuclear explosives to additional countries" is one of America's most critical challenges, the President declared. "Further proliferation would pose a severe threat to international peace, regional and global stability, and the security interests of the United States and other countries."

In effect, the America of Reagan decided to accentuate the previous Carter Administration's focus on proliferation. As during Carter's time, the United States assumed the role of world-wide sheriff. His badge appearing to glint in the desert sun, the former Western movie star, now the American President, seemingly told potential outlaws to stop dead in their tracks and go no further in pursuing a nuclear option. Reagan decided to continue long-standing American goals, ones the previous Carter Administration had also pursued with considerable vigor and sometimes acerbity.

Yet the new team in Washington also wanted to put some distance between Republican policies and those of the past administration. The worldly Europeans had taken particular umbrage at President Jimmy Carter's past moralistic pronouncements on proliferation. Carter's team had pushed hard, possibly too much so, and had goaded some European diplomats to anger and indignation at what they believed was American presumption. Europeans speculated openly why the man they regarded as a former peanut farmer was lecturing them on proper international behavior. Countries like France, Germany and Italy resented U.S. allegations about their nuclear exports. These sales that the Americans called dangerous invariably seemed to affect the Europeans' Middle East and Far East markets and rarely American commercial interests. The United States, not Europe, was the world's leading arms merchant, followed only by the Soviets. In the European view, the Americans ploughed on in their merry way selling whatever they could, including all types of armaments and dual-use technology, and saw nothing bad about it so long as the goods were "Made in America."

Reagan's men sought to smooth over the ruffled feelings that had developed between America and its European allies on proliferation issues, and also to allay suspicions among Europeans that America was using the pretense of "morality" and "world safety" to stop Europeans from selling while the United States grabbed its own piece of the action. In diplomacy, where style is often as important as substance, the new men in charge wanted to radically alter the Carter style and then to modify the substance in smaller doses. Practically, Reagan promised continuity in most areas: opposition to the sale or transfer of dangerous nuclear equipment and technology, full-scope safeguards as a pre- condition for nuclear supply, renewed adherence to the various nonproliferation treaties.

Then, in a new policy twist directed against budding nuclear powers like Pakistan and Iraq and also older ones like India and Israel, Reagan Administration officials drew a line beyond which they indicated it would be unsafe to trespass. They warned that they saw "a material violation of these treaties or an international safeguards agreement as having profound consequences for international order and United States bilateral relations...." In direct reference to those countries which already had nuclear technology, the Administration added the warning that it would "...view any nuclear explosion by a non nuclear-weapon state with grave concern."

Still, the main problem was the Persian Gulf, especially Iraq, still very much in the midst of its war with Iran. That was a hot war where nonconventional weapons were being used, mainly against the enemy's civilian population. As the controversy about nuclear non-proliferation swirled about, the U.S. urged France to follow a policy of restraint in sales. Diplomats suspected that while the era of Iraqi atomic bombs threatening the safety and tranquillity of Middle East peoples was temporarily forestalled, Iraq's strategic vision had not fundamentally changed. Saddam Hussein would have to try again—or turn elsewhere—to find the equipment and raw materials for his "big bang."

The Israeli attack stirred debate about the non-proliferation issue in general. An actual military attack against a potentially dangerous nuclear target, whether from Israel, the United States or another country, raised the question, exactly who was assuming the role of policeman—and what rights did he have? At what point did a nuclear target become dangerous? Where was the cutoff line?

• • •

The Iraqis stuck to their plan. A new reactor remained at the top of the Iraqi acquisition list—an indication of the high priority Saddam Hussein gave to his nuclear program. But the war with Iran was consuming petrodollars faster than oil could be pumped. Fighting a war they had thought would be a walk-over, but had turned into a series of dragged-out defensive battles against a determined foe, the Iraqis needed to focus on projects that could be implemented immediately, were cost-efficient and paid off in tangible benefits on the battlefield.

Following the Israeli bombing, the Iraqis requested that the French provide a replacement for Osirak. The French hesitated, though they were not in a weak position. France had delivered Osirak, installed it, and had it almost ready to become operational, all according to contract. Finances helped determine strategy. France had been paid its money for Osirak and suffered no real economic losses. This, above all, made the French Administration's job of decision-making much easier.

A new contract, not the recovery of costs from the old, was the subject of negotiation. The Iraqis told the French that the new site for a nuclear reactor would have to be safe from enemy bombers. They required that the reactor and other sensitive facilities be moved far below ground. French engineers toured Iraq looking for sites and evaluating cost.

Shortly, a dispute ensued within the French bureaucracy.[1] Iraq's traditional supporters inside the French Atomic Energy Commission, the C.E.A., opposed the more proliferation-conscious officials in the French Foreign Office and in the President's office. Proponents of a renewed sale, arguing that Osirak was for "peaceful purposes" only, repeated shop-worn arguments that the reactor could not spin off enough plutonium for a bomb. (In fact, Osirak may not have been an ideal choice for a bomb program but it wasn't bad.) The French nuclear salesmen, just like salesmen everywhere, could remind themselves of the comforting axiom that invariably crops up in every country when lethal but lucrative high-tech equipment and weaponry is about to be sold: if the Iraqis were going to be doing the buying and were determined to get the goods come hell or high water, why shouldn't "we" do the selling? Why should France suffer a competitive disadvantage? Why shouldn't France reap the financial rewards?

France had the inside track to sell the Iraqis nuclear goods. This was a credit to France's know-how, burgeoning nuclear industry and superb product, reasoned certain French, who believed it right that their country should retain its commercial advantage. Failure to fulfill French responsibilities to Iraq, they argued, could affect future nuclear sales in general, not only to Iraq but to other Third World countries. They also sought to continue French nuclear exports in order to finance France's domestic electrical power program, which was largely based on nuclear energy.

Last but not least, these French friends of Iraq did not want to let the Israelis get away with the destruction of the French-supplied Osirak. The Jews were thumbing their nose at the French. The destruction of Osirak had been treated as a triumph in the Jewish state, even though a Frenchman had died. Israeli Prime Minister Begin had even declared publicly that the French had pursued anti-Semitic policies in their commitment to nuclear sales to Iraq, and should know better, an accusation that was particularly resented in Paris. The entire affair was enough to anger any patriotic Frenchman.

Still, it wasn't all that easy to continue France's nuclear supply to Iraq—neither for the French nuclear salesmen nor the Iraqis. President Mitterrand, though a socialist, sought more, not less cooperation with the new conservative U.S. administration. The U.S. counseled France to slow down her sales efforts, particularly to an emotion- charged and war-prone region. Some French diplomats began to be fearful of an ever-widening Middle East conflagration in which French supplies played a pivotal role. While they didn't like to see France's nose tweaked by the upstart Israelis, nor see valuable reactors destroyed by the to-them outrageous bombing, they were also more sensitive to foreign criticism of French policy than their nuclear colleagues at the C.E.A.

In the end—it took over a year—Mitterrand personally decided the issue by putting his considerable prestige and muscle against re-supply on non-proliferation grounds. He had the support of almost the entire French Conseil des Ministres, or cabinet, with only one known dissenting vote—from Claude Cheysson, the Foreign Minister, who voted against the advice of most of his own diplomats. Cheysson was known for his pro-Arab tilt.

With or without a new Osirak, French and Iraqi relations continued to flourish as the Gulf war raged on. France sold Iraq whatever the French military industry could produce. This included airplanes, bombs, various kinds of missiles, artillery, tanks and also helicopters. France got cheap and secure Iraqi oil in return. The financial pain of foregoing a new reactor project dimmed in the light of expanded military exports.

Getting an atomic bomb was one dream Saddam Hussein didn't want to relinquish. But, mired in a war he had started, Hussein had to find right-now solutions for tactical problems—namely, defeating the Iranians on the battlefield.

CHAPTER FOUR

"Perfume": Samarra's Secrets

"The whole world was there. In the beginning it felt good. We felt like pioneers in the desert....The asphalt dissolved like sugar in coffee."

Bernd Meyer, German engineer, Samarra

SADDAM HUSSEIN dreamed that his surprise attack on Iran in 1980 would bring a lightning victory at minimal price. The first few days after the initial thrust he was flush with conquest. But as several months and then finally a year passed, Iraqi advances against Iran faltered. The Iranians capitalized on superior numbers and the fervor of Islamic patriots to launch human wave assaults. Shortly, it was the Iranians, and not the Iraqis, who captured the battlefield offensive.

Hussein needed a killing weapon to counter Iran's superiority in numbers of fighting men. There were less than 15 million Iraqis in the world, and over 50 million Iranians. His secret hopes had lain with the Osirak reactor and an atomic bomb. Over half a billion carefully invested Iraqi petro-dollars had gone up in smoke with the Israeli bombs. As

Iran's human tidal waves threatened to overwhelm Iraqi troops, Hussein decided to go full-out "chemical." Defenses against it required an investment that few Third World armies, including the Iranians, had made. Since the cost of producing toxic gasses and nerve agent was limited, chemical weapons looked to be a cheap, cost-effective investment that could deliver killing power on the battlefield.

The early weapon of choice was the nightmarish "mustard gas," first used in World War I. That was the same kind of poison gas the Iraqis' backers, the Egyptians, used to attack Yemen during the early 1960s, in the first major use of chemical weapons since World War II. Egypt's Russian-made bombers had sprayed backward Arab villagers with the toxic substance, in an effort to overturn the royalist Yemeni regime, causing several thousand fatalities. The formulae for making mustard gas were published and known, and any good chemist could produce mustard in a laboratory situation. Industrial production would take longer, but Iraqi experts estimated that it could be achieved in reasonable time.

Hussein's scientists synthesized mustard from raw materials in minute quantities in the late 1970s and early '80s, according to Western analysts with whom I spoke, including Julian Perry Robinson of the University of Sussex in England, the West's leading independent chemical weapons researcher. By late 1982, sufficient quantities of extremely pure mustard gas were emerging from the laboratory for Iraq to attack Iranian positions.[1] Iraqi methods were the essence of simplicity: Pour the chemical into an artillery shell and fire it at the enemy. These primitive methods of delivery marked the initial Iraqi forays at least until 1983. With weather and wind currents a key to success, the Iraqis occasionally mis-directed mustard gas shells that fell short and exploded on their own positions. At other times, the shells would land close to Iranian lines but sudden winds drove the cloud of poison gas backwards.

The Iraqis saw these early attacks as successful enough to deserve follow-up. Iranian battle inexperience, and lack of protective clothing or gas masks, contributed to casualties that mounted to the hundreds, some calculated the thousands, encouraging the Iraqis to go further down the chemical warfare road. Serious buying of the implements of warfare began, with Iraqi agents spreading out through Europe. They bought many of their artillery shells from a company in Spain's colorful Basque country. The name of the company was EXPAL, an abbreviation for Explosivos Alaveses S.A., with offices and production facilities in Vitoria, near the Pyrenees Mountains, and sales representatives in Madrid. Western officials discovered EXPAL's role by chance in March, 1984, when a U.N. commission finally sent to visit the scene of fighting at the Gulf certified that Iraq had used mustard gas and possibly the more advanced nerve agent, tabun, on the battlefield. The U.N. team discovered an unexploded Iraqi shell, one loaded with mustard gas, with the words EXPAL written on its exterior, and Spanish instructions stamped on the fuses. The Spanish words read, "Para tiempos de armado inferiores a 6 segundos quitar el tornillo visor rojo peligro, Esp MU 09, LOT 83.01." ("For arming time, less than 6 seconds, remove screw. Red dial reading means danger. Type MU 09. Lot 83.01.") Later, EXPAL representatives denied knowingly having sent shells for poison gas to Iraq.

The Iraqis also required aerial shells for bombs. For these, the Iraqis went to Italy. Hussein's agents asked that the shells not be filled with explosives but delivered empty to Iraq.[2] The name of the company involved was S.N.I.A. BPD, a giant Italian firm headquartered in Colliaferro, outside Rome. S.N.I.A.'s contribution was not substantially different from a number of Italian firms competing for Iraqi business, for goods ranging from ships to guns to battlefield vehicles. The sale marked an early stage of S.N.I.A.'s profitable involvement with Iraqi chemical warfare and missile development.

•   •   •

A few chemical warfare experts in a few Western governments took up the task of tracking Iraqi purchases. With the use of satellites and on-the-ground intelligence, they quickly identified one place in Iraq as the center of chemical warfare production. That was a desert plateau some 45 miles northwest of Baghdad. The sky-high cameras mapped a highway trailing north out of Samarra, cutting like a black ribbon through the heart of Iraq's vast desert. The road forked right after about three miles. Another right, twenty miles further, brought you to a sprawling military-style installation. This was S.E.P.P., the State

Establishment for the Production of Pesticides, the vital center of Saddam Hussein's billion dollar chemical weapons arsenal. U.N. reports later referred to the sprawling facility as the Muthanna State Establishment. S.E.P.P. became the cover organization for the purchase of both equipment and chemical raw materials for chemical warfare.

In 1986, BBC-TV employed the services of Spot Image, the French civilian commercial facility, to photograph S.E.P.P. from the skies.[3] The photo showed what appeared to be tiny Iraqi military huts guarding the entrances. SAM-2 missiles were scattered in the surrounding area. Some of them, it was later learned, were dummies. Enclosed inside the perimeter fence were a dozen squat concrete structures. Also visible were a number of storage buildings, looking like low-slung hangars, three hundred feet in length.

A few of the buildings had short chimneys emitting wispy smoke, noxious fumes of waste from nerve agent and poison gas production. Stored in depots around the edge of the facility, in huge containers, were highly toxic substances which constituted Iraq's weapon of last resort. By 1986, Western intelligence experts found S.E.P.P.'s peaceful pretensions to be, in the words of then-BBC reporter Robert Harris, "frankly incredible."

•   •   •

The companies supplying S.E.P.P. formed a Western European telephone book. With hundreds of millions of dollars in construction costs at stake, there was no shortage of bidders for the work, which ranged from civil construction to providing the sensitive production lines where highly toxic materials would be chemically mixed to turn into nerve agents. But the Iraqis, not the foreigners, were the people in charge, the men who successfully built S.E.P.P., controlled the runs of chemicals through the sensitive chemical production lines and got the plant working.

Most firms used by the Iraqis came from the Federal Republic of Germany. They included Karl Kolb, Heberger, Preussag, W.E.T., Hammer, Konrad, and a series of additional companies called in to fill minor roles. Others hailed from countries as diverse as Australia, Poland, Great Britain, and even India. In the words of one of the European engineers with whom I spoke, Bernd Meyer of the Hammer Company, who joined the project in 1984, "the whole world was there."[4]

Work proceeded well. The Europeans on site—there were up to fifty at any one time—were well-paid. Later, those one or two who would speak to reporters claimed ignorance about chemical warfare production at Samarra. They noted that the Iraqis kept Arab and European workers carefully segregated. Most of the foreigners lived at a residential village some six miles south of the production area—a "village," the site of which was partially chosen to avoid toxic drifts, and also for security reasons. The foreigners made the daily commute of about 15 minutes to Samarra accompanied by an Iraqi guard.

The supplier of most of the sensitive production line facilities was the Karl Kolb GmbH company, with home offices back in Dreieich, a leafy suburban office community about ten minutes' taxi ride from Frankfurt International Airport. The company had served as a supplier of laboratory and technical equipment active to Iraq since the mid-1970s. Its small office in Baghdad included one or two German and Iraqi sales personnel and, at one time, a British engineer. Klaus J. Fraenzel was the Karl Kolb Company's head man on-site in Iraq. Very much an extrovert, Fraenzel cut a swath in Baghdad, sometimes hanging out in the bars of the city's luxury hotels. He had been in Baghdad off and on since 1951. Married to an Iraqi woman, he was known in Baghdad as a superb import-exporter with close connections to some top officials inside the government. According to a German engineer who knew him from Baghdad days, Fraenzel "saved Karl Kolb's life. He got the company the contracts for the Iraqi work and he made Kolb a lot of money."

"He was more than very helpful to the Iraqi government, as well as to Karl Kolb," said another of the German experts who knew him.

Talks to set up S.E.P.P. began in 1981 between Fraenzel, representing the Karl Kolb company, and Iraqi authorities. The German's relationships led to a series of contracts worth over 25 million Deutschmarks to Kolb and millions more to companies working with Kolb or sub-contracting jobs from the firm. Shortly, Kolb decided to do business not in its own name but through a subsidiary set up especially to service Iraq, called Pilot Plant. Pilot Plant had the same managers as the Karl Kolb Company and was based in the same Dreieich office near Frankfurt

Airport. Kolb later set up a third company as well, called Lab Consult, to service the Iraqis.

By September, 1981, the Kolb company and the Iraqis signed their first contracts to build up Samarra's chemical facilities. These authorized the establishment of the installations known as "P3" and "P4," according to official papers I have seen in the hands of German prosecutors. Shortly afterwards, contracts for the installations known as "P5" and "P6" were also signed. The Heberger Company, also based in the Frankfurt area, became civil contractors. One of his workers said about the company's boss, Herr Heberger: "He would build anything, even a cow-manure plant, if it were profitable."

As S.E.P.P. took shape, the Iraqis entered into a new deal with Karl Kolb's subsidiary in August, 1982.[5] This was for the production lines known by their semi-official code names as "Ahmed I" and "Ahmed II." Ahmed I and Ahmed II were names that would bedevil Western intelligence services for years. The analysts thought they were special code designations formulated with great care and deception by the Iraqi military. Similar "code names" were applied to other units, such as "Mohammed," "Ani," and "Ghazi." German engineers with whom I spoke later told me that these code names had a simple origin: "Ahmed" was named for the Iraqi engineer in charge of running the sarin plant. "Mohammed" was the name of the fellow running the tabun plant, "Ani" headed up the mustard gas operations, and "Ghazi" was in charge of CS tear gas facilities.

Ahmed I and Ahmed II, to be installed in the buildings known as P1 and P2, included four high-strength hastelloy units. Hastelloy is a high-strength anti-corrosive metal resistant to toxic materials and indispensable in the production of nerve gas. Each of these units was based on an individual 1,000 liter (264 gallon) reactor. The two "Ahmed" plants were the Iraqi facilities for the production of the nerve agent "sarin" and cost $16.8 million DM, or over $10 million at the time. The facility named "Mohammed" went into the building named P9. Its production line, designed for tabun, cost 3.1 million DM, around $2 million. Both tabun and sarin were invented by German scientists back in the mid 1930s and employed similar production techniques and equipment.

The components at "Mohammed" were similar to those at "Ahmed," but featured a 2,000 liter reactor.

"Modi" was an additional unit ordered by the Iraqis in December, 1983, also for tabun. "Ghazi" was the code name for the Iraqi CS tear gas facility, and had stainless steel components, and a 1,000 liter reactor. Other units included one called "Iesa," consisting of two units of hastelloy.

Some 40 German technicians and engineers came to S.E.P.P. to build the series of buildings, each of them identical from the outside, in the first stage of the contract. The main room housed the machines. A control room, separated from the rest of the installation by thick glass, oversaw the facility. Each building had two levels, half below and half above ground, with stairways on the sides leading to gangways on top. With Iraq in the midst of war against Iran, German engineers attributed this to security measures and did not find Iraqi concerns peculiar or obsessive. They understood that all vital Iraqi economic installations had to be protected. "In the beginning it felt good," one of the engineers told a German TV colleague in a confidential background interview that could not be filmed. "We felt like pioneers in the desert."

But the German engineers also learned that posing too many questions to the Iraqis was unproductive. A Heberger engineer became suspicious when the Iraqis with whom he was negotiating wanted the ramp leading underground to be curved almost like an underground parking facility—so it wouldn't lead straight down into the installation. This could protect the facility against a bomb attack with conventional high explosives and might even serve to ward off a poison gas or nerve agent attack by the enemy. "The obvious conclusion was that this was a project with major security implications," the engineer commented.

Building the ramp curved proved to be complicated and expensive. The Heberger Company ended up constructing straight ramps up and down. But they also added four heavy steel doors—one after the other leading down—in each installation to lessen the effects of a direct hit.

At the end of 1982, Karl Kolb personnel arrived with their equipment. Each building "looked like a witch's kitchen," an engineer told me. Kolb employees informed the other Germans they were installing the production line equipment for the pesticide plant. The Kolb men seemed to know what they were doing. Other German technicians and engineers at Samarra were impressed.

In 1983, Kolb and Heberger got a major new order for four buildings—P9, P10, P11, and P12. The new facilities were bigger than the earlier ones, some 45 by 45 feet square, and would be built above ground, making the construction work faster and easier. Though they were more exposed, they were also multi-purpose. Each unit had a quarantine station. The high-strength glass construction inside these installations came from Schott, a Mainz-based company that was one of Germany's most advanced optical manufacturers and producers of Karl Zeiss lenses, well-known to cinematographers.[6] The company responsible for the critical air circulation and air-conditioning systems was the Ludwig Hammer Company from near Frankfurt.

Hammer's man on-site was Bernd Meyer, a stocky 40-year-old technician from Roemerberg, an hour's drive south from Frankfurt Airport. I met Meyer at his home and discussed his service in Iraq. Meyer was first sent to Iraq in 1982 for a three-week period. Then he arrived in Samarra in mid-1984 on a tour of duty that lasted until July, 1987.

In 1984, Mayer told me, major changes occurred at Samarra. The first buildings—P3 to P6—became fully operational. So did P8. A new, stricter atmosphere prevailed. "We had two identity cards," Mayer explained. "I had to show the first one at Gate 1. Then Gate 1 contacted Gate 2. If I had permission, I then went to Gate 2 where I exchanged my first identity card for a second one."

Several hundred Iraqi security personnel arrived in Samarra that year. They closed off the area and tightened up security. Photography was prohibited. The Iraqis restricted foreigners in their movements and, in particular, forbade them to go near the plants when production was under way. Where individual Iraqis had once been cordial and sometimes talkative, by 1984 they maintained a more discrete, and silent, relationship. They no longer visited informally during off-hours. Iraqi officials placed a red Chevrolet manned by two watchful Iraqis just outside the residential camp. The red Chevrolet became a familiar and ever-present sight to the foreigners.

Mayer later provided German police with a signed document recounting his experiences in Samarra. According to both this document and my own interview with him, his work was carried out in the four project buildings he knew as P9, P10, P11, and P12, as well as in the office buildings and canteens of S.E.P.P. Mayer installed the air-conditioning, plumbing, and the scrubbers in each of these installations, and also replaced the air-conditioning in P3. He got a whiff of what he called "hydrocyanic acid" from P7 and P8 in August, 1985. It had the smell of "almonds." He got sick and couldn't work for two days. Another time he developed what he first thought might be a sun allergy. Spots and patches appeared all over his body—including unusual marks he'd never seen before on the right cheek of his posterior and on his forehead. He went on vacation back home in Germany shortly after and consulted a doctor. The doctor wisely warned him to stay away from toxic fumes at chemical installations. He decided he would not work near that bunker again. He told his German bosses who agreed he could follow doctor's orders.

Once, he jotted down the names of chemicals he saw in bins near one of the bunkers. As he recalled it a few years later, these included thionylchloride, thiodiglycol and possibly diethanolamine, chemicals required in the production of mustard gas and that had been supplied to the Iraqis by several Dutch companies. "I think it was material imported from Holland," he told me.

The Iraqis added an additional measure of security towards the end of 1986. They posted guards, not just at the gates, but at the entrance to each building. The Iraqis also built camouflage structures throughout S.E.P.P. These decoys looked much like P3 to P6 from the ground and exactly like those buildings from the air. In reality, they were mounds of wood and sand. The same trick was used by the Iraqis to camouflage their missile sites during Desert Storm, when many of the sites bombed to bits by allied and U.S. warplanes were dummies.

The Iraqi soldiers mounted SAM missiles around the S.E.P.P. installations, though far from the production area. Mayer saw anti-aircraft and artillery pieces, some of them camouflaged, positioned in selected sites. The Iraqis forbade the Europeans access to the northwest area. This was where a residential village for Egyptian and other Arab workers, referred to by the Germans as the "camp of the Egyptians," was located. Later, the Europeans concluded that the Arabs were the ones working directly with toxic materials. The Iraqi guards, seeking to discourage relationships between the Arabs and Europeans that could lead to security lapses, kept the Egyptians rigidly segregated from the Europeans.

As the plants became operational, problems emerged, stemming from the use of highly toxic materials. Mayer and other Germans said that many of the Europeans entering or working around P3 developed nose-bleeds. The pipes in that facility had to be replaced. Mayer recalled that a pump from P4 totally disintegrated. As he remembered it, that is approximately when the Iraqis and their German helpers began to bring in and install hastelloy-based replacements.

Another time, some chemical materials from one of the plants dripped onto the asphalt floor. A German technician described the effect to Bernd Meyer, who told me: "The asphalt dissolved like sugar in coffee." Maintenance visits had to be coordinated and approved weeks in advance to coordinate with production schedules. The Iraqis parked ambulances at the front of the plant.

The foreigners noticed packs of dogs wandering from place to place throughout the installation. Meyer and the other technicians heard a rumor that the Iraqis were breeding the dogs for experimentation, to test out their poison gas and nerve agent. One day, the dogs all disappeared. Later that day, technicians discovered P5 was completely contaminated. One of the Germans who had been inside P5 said he thought that dogs were being killed by poison gas in an adjacent room or building. However, he had not seen the killing "live" himself.

In 1984, the German government received information that Samarra was a chemical weapons installation. Embassy officials in Baghdad invited their compatriots working at S.E.P.P. to drop by for "friendly discussions," in the words of one of the workers. A few engineers and technicians went. The German officials warned their nationals that there were strong grounds to believe S.E.P.P. was being used to produce poison gas, and cautioned the workers about staying on. With pressure developing from the government, the boss of one firm, Heberger, gave his workers the choice of staying in Iraq or leaving. A few left for a brief time, then returned. All eventually stayed. German officials with whom I spoke in 1990 contended it was not legally in their power to expel German citizens from Iraq, or to forbid them from working at the suspected chemical warfare installation.

The Europeans based at Samarra in those critical years recall that, generally, they had quite a good time at S.E.P.P., which were years well-spent. The attraction was money. Mid-range salaries came to some 4,500 Deutschmark net, about $3,000 monthly at the time. The Iraqis provided the housing and all meals. Provisions on-site were free-of-charge. A particular enticement for the Germans was that the earnings were not taxed by either Germany or Iraq. Salaries could go straight into accounts back home. Many of the workers used the time to accumulate savings and set themselves up for life.

In March, 1984, the Iraqis launched a major chemical weapons offensive against the Iranians. Several hundreds of the Persian foe reportedly died. Most of them were soldiers, a few were civilians.

The German Embassy called in German engineers and technicians working at S.E.P.P. for additional warnings about their suspicions. But there was no hard proof that Samarra was the source. The workers had their own priorities. Not one among them—and this includes non-Germans as well—is known to have voluntarily returned to Europe for reasons of conscience. None refused his salary. Not one of them asked the Iraqis inconvenient questions or, so far as is known, any questions at all. It was better to play dumb. To a man they continued to prosper—and kept their mouths, as well as their eyes and ears, tightly shut.

CHAPTER FIVE

Saddam's Hunt Begins

*"I go home at night, I take a drink, and I think of all
the death those materials can make...."*

Ben Hilbers, Dutch detective

THE WEST'S CHEMICAL INDUSTRIES proved easy pickings for Iraq's chemical warfare agents. Operating discreetly, Saddam Hussein's buying teams scoured Europe and the United States in late 1982 and throughout 1983 and much of 1984, to place the orders for chemical raw materials that Iraq required to get S.E.P.P. and other smaller factories going. The Iraqis wanted to amass enough material for years of operation before anyone noticed.

The Iraqis placed a number of their early orders through Dutch agents. In the mid-70s, the activities of an obscure Pakistani metallurgist, A.Q. Khan, who became known as "the spy who stole the bomb for Islam," caused a major scandal when it was revealed that he had appropriated the centrifuge secrets of the Dutch-German-British nuclear plant at Almelo. Most important, he had gained access to supplier lists and technical specifications. His activities provided Pakistan with the basis for its ultra-centrifuge program, giving it the capability to manufacture enriched uranium for atomic weapons. Beginning in 1983, the

Dutch faced a second major potential embarassment—this time in the supply of raw materials for the production of highly toxic nerve agents and mustard gas in Iraq.

The Iraqis' first stop in Holland was the neatly laid out Dutch seaside city of Terneusen. Terneusen's factories seem to merge with the sea at Wester Schelde, just to the north of Belgium, where the small Dutch city is located. The area is thick with industry. Oil depots sprout from the ground like giant mushrooms. Wisps of smoke curl out of the stacks of industrial chimneys. At the center of town is a modern shopping mall with quaint Dutch restaurants and streets blocked off from traffic.

The company that had agreed to supply Iraq was called K.B.S., and it was not a manufacturer but a trading company. Its offices were in an oblong office complex just outside the town center. A strapping, ruddy six-foot-three former Dutch Army officer, J.A. Bravenboer, headed the company. His number two and commercial manager was a Jordanian, M.L. Sakhel. Sakhel did most of the travelling to the company's clients in the Middle East, including Iraq, and had established a warm relationship with his Iraqi customers. He was out of town when I met Bravenboer.

Bravenboer was a bit nervous when we met but eager to set the record straight. He said he was glad that a journalist had come to check out the facts directly with him. He displayed some contradictory concerns both about chemical warfare and his very practical desire to stay off Iraqi blacklists—the same kind that the Iraqis drew up for companies dealing with Israel—if he refused to service Iraqi chemical programs or somehow insulted them. Still, he declared, he wanted to clear matters up and tell the "true story."

Bravenboer's small trading company had been a regular supplier to the Iraqis from the mid-70s, originally dealing with the Chemical Importation and Distribution State Enterprise in Baghdad, known as A.C.M.A. A typical order from A.C.M.A.—one that Bravenboer showed me was placed in November, 1976—was for 250 liters of ammonia solution, small amounts of trisodium phosphate and sodium hydroxide, and 1,500 liters of toluene.

Bravenboer said that serious contacts between his company and the Iraqi State Establishment for the Production of Pesticides, or S.E.P.P.,

A.C.M.A.'s successor, were made in late 1982. Iraqi buyers visited Terneusen in 1983. Among them was the man who signed many of S.E.P.P.'s orders to the company, Dr. Al Ani.[1] Bravenboer refused to identify other Iraqis with whom he had dealt, a violation of commercial discretion that could cost him business. These visits resulted in orders for a number of chemical raw materials.

Shortly, the quantities involved in Iraqi orders jumped dramatically. Included were large quantities of thiodiglycol. This chemical is the key raw material for the production of mustard gas. Said British chemical warfare expert Julian Perry Robinson about its importance, "You add some spirits of salt to it, shake it up, and you've got mustard gas." In late 1983, K.B.S. supplied some 500 tons of thiodiglycol to Iraq, purchased from a subsidiary of the multinational corporation, Phillips Petroleum, located in nearby Tessenderloo, Belgium.

Reports of poison gas usage were already coming in from the Gulf battlefield, but the Western press, denied access to the area and generally wary of a propaganda campaign incited by the fundamentalist-led Ayatollah's regime in Iran, stubbornly refused to give them much credence. The Iranians, victims of the attacks, flew tens of the wounded to Europe where they could receive high quality hospital care and also be put on display for Western photographers and TV cameramen. Blistered and scarred Iranian men and women in hospital garb peered out from their charbas of suffering. There seemed little doubt that poison gas and nerve agents were becoming an integral part of the Gulf War.

In February, 1984, the Iraqis had ordered over 50 tons each of monochlorobenzene and ethyl alcohol from K.B.S.[2] Both are ingredients in the production of the nerve agent, tabun. K.B.S. made its purchases from major chemical firms in West Germany and Czechoslovakia and supplied the materials to Iraq.

About a month later, K.B.S. received a gigantic order. This one set the alarm bells ringing in Bravenboer's head. The order was for another 500 tons of thiodiglycol, and also massive quantities of other potentially dangerous materials: 250 tons of phosphorous oxychloride, or POCL3, a vital component in producing the deadly nerve agent tabun; and 200 tons each of two precursors, trimethyl phosphite and potassium fluoride, for the even more lethal nerve agent sarin. Similarly large orders were received for dimethylamine, an ingredient for tabun; sodium fluoride, which can help manufacture sarin; and isopropanol, also used in producing sarin. Significantly, the Iraqi orders were noticeably lacking in what chemical industry representatives pointed to as purely pesticide-oriented raw materials—such as toluene, nitrobenzene, or vinylchlorides.

Only one item was actually banned for sale without explicit permission. That was POCL3. Bravenboer told me that when he saw POCL3 on the Iraqi shopping list delivered to his firm he got nervous. He had read about the allegations of Iraqi chemical weapons use and he became suspicious that the enormous quantities ordered by the Iraqi agents could be diverted to nerve agent and mustard gas production.

Bravenboer checked with people he knew at the T.N.O. laboratory used by Dutch governmental authorities in Delft. A friend of Bravenboer—an expert in chemistry—studied the orders and remarked, "There's enough there in those orders to cover the entire Middle East in pesticides—or poison gas and nerve agents." His friend added that the Iraqi shopping list would keep Iraq in poison gas and nerve agent production for a good five years.

Bravenboer said he then went to officials in the Dutch Foreign Ministry in the Hague for advice. They told him that the materials ordered from his company could indeed be used for poison gas and nerve agents. Bravenboer related that he then refused to supply some of these chemicals to the Iraqis, beginning in the spring of 1984. Dutch export controls included thiodiglycol and trimethyl phosphite, though not yet potassium fluoride or dimethylamine. Phosphorus oxychloride, the renowned POCL3, was definitely not to be supplied.

Bravenboer felt he was walking a tightrope between the Dutch government and his Iraqi clients. He checked around to see which companies had the chemicals, but he stalled on filling the order. He told the Iraqis that he was having trouble obtaining authorization from the Dutch government.

Dr. Al Ani, representing S.E.P.P., tried to assure Bravenboer in writing that the raw materials would be used for civilian purposes. In a telex dated the 20th of March, 1984, Al Ani claimed that the long list was for peaceful products, among them: rubber, drugs, pesticides, fertilizers, paper, vegetable oil, batteries, dry cells and petrochemicals. "So continue with your tradition of supply [to] the Iraq chemical industries sector," Al Ani urged.

The Iraqis believed that Bravenboer would play the game by Iraqi rules and provide them, as before, with their vital raw materials. But, by March, Bravenboer was responding to Dutch and not Iraqi governmental pressure. "For us it was an easy decision to cancel, once we knew the facts," Bravenboer contended. He faced two problems. The first was not to insult the always sensitive Iraqis, who were his best customers. He wanted them to stay happy and he did not want to risk getting on a future Iraqi blacklist. The second was to cancel his own orders, many already placed, with chemical company suppliers.

He said that he succeeded on both fronts. Together with Dutch officials, Bravenboer skirted the issue in replying to the Iraqis. He told them the Dutch government would not approve his selling chemical raw materials if the destination were Iraq or Iran. Though he personally wanted to maintain good relations with Iraq, he asserted, he placed responsibility for the cancellation and non-fulfilment of orders on the Dutch government.

He had one fierce argument with a supplier, the Alcolac Company of Baltimore, Maryland. That company, said Bravenboer, wanted to get paid whether the order was cancelled or not. Bravenboer stood his ground. In 1986 and '87 Alcolac made its own lucrative deals directly with the Iraqis. The company was charged and convicted by the U.S. government for illegally shipping thiodyglycol to the warring gulf countries. (The company was non-partisan in its supply and sold the same kinds of chemical substances to Iran, too.) Other sub-suppliers appreciated the perils of hostile relations with the Dutch and other governments, and went along with the cancellations.

Bravenboer's version is that he backed out of the deal based on his own initiative. Bas Ter Haar of the Dutch Foreign Ministry offered a slightly different chronology. He told the BBC, for the television documentary on which I worked, that his government received a warning from "Western intelligence" in the spring of 1984: Three Dutch companies were supplying chemicals to Iraq that were being used by the Iraqis to make chemical weapons. The Dutch government then took the lead and intervened with the companies in question, including K.B.S. The Dutch authorities, like other Western European suppliers, had only general guidelines in place for their chemical industry proscribing the most dangerous chemical raw materials. Apparently, as I learned from chemical experts, the West hadn't wanted to put Third World countries on the alert as to which chemicals they might require, and the problem lay dormant. With the use of chemical weapons in the Gulf confirmed by the U.N. commission's visit to the battlefield in the spring, the Dutch first promulgated detailed regulations for chemical weapons exports in April, 1984, and expanded the list of raw materials in November.

Bravenboer had justification for worrying whether the Iraqis would stay customers. Back at Sa'ad headquarters in Baghdad and S.E.P.P. at Samarra, the Iraqis waited impatiently for their goods. By chance, the Iraqi Ambassador invited Bravenboer to the July 17th, 1984, Independence Day reception at the Iraqi embassy. Bravenboer made a special point of explaining his problem there to the Iraqi Ambassador who, he said, was "very understanding," more so than the officials in Baghdad.

Bravenboer had a feeling that there could be a lot more orders on the way—he hoped for items not on a blacklist. As it turned out, Bravenboer never broke the law and did not irretrievably place his Iraqi business in jeopardy. He continued as a favored supplier of chemical products and raw materials to Iraq. Later that same year, K.B.S.' commercial manager, M.L. Sakhel, visited the Middle East, and the company supplied the Iraqis with substantial quantities of two chemical raw materials that never made it onto the Dutch government's proscribed list of raw materials: some 10 tons of dimethylamine HCL, a precursor of tabun, and a similar quantity of isopropanol, a sarin precursor. His company also supplied small amounts of items that could be used by the Iraqis for experimentation in the production of psycho-chemicals but were not on any banned or warning list and were totally legal.

Of course, with all that business at stake, how could Bravenboer be expected to know everything?

•   •   •

The route from Terneusen links up with a superhighway in Belgium and continues northward towards the Dutch capital in the Hague. Early in the winter of 1986, I went to see the officials in charge of the economic investigation unit and had a chance encounter with the detective on the case, Ben Hilbers, who walked into the room after the more senior officials had departed. He is the kind of guy journalists don't always get to see. A wavy-haired and genial family man in his early 30s, he headed the break-through investigation into chemical weapons sales, visiting companies and then raiding them, examining papers, and coordinating information in Holland, France, Italy and elsewhere. Hilbers was profoundly disturbed by his investigation into chemical raw materials shipments to Iraq. "I go home at night, I take a drink, and I think of all the death those materials can make," he confessed when we had a moment alone together. "So I keep doing it, and I've worked hard on this case."

Many of those middle-level officials dealing with European supplies of chemical warfare agents to the Middle East were detached from the realities of far-off warfare. Not Hilbers. He internalized the war's meaning. He kept reminding himself of the consequences of these materials falling into Iraqi hands. Some men were murdering others with Dutch-supplied raw materials and he felt a personal responsibility, even anger and outrage.

When I later tried to contact Hilbers by telephone, Dutch authorities cut us off and forbade me from talking with him. Governments never like journalists talking to people who handle raw data. I met several other officials in Holland but none of Hilbers' quality.

From the Hague I drove eastward, skirting Amsterdam to get to Arnhem, a small city on the border. A company in Arnhem called Melchemie received sizable Iraqi chemical orders. It operated out of a modest downtown office near the center of the city.

Melchemie, like K.B.S., was a trading company and a regular supplier of raw materials to the Iraqis. The company's 1984 business with Iraq was on the order of ten million dollars, a sum that represented a substantial part of its chemical division's business. The company traced its commercial relationships with Iraq to 1969, and claimed to have delivered materials to all important Iraqi state organizations since that time.

As an indication of Iraq's importance in the company's commerce, Melchemie opened an office in Baghdad in the early 1970s headed by an Iraqi employee.

By the time I got to Arnhem, the company was under investigation by Dutch authorities for illegal exports. The Dutch prosecutor, a Mr. Tiedkin, discussed some of the details with me. He showed me an Iraqi chemical materials order to the company but would not allow me to photocopy it. He was a decent enough man. I remember my embarrassment when he caught me trying to sneak the order out of his office to photocopy it.

That start was inauspicious. I called Melchemie from the court building, asked for the general manager, I.O. Zandkamp, and got him on the line by informing the secretary I was calling from the Arnhem prosecutor's office, where I was visiting. When he came on the line, he agreed to see me within the hour.

"We are just traders," I.O. Zandkamp said during our meeting in Melchemie company offices. "We have no technical ideas. The customer can use chemicals as they want, that is not of interest to us."

Zandkamp acknowledged that S.E.P.P. and the Iraqi Ministry of Industry were regular customers. I was not able to obtain a precise list of raw materials Melchemie sold to S.E.P.P. in 1982, 1983 or the first months of 1984. But on March 9th, 1984, Melchemie received a huge order—for quantities of chemical raw materials even greater than those to be supplied by K.B.S. The order from the Iraqi Ministry of Industry, State Organization for Chemical Industries, flimsily designated the intended uses of the materials and looked like this:

Engineering Plastics/Insecticides Thionyl Chloride ....1000 Tons
Etching Glass/Petrochemicals KF/KHF2 ....20 tons
Plasticisers POCL 3 ....60 tons
Fluorinated Plastics HF ....5 tons
Textile dyes/Pharmaceuticals Pyradine ....15 tons
Safety Matches/Pesticides Phosporus ....100 tons
Pharmaceuticals 0-Chlorobenzaldehyde ....30 tons
Organic Solvents/Isopropyl-Alcohol ....150 tons

British expert Julian Perry Robinson noted that "the list is strongly suggestive of chemical warfare agent production. In that case, two different types of nerve gas: the phosphorous oxychloride, suggestive of tabun; other ones, highly suggestive of sarin. The presence of the potassium fluoride would, I think, rule out application of those chemicals in pesticides."

This was a shopping list for chemical weapons. The civilian end uses mentioned by the Iraqis were either untrue or subject to doubt. The real Iraqi use of the listed materials would be as follows:

Thionyl chloride (with 1,000 tons) could be and probably was used for the making of mustard gas. Additionally, it would be useful in the production of the sophisticated nerve agent, sarin. One thousand tons was enough to feed Iraq's chemical weaponry production for several years.

KF/KHF2 was for sarin. Likewise with HF and isopropyl alchohol. O-Chlorobenzaldehyde is a key ingredient in making CS, or tear gas, another essential element of the Iraqi chemical warfare program.

Only one item in the order was unconnected, apparently, to chemical warfare. That was phosphorous. It could be used in certain kinds of bombs but also for kitchen matches. The Iraqis ordered enough to light a fire in every stove in Mesopotamia.

Though regulations were later tightened up by Western governments, all the raw materials on the shopping list were legal at the time of the order save one. POCL3, phosphorous oxychloride, the same chemical material the Iraqis tried to get from Bravenboer, was on the banned list of the Dutch government. This was because it was well-known as an essential ingredient in the production of tabun.

Melchemie promptly filled everything they legally could in the order—all but the POCL3—shipped it, and made a nice profit. It was another case of capitalist enterprise versus a well-meaning but lethargic bureaucracy that had yet to respond to a problem. The company's later estimates of how much they made and those of governmental investigators varied widely. The company said it profited a few thousand Dutch guilders; official Dutch investigators told me that they believed the real number was closer to a few million.

The most lucrative part of the order was POCL3. How to deliver it required crystal-clear thinking followed by clever foot work. Here's what Melchemie did, as reconstructed from my conversations with I.O. Zandkamp, general manager of Melchemie, Ben Hilbers, the detective on the case, several of his superiors at the Dutch government economic control unit, and the local prosecutor in Arnhem.

Bas Weijman, the company official responsible for exports in the company's chemical division, first contacted a variety of European companies, among them Bayer in Germany, to get the order filled. The major companies refused to send raw materials to either Iran or Iraq. He then tried firms in the Soviet Union, India, and elsewhere, still without success. The worldwide alert in effect had its influence.

Weijman informed Iraq that he had some problems placing the order. In a May, 1984 letter, S.E.P.P. replied to Melchemie in writing. "We know this product is listed in your country and therefore we suggest you to buy from Italy [sic]."

Now the conspiracy developed. Further communication with S.E.P.P. about the Italian route was mainly by telephone. What was written was later seized by Dutch governmental investigators.

On July 2nd, Melchemie apologized to S.E.P.P. for the delay in finding the raw material. Weijman wrote, "You certainly know that the products in question are subject to obtain export license from the government in the exporting country. This explains the unusual delay in answering to your enquiries and to request you to understand [sic]."

Shortly, the Melchemie sales executive hit paydirt with a division of the giant Italian firm, Montedison, in Milan, a company with which Melchemie officials claimed to have had a decade-long association. Melchemie's official contact was Enrique Gagliardi at the Ausidet division.

On October 10, 1984, Weijman flew to Milan for a one day meeting. He booked a room at the American Hotel in Milan. In addition to Gagliardi, a second contact man at Ausidet, a Dr. Michelis, was involved in the negotiations.

With the embargo on Gulf War military sales already in effect, the Italian government had the same basic list of proscribed exports as did the Dutch. But the list didn't bother Ausidet at all. In fact, as Enrique Gagliardi told me by telephone from Milan, speaking bad French, he and Ausidet didn't even know about it. Gagliardi said he was an experienced salesman. But he contended he and his colleagues at Ausidet had no idea that POCL3 was banned, and no knowledge at all that it could be used as a key precursor for the production of nerve agent.

Ausidet and Melchemie speedily concluded an agreement. Ausidet would order the raw materials from a French chemical company, Artochem. The materials would be shipped from Artochem, by truck, to Venice, Italy. From there they would travel by cargo vessel to Iraq.

The plan was clear. No proscribed materials would ever enter Holland. The role of Melchemie would be deliberately underplayed. Dutch governmental regulations would be neatly circumvented. But to protect themselves, Melchemie asked for, and got, assurances in writing from S.E.P.P. that the material was to be used for peaceful purposes. A May letter from S.E.P.P. to Melchemie stated that the potentially lethal POCL3 "was needed by one of our cement companies."

Melchemie company director Zandkamp explained in the interview I had with him that, "If it were guaranteed that the product is for peaceful purposes, then our opinion is we are free to deliver." His claim of innocence through ignorance was a preparation for the upcoming legal battle.

Were Melchemie officials aware that POCL3 was a tricky cargo, the delivery of which would be illegal? The extent of their knowledge is indicated in a letter Melchemie put in writing to S.E.P.P. on October 16th: "As we have no export permit from our government, we suggest that the financing for this product is done in the same way as we agreed for order KHF2 and KF [potassium hydrogen fluoride and potassium fluoride]. This is the only way to ship POCL3 without complications."

Potassium hydrogen fluoride and potassium fluoride are also nerve agent precursors. Like many other raw materials connected to chemical weaponry, they weren't on the banned Dutch government list. Still, Melchemie wanted to make sure the payment would take place outside the borders of Holland. The money for the order was to be deposited into a West German bank account.

The shipment of POCL would get to Venice and then be sent in six separate consignments of ten tons each, from Italy to Turkey and then by land to Baghdad. The first shipment was loaded onto the S.S. Aetos and left Venice on December 20th, en route to Mersin, Turkey. The Aetos returned shortly and carried a second shipment a week later. The two containers were then moved by truck, arriving in Baghdad on January 5th and January 7th, 1985, respectively, according to receipts of delivery I saw in the possession of the Dutch investigators.[3]

By February, the Dutch government got wind of suspicious activity and began to track Melchemie. Officials swiftly gathered enough evidence to justify a raid. They sought permission from higher authorities and got it.

On the morning of February 26th, 1985, fifteen Dutch agents staged a lightning raid on Melchemie company offices in Arnhem and the homes of three key company officials, including sales executive Bas Weijman, seizing documents relating to the illegal trade. The action effectively put a halt to the shipments to Iraq and interrupted Melchemie's commercial contract with the Iraqis and also with Montedison in Italy.

The reaction from Baghdad came less than two weeks later, on March 9th. Never ready to take a rebuff lying down, the Iraqis frothed with surface outrage over the unexpected intervention. The Iraqis threatened the Dutch government with drastic action. "In case your government not stopping actions against our country, blocking our economy and our good reputation, we foresee serious consequences for our bilateral relationship between our two countries," the Iraqis wrote to Melchemie. The Iraqis also sent copies of the letter to the Dutch Embassy in Baghdad and the Dutch Foreign Ministry in the Hague.

The company asked the Iraqis for further written assurances promising a civilian application and barring military use of the POCL3, and even asking for the recall of the shipment. The Iraqis, under pressure and with their honor challenged, suggested that they return the goods.

A curious exchange of letters followed. Weijman of Melchemie wrote Dr. Al Ani of S.E.P.P.: "We appreciate your sympathizing with us by offering your willingness to have returned the two containers of POCL3 which are as per your sayings still in the port of Aqaba. We would appreciate to know at what conditions you can put them at our disposal on basis fob Aqaba or candf italian port....[*sic*]"

The letter was transparently a deception. The goods were never in the Jordanian port of Akaba at all. They had been delivered via Mersin, Turkey. The Dutch authorities had in their possession signed receipts—both from Turkey and Iraq.

A few months later, the Iraqis ostensibly returned the goods to Italy. Dutch governmental investigators visiting Italy doubted the same shipment was returned. They didn't trust the work of Italian customs authorities, pointing out that only a quantity check was made on the returned goods. No one in Italy had ever checked the container itself.

"It's all a storm in a glass of water," Zandkamp told me in Arnhem. Melchemie, he said, had suffered financial loss: "We're no longer invited to bid on projects in different countries," Zandkamp complained. "We've lost between three and five million dollars in business.

"Anyway, in our opinion it's a bit hypocritical that the Dutch authorities are so eager on these listed products," he added. "All over the world there are many producers, and you can't close the market."

Only one company in Holland (Monchy) refused to have much to do with the Iraqis. Otherwise, the Iraqis got on fine, benefitting from the leniency displayed by the Dutch court and, more indirectly, the world community that refused to outrightly condemn Iraqi actions.

Melchemie got a bad name both in Holland and elsewhere for its dealings. Though the conspiracy was clear, the Arnhem judge let the plotters off with a slap on the wrist—a fine of some 100,000 Dutch gilders, about $40,000 at the time, for their schemes of economic evasion. There was no fine for the most outrageous aspect of Melchemie's provision, the supply of POCL3 to Iraq at a time when there were already battlefield reports of the use of nerve gas against Iran. The judge ruled that this supply of POCL3 had come not from Holland but from a second country, Italy, and had purportedly been returned to the suppliers. Therefore, Melchemie did not bear legal responsibility before Dutch courts for delivery.

The rest of the massive order from Melchemie arrived safely in Iraq and was transported down to S.E.P.P. Good detective work by Hilbers and a green light from the economic powers enabled the Dutch goverment to interrupt the flow and stop the perpetrators. Zandkamp of Melchemie appeared righteous when he complained about the fuss. He didn't like being singled out. "Why should Holland set an example— and why should Melchemie be the one to suffer?"

Why? No special reason. If the Iraqis couldn't find the ingredients in Holland, they might find them elsewhere. Or they would make their purchases through intermediaries. Melchemie's attitude—and its excuse—was the same as that of many other suppliers. The truth is that Melchemie hardly suffered at all while Iraq, aided by supplies from Melchemie and similar firms, took decisive strides forward in its quest for self-sufficient chemical warfare production.

CHAPTER SIX

1984

"The Iranian enemy is an insect. The Iraqi army shall
take great pleasure in using an insecticide to wipe
them out."

Major General Maher Abdul Rashid, Iraqi Army, 1984

1984 was a crucial year in one respect not foreseen by George Orwell.
It was the year that the Iraqis began to use toxic agents in abundance.
Chemical weapons came into their own as a force in modern military
and political affairs.

In the spring, a U.N. investigating commission was sent to the Gulf.
Its multi-national members wandered through the battlefields looking
for evidence to determine whether Iranian allegations about poison gas
use were true. The unit analyzed dirt samples and one or two unexploded bombs. The members concluded that they could definitely report
the use of mustard gas. With somewhat less certainty, they could also
report the possible use of tabun. The experts sent their report to the
Secretary General, who issued it to U.N. members. Many representatives privately deplored this barbaric revival of a means of warfare that
had marked an earlier part of the twentieth century. Even so, there is a
difference between privately deploring an act and outright condemnation of it on the stage of the world.

The Iraqis' public stance in response to the carefully-hedged wording of the U.N. team's conclusions was classic Orwellian doublespeak. In 1984 (and as late as May, 1988) Iraqi representatives consistently denied that their forces were using poison gas—even as they were manufacturing both mustard gas and nerve agent in secret desert factories and using these substances to kill people. The Iraqi denials soothed the consciences of Western governmental sympathizers who preferred a victory for Iraq to one for Ayatollah Khomeini's Iran. It enabled the Iraqis to continue their policy of realpolitik, deploying whatever battlefield weapons would kill and terrorize the maximum number of Iranians and their Kurdish allies. The U.N., with the tacit consent of the West, issued no formal censure.

But, occasionally, the shell of obfuscation got shattered. In an informal statement issued in Baghdad in 1984, a hitherto little-known Iraqi general, the commander of Iraq's powerful Third Corps, Maher Abdul Rashid, speaking in typically metaphorical Arabic, advocated the use of poison gas and nerve agent. His language was the kind that, while not direct, had crystal-like clarity for his audience in the Middle East. The Iranian enemy was a "foreign pest," Major General Rashid declared. And since the Iranians were only "insects," the Iraqi army "shall take great pleasure in using an insecticide to wipe them out."

The insecticide, of course, was nerve agent. General Rashid's carefully chosen words justified Iraqi planes spraying Iranian troops and Kurdish villagers with the two kinds of nerve agents they were manufacturing: tabun and sarin. Al Rashid's oratorical flourish was a war cry reflecting the Iraqi regime's true attitude, not only about the use of chemical weapons, but about the value of human life. Iraq's unabashed willingness to use poison gas in battle changed the context of chemical weapons proliferation. Rashid's candid admission pointed to a danger faced by a somnolent world community.

Western countries made their own discrete moves to slow the chemical weapons traffic. Governments in North America, Europe, Japan and Australia expanded their list of key chemical raw materials that needed to be watched and required special licenses or permissions for export to the Middle East. But, while Western countries did not want to be Iraq's blatant accomplices in poison gas use, Iraq was a powerful, wealthy nation, a member in good standing of the Third World club, a prominent leader of O.P.E.C., the oil exporters' organization, a leading Arab country, and above all, a superb market. With the war dragging on, more goods could be sold, profits could be made, and there was a limit to how far the West would go in pushing its companies to stop the chemical weapons traffic.

· · ·

1984, the year that most signified the spread of chemical weapons, also almost saw a breakthrough in halting its manufacture. The quest to ban chemical weaponry had long since become a regular part of the work at the on-going Conference on Disarmament held in Geneva, Switzerland. Through the years, Soviet and American negotiators made some progress on the issue. Efforts to more effectively control the spread of chemical weaponry by creating a Chemical Weapons Convention had begun in the 1960s, and intensified under the leadership of U.S. President Richard Nixon. But, by the early 1980s, no agreement had been signed. Practical difficulties in regulating the chemical industry and the reluctance of most states to open up their chemical industries to foreign inspection inhibited an internationally enforcable ban on the production of chemical weaponry. (The treaty finally was completed and signed in 1992.)

On April 18, 1984, the United States tried to break the deadlock at the Conference on Disarmament talks in Geneva. The U.S. initiative was bold but had an element of the surreal. The smartly tailored Vice President of the United States, George Bush, making a personal appearance, had a 66-page draft treaty on chemical weaponry tucked in his briefcase. Speaking from his seat to the crowded room, Bush, though never a great orator, spoke cogently and articulately. He called upon the world to resolve that "the growth in the number of the most dreaded weapons of modern warfare must not simply be slowed; it must be reversed. In the matter before us—chemical weapons—they must be banned, totally banned."

Bush, in strongly affirming American policy to outlaw chemical weapons, suggested a radical path: he proclaimed American support for full-scope challenge inspections of his, or any other nation's, chemical facilities, including production lines. He said the United States was ready to open its factories if other countries would do the same. "Let's face reality," the Vice President said. "Chemical weapons are not difficult to hide and they're not difficult to produce in a clandestine manner. Many states have the capacity to do this. We can rid the world of these weapons only if we make it impossible for anyone, for ourselves, to do such things without detection."

Bush's words sounded an alarm about chemical weapons in an impressive way but the event that people remembered most is not what he said but what happened when a cameraman dropped his camera from the public gallery. In the words of an observer, "half a dozen sober-suited men around Bush suddenly whipped out handguns."

The American Vice President's speech drew a cautious, though not entirely negative, reaction from the Soviets. The head of the Soviet delegation at the Geneva talks, Viktor L. Issraelyan, said he had doubts about America's "political will" to ban lethal chemical weapons. But while professing skepticism, he promised that the Soviets would seriously study the American proposal; rhetoric was one thing but actually achieving concrete arrangements another. The Novosti news agency was more critical of Bush, claiming the U.S. proposals meant "asking nations voluntarily to sanction intelligence activities by the other side on their territory.... In reality the U.S. intention is to torpedo the possibility of an agreement."

Was the U.S. Administration bluffing, possibly trying to sanitize its image after Congress had recently refused to sanction the U.S. Army's own chemical weapons modernization program? Bush's proposals received minimal press pickup at home where they weren't taken very seriously. The little reported was concise and, in at least one particular case, caustic. Columnist Mary McGrory, an old Washington hand who relished in excoriating President Ronald Reagan's policies, didn't bother to couch her language in diplomatic niceties: "What is it, a cloud, a UFO? No, it's a dove. It's Ronald Reagan making his maiden campaign flight as a peace candidate."

McGrory called the proposal "vintage Reagan arms control," taking care to explain what she meant: "That is, it is a fishy proposition, to be sold by a suspect salesman and wrapped around a scheme to make more of the weapons that the treaty being sought is supposed to reduce." Noting that Bush only a year before had cast the tie-breaking vote to push a bill authorizing the production of nerve agent through the Senate, McGrory remarked that picking Bush to go to Geneva is "in the great Reagan tradition of picking a negotiatior whose record suggests that he is only kidding as he opens his samples case.... Just on the face of it, he is not a fanatic in the cause of ending chemical warfare."

On the face of it, Bush's lofty words at Geneva, addressed first and foremost to the Soviets, were impressive. He referred to the future safety of the world's children, whether they lived in Vladivostock or Leningrad or Peoria, Illinois, or Paris or London or Caracas or Belgrade. "Every single family, a child if he knows about it, is scared to death of chemical weapons.... We come here trying to address ourselves to perhaps the most fundamental question on arms existing in the world today—that is, how do we, as civilized, rational people, eliminate, ban in entirety in a verifiable way, all chemical weapons from the face of the earth...."

Bush may have sounded sincere but his geography was unwittingly off. As the Vice President spoke, the main danger in the spread of chemical weapons technology lay not in the conflict between East and West, but in its creeping advance down the North-South political axis. Specifically, the peril lay in that area to the southeast of Europe and the south of the Soviet Union called the Middle East. His message lacked bite in that he ignored the proliferation that had already occurred and the chemical warfare in progress. Iraqis were dousing Iranian soldiers and civilians with noxious and toxic substances. As they did so, they were "conventionalizing a means of warfare that had up to now been forbidden," a Western military figure told me at the time. "They are making chemical weaponry part of the battlefield equation."

•　　•　　•

The Iranians bitterly denounced the Iraqis for "genocide" against their civilians. The Iranians at first transported their poison gas victims to hospitals in Europe to be treated and to help them gain sympathy for their suffering and score political points. The visits produced neither medical miracles nor votes for the Ayatollah and his Islamic militants at the United Nations. There, the Arab bloc constituted a potent political force and prevented condemnation of Iraq.

The Iranians saw themselves as victims—of Saddam Hussein's non-conventional chemical warfare and missile attacks, in which they lost thousands of lives, but received little Western sympathy—and of a world which feared their religious fanaticism and which, they believed, wanted to deny them their sovereign and rightful place among nations. Both the West and the conservative Arab regimes situated on the Gulf, as well as Saudi Arabia, wanted to hold the line against the spread of Islamic fundamentalism. The Iraqis' poison gas and missile attacks caught the Iranians unprepared and unprotected by even the most elementary anti-toxic protection.

I walked into Iranian consulates in London and Bonn in 1986 and '87 to speak about their concerns about poison gas. The soft-speaking Iranian diplomatic representatives claimed that poison gas and non-conventional weaponry was un-Islamic, its use was blasphemous, and that Saddam Hussein was a barbarian and a heathen. They swore that their own country would never use poison gas because that would be to defile Allah and Muhammed, his chief messenger.

The Iranians, though, decided that public relations gestures and protests did not produce battlefield victories. Behind those usually closed embassy doors, the Iranian military and the pasdaran were preparing the way for the use of non-conventional weapons that could hit back at the Iraqis. The pasdaran created their own buying structures that operated independently of the Iranian Ministry of Defense. Some of the buying occurred through Iranian embassies situated abroad: for example, in the tightly guarded embassy in Bonn. There, Kharim Ali Sobhani, ostensibly a junior diplomat assigned to the mission, led a wave of buying in Western capitals which rivalled Iraqi efforts. (He was found out and asked to leave by the normally tolerant German government, which had strong trade relations with Iran.)

By 1985 and 1986, a new mindset came to Iran. The Iranian leaders—like the Iraqis—now sought the kinds of quick fixes that would produce big scores on the battlefield. In addition to considering the future possibility of a nuclear option, they were engaged in an immediate and practical push for missiles and also looked to develop a chemical weapons force to retaliate in kind.

The Iraqis, though caught red-handed, were not forced to pay a political price for their outlaw attacks. Not surprisingly, the more remote the war, the less the concern. A few years later, this unwillingness to make Iraq pay a price led to attempted Iraqi genocide against the Kurds, Iraqi citizens, as well as against Iranians and possibly even Shi'ite sympathers of Iran. Laissez-faire attitudes convinced Saddam Hussein that he could get away with the invasion and annexation of Kuwait. It led to Desert Shield and Desert Storm.

Even as the Soviets and Americans were debating the fine points of a chemical weapons ban at Geneva, the non-conventional weapons option had spread to the states of the Middle East. Among those acquiring chemical weapons were some of the most radical states in the Arab world: Libya, Syria and Iraq. Egypt also had an advanced program, and had in fact used poison gas in their war to support republican forces in Yemen during the 1960s. Israel, too, was believed to have acquired a chemical weapons capability.[1] While the politicians debated the fine points at Geneva, many Third World generals (including the Iranians and not just the Iraqis) proceeded to envision more practical steps. They saw chemical weapons as an option they could afford, could develop, and could integrate into their order of battle. The phrase that chemical weapons were actually "a poor man's atomic bomb" gained currency.[2]

The challenge in 1984 was substantively different from that of a decade before, when a chemical weapons ban was first broached. In 1984, because of Iraq, the use of nerve agent and poison gas gained a shadowy but growing future legitimacy. The Iraqis showed that waging a war with chemicals could be done, and that you could get away with it.

CHAPTER SEVEN

Men of the Pentagon

"We had thousands of pissing matches with the Allies. It was all in the game."

Dr. Stephen Bryen, formerly head of Department of Technology Security Administration (D.T.S.A.), The Pentagon.

As the planners in Washington and other Western capitals looked about them in the first years of the 1980s, they saw a world where nuclear deterrence had kept the peace between the Superpowers. A Third World War hadn't occurred. The possibility of one happening was remote. The awesome power of the atom had reduced the scale of conflict into rebellions, terrorism, civil strife. Those nations that had declared they had nuclear arms were the five permanent members of the United Nations Security Council: the United States, the Soviet Union, the United Kingdom, France and China. These powerful countries formed a nuclear cartel. A few nations like Israel and India also had nuclear capability but would not openly proclaim it, and formed a second group "at the fringe": tolerated, but not accepted to full club membership by the cartel.

The United States' own interest in assuring its dominant position in the nuclear club and maintaining the club's "exclusivity" colored the view from Washington. The new Reagan team decided on two steps in 1981: first, to embark on a huge military build-up aiming to achieve not parity but supremacy over the Soviet Union in strategic arms. It would take trillions of dollars and years to accomplish and plunge the United States into incredible debt, possibly affecting the quality of life of future American generations.

In addition, the Reagan Administration determined to re-enforce the exclusivity of the nuclear club by firming up the entrance barriers, especially to a new generation of dictatorial and sometimes fanatical Third World nations. Ownership of nuclear bombs, hazardous enough in the First and Second Worlds, could be downright catastrophic among Third World nations led by dictators who operated from a narrow power base. This was because of their inherent instability and what Washington believed was the unpredictability of their decision-making.

As the Reaganites tried to carve out a new position in arms control policy, one well-informed official at the State Department's Arms Control and Disarmament Agency summed up the situation this way: President Reagan, he said, will "get rid of about eighty percent of Mr. Carter's rhetoric, and keep about eighty percent of Mr. Carter's policy."

The other twenty percent, however, included a major new element, one that would become a hallmark of the drive to halt nuclear proliferation and the spread of dangerous weaponry throughout the 1980s. This policy became explicit in a Presidential memo issued to the relevant departments of government in November, 1982. The Reagan Administration would seek to embargo not just atomic bombs but the means to deliver them. The President's basic instruction: find ways to hinder the proliferation of nuclear-capable missiles, including those ostensibly for non-military use, such as space launchers.

Just as the nascent "Star Wars" program would, by the mid-1980s, attempt to render missiles impotent by preventing the rockets from reaching their targets, the Reagan Administration sought a policy that bordered on technological denial to prevent errant Third World nations from being able to launch the missiles in the first place. While the Americans did not believe they could stop the sale of all such missiles to the Third World, officials felt they could severely inhibit the spread of manufacturing technology. The U.S. did not want to see a series of independent missile production centers cropping up. In short, American diplomacy took aim at the spread of the nuclear-tipped missile.

Surprisingly to some, the Reagan Administration attracted a select few of the "best and brightest" to its ranks to help control sensitive exports. Among them: Stephen Bryen and Richard Speier, both in their forties, both dedicated to halting dangerous weapons traffic or what could manufacture the means of mass destruction. Speier and Bryen played vital roles in pushing for new programs and policies. Each dealt with separately defined domains:

• Bryen headed the Department of Defense's export licensing review group and was in charge of Pentagon relations with C.O.C.O.M., the Paris-based Coordinating Committee for Multilateral Export Controls, which worked almost as a second arm for NATO countries blocking sensitive exports to the Eastern bloc.

• The Pentagon assigned Speier the job of conceptualizing what would become "M.T.C.R.," the Missile Technology Control Regime— designed to curb the stem of dangerous missile exports and particularly to halt the spread of missile-making technology, especially in a North-South context, to Third World countries.

The separate areas overseen by Bryen and Speier comprised overlapping American concerns.[1] The Americans did not want all kinds of advanced weaponry—especially but not exclusively nuclear goods— spreading into the hands of unpredictable and untrustworthy Third World autocrats, nor did they want the Soviets and their allies to acquire the West's most prized technology.

C.O.C.O.M. and M.T.C.R. each had striking flaws. C.O.C.O.M., a fully developed technological listing of sensitive items, applied only to Soviet, and not Third World sales, and left a gaping hole through which the West's most advanced technology could be sold to the highest bidder. M.T.C.R., on the other hand, consisted only of guidelines and had no actual enforcement provisions. Additionally, M.T.C.R. contained a "grandfather clause," which provided an escape hatch for those nations that wanted to signal their respect for international agreements, but simultaneously sought protection for their commercial interests from immediate damage. The "grandfather clause" referred to missile deals signed before the M.T.C.R. treaty came into force. Contracts already signed could be continued just as they were.

•   •   •

Car-tinkerers like to fix defective systems. Dr. Stephen Bryen is a car-tinkerer. He grew up in the New Jersey meadowlands where his father tinkered before him. Even when getting his Ph.D. at Tulane University in New Orleans, he loved to fix engines and get a car into running shape. In 1981 he had a 1974 Chrysler that he'd bought for $100. His father told him it was worthless. He fixed it up himself. The same year he became Deputy Under Secretary of Defense for Trade Security Policy, and later headed up the technical investigation and enforcement arm of Pentagon policy as director of the Defense Technology Security Administration, known as D.T.S.A.

D.T.S.A.—which Bryen succeeded in forming in 1985—processed as many as 40,000 export licenses annually. Bryen pioneered cooperative agreements with non-aligned and neutral countries such as Sweden, Switzerland, Finland, Austria, India, South Korea and Singapore. He personally handled and supervised C.O.C.O.M. negotiations in Paris. In 1984, the Defense Department awarded him its highest civilian medal, the Distinguished Public Service Award. He got it a second time in 1988.

Shortly after entering the Pentagon he had a stroke of good luck. Though a neo-conservative Republican himself—he had been foreign policy advisor to New Jersey's Senator Clifford Case and later a staff member on the Senate Foreign Relations Committee and director of its Near East subcommittee—he and the the newly-elected socialists under President François Mitterrand in France quickly found common ground. Bryen discovered that the French government had a KGB spy producing a wealth of information, including documentation, that arrived regularly at the intelligence division of the French Defense Ministry in Paris. This spy, code named "Farewell," provided specific lists of technology that the Soviet Union was obtaining illicitly from the West. The lists revealed how the Soviets were stealing Western high-tech weaponry, where they were getting it, what they had or were about to get, and how they were adapting it.

Bryen nurtured this French connection. "Farewell" became a joint French-American operation. All that treasure of priceless Soviet data flowed into Paris and Washington by 1982 and '83. For a period of years, the French Defense Ministry and the Pentagon, largely through the person of Bryen, shared a steady stream of information and documents that pinpointed a concerted campaign by the Soviets to identify the cream of major Western high-tech advances, to steal it outright, and then to adapt it for Soviet purposes. "Farewell's data showed how technology could be diverted—and how we could stop it," Bryen recalled. "It gave me the impetus to be able to push for a strong, well-coordinated export policy that would deny the Soviets what they were getting from many Western countries."

Buttressed by Farewell's material, Bryen struggled on the bureaucratic front with increasing success. In 1983, he pushed hard and got some reserve officers assigned temporarily to his office. The review of militarily-sensitive export licenses in the Pentagon had been handled by the Department of Research and Engineering, then under Richard Delauer. Bryen and Delauer fought each other for bureaucratic turf. It took two years, but by 1985 Bryen won the battle to gain control of the license review process, arguing that "R & E was screwing up" and that a single authority was required. That same year D.T.S.A. came into being.

Fights persisted within a broader context in the U.S. government: State versus the Pentagon versus Commerce. Each department of government responded to its constituencies. Commerce wanted to sell American goods, the Pentagon sought to maintain a monopoly on American military sales and to make sure no American secrets or power were betrayed; and State liked to put a good face on it all and explain it to U.S. allies. "Commerce wanted credible export controls," Bryen conceded. "But they didn't want to be bombarded by requests or complaints from exporters."

Once agreement was reached internally on American policy, the focus switched to C.O.C.O.M. headquarters in Paris. There, Bryen and his staff could begin to argue individual cases with other C.O.C.O.M. members—for example, about sales of possibly strategic goods at the Moscow Trade Fair. Bryen made other countries aware that the U.S. cared about goods that were designated "sensitive" and didn't want them sold to the Soviet Union or other potential enemies. There were constant fights over which equipment could be sold. In Bryen's words: "We had thousands of pissing matches with the allies. It was all in the game."

The agreement defined three categories for controlled goods. One was G.E., which meant "General Exception." The second was F.C., for "favorable consideration." The third was A.E., for "administrative exception." G.E. meant a company had to have unanimous C.O.C.O.M. agreement before it could sell a controlled item. F.C. meant that a sale could be banned only if there were specific grounds, or for cause: e.g., specific information that it was dangerously proliferating technology or a part of a dangerous sales unit or system. A.E. goods didn't have to be taken to C.O.C.O.M. for approval, but rulings about their sale were made in the individual home countries. In Bryen's words, "it was basically very rare for anyone to say 'no' about A.E. goods." In the end, the U.S. wanted to eliminate it as a category.

Arguing with the Europeans was half the work. Bryen: "We had to be imperious at times. But we were nice about it. We tried to be tough but we listened carefully." Actually attempting to enforce the agreement was the other half.

Bryen believes his biggest accomplishment in the Pentagon was creating D.T.S.A. The second: making C.O.C.O.M. work. But the key to success lay in the person of Farewell, that carefully cultivated French-American secret. The Americans were able to pinpoint what technology the Soviets were getting and from which Western power because of Farewell. The Americans only mildly objected that the "good French" in the Defense Ministry on Rue Sainte Dominique in Paris were at the same time selling helicopters and Mirage fighter jets to the Sandinistas in Nicaragua, the group considered by Reaganites to be enemies of the United States and peace and order in Latin America.

Then the spy got caught. The Americans believe Farewell created the opening for his own farewell by blabbing or bragging to his girlfriend what he was doing. She got scared or bewildered or she was simply treacherous and reported him to the authorities. Farewell was arrested and executed by the Soviet authorities.

In 1987 Bryen got himself a used Ford LTD from Hertz, paying $5,500 for it. It was one car that didn't require that much tinkering.

• • •

In the spring of 1983, a key man was added to the negotiations and disarmament team at the Pentagon. His name: Richard Speier.

A Harvard graduate in physics, Speier obtained a Ph.D. in political science from the Massachusetts Institute of Technology. He worked his way up the line of governmental bureaucracy. He was a staffer at the State Department's Arms Control and Disarmaments Agency, where he worked on nuclear non-proliferation during the Carter Administration. Speier got disillusioned with the limits of what could be accomplished by American attempts to unilaterally impose nuclear arms control concepts. He turned to the National War College for additional course work and training in the nature of modern weaponry. There, he studied the practical possibility of limiting missile proliferation.

In the winter of 1982-83 Speier made the switch to the Department of Defense, where he became the Pentagon's man on missiles. His assignment was to implement the President's desire to hinder the spread of nuclear-capable missiles: to analyze the hardware that could be banned, to design the policy, to help coordinate that policy with a number of other government departments, to assess the role of Western allies in implementing the policy, and even to draft a future treaty.

Speier was an anomaly. He had early on decided to make government service a career. With his dull suits, his occasional suspenders, his striped Ivy League ties, his dapper mustache, he looked like a functionary who had to survive, happily or unhappily, within a large bureaucracy.

In fact, Dick Speier had the expansive soul of a romanticist. Speier spent much of his leisure time in small theaters; his favorite playright was avant-garde theater writer and director Richard Foreman. He cared for his family, husbanded his vacation time, but as he drove back and forth on the Washington parkways from his home in Virginia, his mind conjured up those images of the absurd that directly related to his assignment: those thousands of screws and bolts and sub-systems that converged to make a missile.

From external appearances, Speier's job at the Pentagon lacked clout. His tiny windowless office was impossible to locate without a guide. It was piled with papers. The bare cubby contrasted sharply with the carpeted, windowed office of an undersecretary. Speier's was tedious, low-prestige work, with very little press attention in the early years. In fact, public focus on what he and his colleagues were doing could be the absolute kiss of death. He was thus often content to be left to his "room without a view" in the Pentagon maze.

His mind was left free to roam amidst the paper clutter of his office, occasionally fortified by instant coffee brewed from water heated on a corner kettle. He persistently analyzed how to control the manufacture and sale of missile components and sub-systems in ways consistent with the President's memo of instruction. Hours of hard concentration were interrupted only by the occasional staff meeting. Speier's work boiled down to defining how to prevent the acquisition of killing capability by errant states. He focussed hours of thought on what many might consider abstruse technicalities—such as the welding of finely fitted castings into objects that, in many cases, he became determined to ban, or which metal shapes could fit with others without necessarily shaking the peace and well-being of the world.

Speier, as imaginative in his work as he was conventional in his appearance, was a fighter. He became the apostle of an expanded concept in arms control: stopping the spread of long-range missiles capable of carrying dangerous explosives in unconventional warheads. This was a direct off-shoot of the drive to limit nuclear capability and epitomized the problem. The technology for both peaceful space flight and deadly missiles is the same. Speier fondly told me how President Kennedy was asked the difference between an Atlas rocket that put astronaut John Glenn into orbit and one armed with a nuclear warhead. Kennedy replied: "Attitude."

Until 1985, Speier's aim was unambiguous. He delineated the general principles previously approved and tried to specifically define them. Then he had to get agreement on those definitions from his own Administration, including three departments of government, and the major industrial countries of the Western world. If he got that far, he hoped, then Western governments could control the proliferation of missile capability.

Speier played a key role in drafting what would become known as the Missile Technology Control Regime—pushing it through the American bureaucracy and convincing America's allies to go along with it. As Janne Nolan of the Brookings Institution in Washington, herself an expert in missile politics, said to me, "Dick showed what you can do, what a complete zealot or dedicated public servant, depending how you look at it, can get done in this town.... What he created was a modest initiative but a real revolution."

The drafting went on throughout the early 1980s. Within the U.S. government, an inter-agency grouping, including the Pentagon, A.C.D.A., the State Department and the Commerce Department, began to handle the problem. By 1985, the direction and guidelines had jelled enough to provide both the U.S. government and its allies with a basis of action to limit the spread of missile technology. Participating governments acted informally as if the agreement were in effect. The formal signing took place in 1987. But Speier, in a Pentagon interview, said the treaty had "bite" from as early as 1986. At that time, a luncheon speaker at an American Institute of Aeronautics and Astronautics meeting denounced the growing control on rockets as something that was already hampering business and would "ruin the balance of payments."

It took until the spring of 1987 to iron out the wrinkles. Speier and his colleagues on the same M.T.C.R. task force broke missile technology down into two separate categories. These categories became annexes to the agreement. The first category defined the most dangerous elements. Falling within it were complete rocket systems, including ballistic missile systems, space launch vehicles and sounding rockets. The transfer of category one equipment to second nations, said the U.S. government, "will be authorized only on rare occasions and where the government obtains binding government-to-government undertakings...." Additionally, on sales of American equipment, it "... is understood that the decision to transfer remains the sole and sovereign judgment of the United States Government."

Category two items were less sensitive, and the legality of shipping them was mainly a judgment call where they fit within the overall systems. This category included individual items like propulsion components and propellants, flight instruments, flight control systems, missile computers, avionics equipment and test facilities and equipment.

The seven most powerful industrial nations—the ones that meet annually in an economic summit and are known as the G-7—subscribed to the agreement. They were: Canada, France, the then-Federal Republic of Germany, Italy, Japan, the United Kingdom and the United States. They agreed to "a new policy to limit the proliferation of missiles capable of delivering nuclear weapons." These countries agreed "to control the transfer of equipment and technology that could contribute to nuclear-capable missiles" and "to limit the risks of nuclear proliferation by controlling transfers that could make a contribution to nuclear weapons delivery systems other than manned aircraft." The G-7 believed they had the industrial might to back up their will to control the development of space and missile technology.

The Missile Technology Control Regime officially came into being on April 16th, 1987. The M.T.C.R. documents were deposited with both houses of Congress. In a statement issued by the Assistant to the President of the United States, the Administration noted that all seven participating governments "...have agreed to common guidelines... a common list of items to be controlled," and would act in concert "to prevent commercial advantage or disadvantage for any of the countries."

Speier pointed to the fact that the M.T.C.R.'s guidelines provided a resource to governments to enable them to determine what was, and wasn't, illegal or dangerous. In his words, "the export controls make your diplomacy work better." According to him, "there was a lot of diplomacy in getting the regime to work"—both between governments and inside each of them.

As might be expected in a national capital where back-biting is a favorite local pastime, M.T.C.R. got a lot of criticism. "M.T.C.R. is a treaty in search of a problem," one person told me. The truth is there were many problems with the agreement, the main ones being the lack of enforcement procedures and the grandfather clause—whereby any projects or contracts started before the treaty came into effect could be continued—but the very fact the agreement existed could help slow the missile race.

Each American governmental unit had its duties. State would consider the diplomatic implications of each sale. Officials at the State Department's intelligence branch had cast a professional eye on missile-related exports for a long time—since the years of the Kennedy-Johnson administrations. The Department of Commerce would measure the effects on American business. Officials there wanted to be sure the United States was not undercut competitively.

The structure of control in other countries varied. In the U.K. and France, foreign office personnel—those normally handling C.O.C.O.M. East-West trade controls—also handled nuclear and missile obligations. In Italy and Japan, those special offices responsible for strategic trade controls were assigned M.T.C.R. supervision. In Germany and Canada, a mix of offices assumed supervisory responsibility. In the U.S., the Commerce and State departments handled strategic trade while the Pentagon was in charge of nuclear-related matters.

Speier and Bryen were unalike. Bryen was an activist, a guy who defined the guidelines and then got the job done. Speier occasionally "spun wheels," in the words of someone who had worked with him, but he had noble aims, good concepts and a meticulous schedule. Some less tuned than Speier to the rising perception of the danger of missile proliferation thought him a fanatic. In the words of one of his colleagues, he was "a one-man band" in pushing the concept of missile control through the Administration and past the bureaucracies of America's closest allies.

Speier described his own role more modestly. "Non-proliferation as a whole was ready for a turn," he told me, "And the missile area was the next step."

What Speier accomplished was "neither the City of God nor did it cure the common cold," in Janne Nolan's words. But it did push the United States and its anti-proliferation weapons policies a step forward.

•   •   •

The West had been aiming to put a clamp on missile technology for a good cause—to stop nuclear proliferation. But by the time the missile agreement came into effect in 1987, the grounds had shifted. Other non-nuclear technologies dominated the world's battlefields. The Iraqis had used chemical warfare against Iran and occasionally directed their weapons against defenseless Iraqi Kurds.

Less than a year after M.T.C.R. was ratified, the "War of the Cities," a missile battle, and the use of poison gas helped force an outcome to the Gulf War between Iran and Iraq. The cruel deaths pointed the way to the danger of proliferation in the years ahead. Specially designed warheads could store nerve gas or toxic biological strains. Those were the kinds of warheads that Iraq's SCUD-B missile could realistically carry. That was also the kind of technology that had to be denied to Third World tyrants like Saddam Hussein or Ayatollah Khomeini.

Speier sometimes wondered if he was effective. Could he really do the job? Or was he more like the little boy with his thumb in the Dutch dike who, as the story goes, waits there with trepidation "as the hole's been opened up and the water's begun to run." How do you block the spread of knowledge, especially when it is poisonous and destructive? Once the genie is out of the bottle, how do you stuff it back?

Both Dick Speier and Steve Bryen were part of a tiny team of American officials actively involved in the battle against proliferation. They sought to block the spreading use of chemical agents, the specter of solid-state missile technologies, and the terrorizing use of poison-filled missiles to kill enemy civilians. Each day they devised, reviewed or enforced new tactics and strategies for resisting or just impeding what might otherwise be inevitable.

Speier, a civil servant, remained in his Pentagon job through the beginning of the '90s, playing a key role in the Bush Administration to map out missile technology policy. Bryen, an appointee, left the Pentagon in 1988 to form his own Washington-based consulting firm.

CHAPTER EIGHT

The Saga of Sa'ad-16

"Here is the requested confirmation. Our conclusion is that the merchandise can now be exported without further correspondence."

Dr. Guenter Welzien of German governmental export licensing office, letter to MBB's partner, Gildemeister, 1983

IF THERE WERE A COMPANY that symbolized modern Germany, both its spectacular achievements and its links to the sordid past, that was Germany's leading armaments and aerospace firm, MBB. MBB, which stands for Messerschmitt-Boelkow-Blohm, was an industrial giant headquartered in Ottobrunn, a Munich suburb. The idea of creating MBB as a single industrial powerhouse was the brainchild of the late Bavarian prime minister, the conservative leader, Franz Josef Strauss, who talked two brilliant design engineers with separate companies, Willie Messerschmitt and Ludwig Boelkow, into merging. A photograph famous within MBB's corporate headquarters shows the founding fathers, Messerschmitt and Boelkow, beaming happily together at the 1968 Paris Air Show, where their two firms had just combined to become a conglomerate.

The two men knew each other from World War II, when Boelkow had worked for Messerschmitt. Theirs was not a totally new partnership but an old association renewed that, like the company itself, had its roots in Nazi Germany. MBB swiftly became an additional symbol among those that had already made Germany and Bavaria renowned: superb beer, hard work, faithful enterprise, attentiveness to detail, and belief in God, in approximate order. It was as sacred a Bavarian institution as any, possibly rivalling the Catholic church in prestige and popularity.

Willie Messerschmitt was one of the modern world's most outstanding technical geniuses. Born in Frankfurt in 1898, he was only four when the Wright brothers took to the North Carolina air in 1902. As a 15-year-old schoolboy, he fell in love with the idea of flight and aviation. World War I showed the new technology's potential for military purposes. After World War I, with commercial flight still in its infancy, Messerschmitt, still a student of engineering, struck out on his own and founded his company in 1923.

Within a decade he turned to warplane design. In 1934 he built the ME 108, with retractable landing gear, flaps and slats, one of the world's most advanced aircraft at the time. His ME 109 light fighter, designed in 1935, became the Luftwaffe's standard fighter. German industry eventually built some 35,000. In 1942, Messerschmitt developed the ME 262, a German jet fighter, of which about 1,500 were produced before the end of the war. It had a speed of over 500 miles per hour, 120 miles faster than any aircraft possessed by the Allies. His ME 238 had the same pulse thrusters that were used in the V1 winged bomb. The ME 163 attained a speed of over 600 miles per hour in 1942. It was powered with a liquid-fuel rocket engine.[1]

Ludwig Boelkow, born in 1912, was the other essential force in MBB besides Messerschmitt himself. Boelkow was one of the design geniuses behind Germany's development of both jet and rocket engines. In 1939, following his studies at a technical school in Berlin and a degree as a mechanical engineer, he joined the Messerschmitt Company. His specialty was high speed aerodynamics. He first worked on Willie Messerschmitt's jet, the ME 262, and then its successors. His capture after World War II led to his interrogation by American forces at Oberammergau, but Boelkow was never charged or tried as a war criminal. Following the war, he started his own engineering firm and proved himself a genius in developing advanced missiles, aircraft, and other armament.

The Allies initially wanted to keep Germany de-militarized and weak after World War II, as they had tried to do after World War I through the Versailles Treaty. Back in the 1920s, the German military evaded Allied restrictions by using surrogates. Germany developed its submarines, tanks, guns, and other weaponry in neighboring countries such as the Netherlands and Sweden, working with armaments and aircraft manufacturers such as Bofors and Fokker. Surprisingly, the German army also secretly undertook joint projects with the newly-constituted Soviet army during the '20s, including one to test poison gas.

After the Second World War, the victors took their cue from history and initially forbade German military rearmament. They had support from the overwhelming majority of Germans inside Germany itself, who were sick of war. As Germany headed down the economic road that would shortly make it Europe's strongest economic power, East-West relations deteriorated. The Allies felt they needed Germany's might wedded to the Western coalition in order to fight what they perceived to be the rising menace of Communism. By 1955, West Germany fielded an army, was integrated into the Western alliance, and officially entered NATO.

The Messerchmitt firm was initially affected by the ban on armaments and aircraft production. Willie Messerschmit, forbidden from producing additional aircraft in Germany, emigrated to Spain, where he designed the HA-100 and built 200 trainers and the HA-300 supersonic fighter, Spain's first jet aircraft. He also developed ties to Austria and Switzerland. His efforts became successful in that his non-German companies were already building jets for NATO by the mid-1950s without protest from any member countries, including the United States.

Both Boelkow and Messerchmitt also tried their hand in Egypt. Both turned up in Cairo during the 1950s attempting to develop aircraft and missiles for Egypt, which then had the leading Arab army. The Egyptians urgently wanted to develop themselves as a military power. At first under King Farouk, and then under the revolutionary leadership of Gamal Abdul Nasser, they recruited Germans, many of them ex-Nazi officers, to build their forces. The Messerschmitt Company and Egypt signed a contract on November 29, 1959. From that point, German engineers poured into Cairo. "Project 36," Messerschmitt headquarters, was a white factory building just on the outskirts of Cairo. Part of it was devoted to building fuselages for supersonic aircraft, other areas were pinpointed for the design of the ME 300, to be built under special license in Egypt. Egypt manufactured the trainers but, reported MBB promotional material, "the lightest Mach-2 fighter ever built, the HA (ME) 300 of 1964, was flown only as prototype: series production in Egypt never started."

At nights, the Germans often hung out together at Shepherd's Hotel, not far from the banks of the Nile River. Work proceeded apace. The Germans liked Egypt, were well-paid, and the Egyptians liked them.

Among those enchanted by Egypt was Ludwig Boelkow. He fell in love with the country, its history, the Nile, the sun, its contemporary ambiance. In Egypt, Boelkow became a solar energy buff. He became fascinated by the possibilities of applying his technical skills to creating a clean, smoke-free world of pure solar power. But first he had to finance such a quest, and that came through "regular" business.

In late 1989, I met Boelkow, retired, in his tiny office about a mile down the road from MBB, in Ottobrunn, the Munich suburb. He had become a role model in modern Germany: an enormously successful industrialist, a man of action looked up to as a visionary, a fighter in both peace and war, an entrepreneur believed to be one of those most responsible for having helped to take Germany from the ashes of World War II to transform it into Europe's mightiest and most prosperous nation. At the time MBB was already involved in the export scandals that would accompany its demise. There was considerable, not particularly well publicized concern about its ties with Egypt and its associations with Iraq. Boelkow was convinced the United States was behind the outcry. "It's all a question of competition," he said. "The Americans don't want us in the market. I can smell it. That's the reason for the fuss."

•   •   •

In the aftermath of World War II, many Germans felt exports were the key to the country's future prosperity. Sales became a lofty goal with an importance approaching the sancrosanct. German companies made money and carved out ever-bigger niches in the markets of Europe and the world. The emphasis on balance sheets, economic growth and Gross National Product got so pronounced that some home-grown critics complained that Germany didn't have a soul. Germans, they said, worked so hard they never found the time to get one. Even after joining NATO, many Germans remained reluctant about re-engaging in military production. But soon, Germans began to produce high-technology military items for themselves. It didn't make economic sense to do otherwise. Soon German companies also found that it didn't make sense to sell to the German army if they couldn't also be competitive internationally.

Among Germany's Third World clients was Iraq, one of the Arab countries that had plenty of petro-dollars to burn and also military and political ambitions to fulfil. The Iraqis' main supplier of missiles through the 1970s, the Soviet Union, would not encourage the Iraqis to develop their own production capacity. The Iraqis craved missile independence. So, the Iraqis looked elsewhere for help in becoming a missile power.

What more logical choice than Germany? Germany had a rich tradition of aeronautical engineering and rocketry. The Germans had given the world much of the expertise for un-manned flight, going back to the V-1 and V-2 rockets.

And within Germany, what more logical choice than MBB? Through MBB, the Germans sought to revive the skills of a generation past and grab their fair share of a booming worldwide market, the kind that could warm any entrepreneur's heart.

•   •   •

Though its roots rested in the Nazi period, MBB blossomed in the free and democratic atmosphere of the Federal Republic. MBB was owned by two state governments, Bavaria and Hamburg, several of Germany's leading banks (including Deutsches Bank), the industrial giant Siemens, and had some limited foreign ownership: the giant French corporation, Aerospatiale, had a small share of the concern. The board of directors—the Germans call it a supervisory council, reflecting the semi-public nature of the enterprise—was a microcosm of powerful local, national and even international interest groups. It was invariably headed by the Prime Minister of Bavaria. For the early years of the company's existence that was Franz Josef Strauss, a conservative of national stature within post-war Germany who was instrumental in providing MBB with political backing. Strauss, who was both staunchly pro-West and a strong supporter of Israel, helped give MBB international respectability. The company's deputy chairman was always a labor movement official, someone associated with the giant German trade union, I.G. Metall.

The company had 40,000 workers, and offices scattered throughout Germany. Top management liked to regard the conglomerate as the vanguard of a highly technological army. MBB's partnerships formed a list of modern Europe's most prestigious military and industrial projects. MBB got contract work from NATO, the German government, and even some American SDI projects. These ranged from civilian plane projects like the Airbus to military fighter plane projects like the Tornado, and to rockets called Hot, Milan and Roland. One thousand employees worked at MBB's military production and testing center for missiles and rockets at Schrobenhausen, one hundred miles to the northwest of Munich. The munitions department featured some of the world's most sophisticiated warhead development, a lot of it based on a dispensing module called the MW-1. This included the MUSA multi-fragmentation mine for mixed-area targets, the MUSPA multi-fragmentation mine to engage aircraft taxiing for taking off, and the STABO runway cratering bomb.

The company also produced components of the U.S.-designed and built Patriot missile, which later became the "star" of Desert Storm in 1991, provided to both Israel and Saudi Arabia to counter the SCUD-B. The company was responsible for the final assembly of the missile for European clients, including the U.S. Army in Germany.

MBB, in brief, marshalled great power and influence within the Federal Republic and also outside it. "The company is an international player in space and advanced weapons," German friends told me, cautioning me that MBB functioned very much within Germany's complex political structure. According to Alois Schwarz, the respected deputy chairman of the MBB board of supervisors, with whom I spoke at length, MBB management informally committed itself in the mid-1980s to submit any military projects designated for non-NATO clients to the board of supervisors for informal consultations and approval.

But there was less to MBB than met the eye. The firm had persistent economic difficulties. The company's balance sheet was not nearly as impressive as its far-flung manufacturing projects. Among insiders in the German armaments industry, it had a mixed reputation. I spoke with a leading German arms dealer, Gerhard Mertins, whose sales to Saudi Arabia and other countries had netted him millions, and whose reputation was that of, not just a salesman, but the eyes and ears of the German government and its intelligence service in the Arab Middle East. He was critical of MBB. "They never really made a profit, so their specialty was mergers. That's how Messerschmitt became what it was. Their own sales couldn't build them a cash balance, so they kept diluting themselves, their own ownership and control over their destiny.

"And they were always just a bunch of individuals, not like some other German companies, such as Daimler-Benz, where there was a dedication to the good of the company. At MBB, everyone just cared about himself, his area, making the deal for what he could do. Often they'd start a project and then walk away from it. I never liked them and I still don't."

•   •   •

Iraqi leader Saddam Hussein approached MBB in the early 1980s to help the Ba'athist leadership build the Third World's most modern research center for missiles and rockets, what became known as Sa'ad-16. Hussein sought long-range industrial independence that would give him the wherewithal to build his own missiles. MBB and the Iraqis entered talks in 1982.

MBB, using the Sa'ad facility, could develop rocket propulsion, wind tunnels and firing chambers, and could eventually gain access to a credible range for testing, all things that the company couldn't do easily in Germany itself.

As one veteran of corporate missile competition (who requested that his name not be used) suggested to me, if MBB played its cards right, the German company "had the option of using that advanced missile research base in far-away Iraq to develop technologies and sub-systems far from the prying eyes of their own country's politicians and far from nosy journalists."

Many of the documents involved in these Iraqi-German negotiations came into my possession and some people within the company told me what happened. What emerges is a tale of deception, sophistry and legal (but not illegal) deceit—an object lesson in how to get around the regulations imposed by your own government without breaking the law.

The place chosen by the Iraqis for their "laboratory" facilities to develop missile expertise was the sleepy university town of Mosul. Some 230 miles northwest of Baghdad, Mosul is Iraq's third largest city after Baghdad and Basra. The city sits on the right bank of the Tigris River at one of its widest points. Aside from its role as market for the region's agricultural products—wheat, barley, cereals, sheep—Mosul is famed for its skilled metal workers, many of whom hail from Iraq's Christian Orthodox community. The city connects Turkey to the north with Baghdad to the south and has rail and road links with Aleppo in Syria.

The choice of site was deliberate, part of an effort to scatter manufacturing and research sites around the entire country and not just in Baghdad. The missile center was designed to be on the outskirts of the town. It became known as "Sa'ad-16." "Sa'ad" means "happiness," "welfare" or "well- being" in Arabic. It can even mean good luck. Sa'ad-16 functioned under the general auspices of the Sa'ad General Establishment, an Iraqi governmental company responsible to the Ministry of Industry. Sa'ad's general manager at the beginning of the negotiations was M.B. Namody. H.A. Dahan took up the position in 1985.

MBB set up a wholly-owned subsidiary to handle the deal, MBB TransTechnica. Ostensibly a "technology transfer" company, as its name indicated, its real purpose was to create a protective shield between MBB and the Iraqis so that the conglomerate could distance itself from the project should the need arise. "The project actually involved practically every division of the company" ranging from aerospace to military departments, according to one MBB official with whom I spoke, who explained how Sa'ad-16 could provide Iraq with the foundation for that country's advanced missile development and any future efforts Iraq might make to launch satellites into space.

MBB chose an outside partner as civil contractor. This was Gildemeister, a tool and weapons manufacturer located in Bielefeld, a small city in central Germany. Gildemeister, not MBB, became Iraq's official liaison, responsible both for constructing the facility and delivering all equipment properly licensed to Iraq. This company offered a protective shield between MBB and legal responsibility for sensitive exports to Iraq. Following MBB's model, the Gildemeister company's management set up its own subsidiary, Gildemeister Projecta, to handle the job.

MBB dispatched two officials to Baghdad in mid-February, 1983, to clinch the deal. Both were young men: Josef Scheidle, 42, and Erich Ludwig, 37. As the two flew into Baghdad, the Iran-Iraq war was underway. Yet Baghdad was still remarkably peaceful and untouched by war. The battle sites were some two hundred miles away in Basra and by the Gulf.

With a first-stage 400 million DM contract at stake—some $250 million at the going exchange—the negotiations had to be undertaken with utmost discretion. This was partly because of potential problems with the German government. Since the Gulf was a "hot" area with an on-going war, there was always the possibility of a weapons embargo, even for a "research facility." Also, MBB faced competition from companies within Germany. Scheidle memoed his superiors that the state-owned Fritz Werner Company, also a weapons supplier, was favored by the Iraqis for the research and development contract. Fritz Werner had already proposed that the Iraqis modify an existing weapons system: namely, a 122 mm. artillery missile including the launcher and Sam 7's.

Scheidle proposed an agreement in stages, with a "framework agreement for technical assistance," including common development in defense technology, as the first step. He got two executives in MBB's corporate division, with overall responsibility for military projects, to write directly to the Sa'ad General Establishment on July 21st, 1983 to assure the Iraqis this was an all-company effort that involved the West's best armaments and missile expertise. "MBB has considerable experience in international joint ventures in the field of development and production of defence systems over a long period of time," the company explained in a formal letter written in English to Sa'ad. "MBB is pleased to inform you of its capability and willingness to cooperate with you in certain projects."

The MBB officials, implying as much as was explicitly stated, assured the Iraqis that "due to its experience in national and international cooperation, MBB is in the position to extend and to complete its know how for certain projects by incorporating further specialized companies."

In effect, MBB promised the Iraqis the cooperation of its extensive network of daughter companies and sub-suppliers. By mid-summer, MBB and Gildemeister wrapped up the deal. On August 25, 1983, the Iraqis provided confirmation to Gildemeister Projecta. The letter came from H.A. Al-Dahan, the director general of the Iraqi State Organization for Technical Industries, the Sa'ad General Establishment, and was marked confidential. "We are pleased to inform you that we intend to grant you the contract for project Sa'ad-16," Al- Dahan declared, stipulating the following Iraqi conditions:

"1. Setteling [sic] the subject of finance and the commercial and contractual conditions, as well as the total cost of the contract.

2. That the basis for technical assistance and cooperation in reaserch [sic] and development projects with your partners MESSERCHMITT—BOLKOW—BLOHM [sic] are defined.

We hope that you will do your best in obtaining the best possibilities of finance.   Thank you.

H.A. Al-Dahan

Director General"

Gildemeister Project and MBB signed on the 16th of September, 1983. The MBB-Gildemeister contract, and then the Gildemeister contract with Iraq itself, would involve continuous MBB aid to Iraq from the date the contract was signed until a point just short of completion in 1989.

Lots of money was at stake. Sa'ad-16 became a commercial bonanza. At least 28 German companies became sub-contractors to Gildemeisteror MBB in providing the Iraqis with equipment and training. Among them were many of Germany's finest and most venerable: Degussa, which had been a successful poison gas producer in World War II, provided the facilities and training for labs 102 and 113. Aviatest, a division of the powerful Rheinmetall, provided the wind tunnel. An Austrian company, Bowas InduPlan Chemie from Salzburg, played a role in a number of the explosive labs.[2]

The Karl Kolb Company, already well-established in Baghdad from its chemical sales, got into the act at Sa'ad-16 as a sub-contractor with close to four million DM of equipment "for material tests." Other companies involved in building Sa'ad-16 included the Carl Schenck company from Darmstadt and both Henri Hauser and Varian from Switzerland, all of which would figure in other projects using dual-use technologies for mass destruction weaponry. The overall plans for Sa'ad-16 were drawn up by Vienna's "Consultco" or "Consultation— Projection and Coordination of Buildings and Plants" company. A Consultco spokesman replied to Stern Magazine's questions, "It is true that we carried out the overall planning. However, this is a civilian project of Mosul University."

Even a cursory look at some of the commercial documents that came into my possession shows that from its inception the Mosul R&D project was a military operation. For example, the simulated flight shooting range, Lab 0614, a vital link in the push towards mastery of missile technology, could serve no other purpose. The overall cost of the lab was quoted by Gildemeisterto Iraq at 33,691,366 DM, or over $20 million. "Necessary supplements" to this range came out at 8,735,600 DM, or over five million dollars, with an additional 5,423,200 DM, or more than three million dollars, for options.[3] Overall, this single laboratory's price came to a cool $25 million, according to initial offers. American companies played a big role in the control systems: the Iraqis ordered computers for Lab 0614 from the Digital Equipment Corporation, based in Massachusetts.

In toto, the original proposal for technical equipment to this "peaceful Iraqi research project" to be supplied by MBB to Gildemeister

Projecta and Iraq came to over 100 million DM, some $70 million. That proposal was later whittled down to 77 million DM, over $50 million. Once the building construction and plant installation was thrown in, the overall project was worth over 400 million DM, or well in excess of $250 million.

Udo Philipp, as MBB spokesman, admitted to me after I got to know him some time after our first meeting in 1989, that he had to learn how to "turn the truth"—that is, to lie—with a straight face. A former star reporter with ZDF, Germany's national TV network, he first told the press that MBB was only cooperating in building "...a development and research laboratory which will closely cooperate with Mosul University, among other things."

The documents that I obtained told a different story. Incredibly, items for the Mosul project got license approvals from the German government as civilian goods, and I could find no notation in any German records to which I gained access that the project was ever identified as a military one.

One of the Iraqi authorities' greatest concerns, as early as 1985, was that Sa'ad-16 would somehow be classified by the Americans as a "nuclear" project. That could cause a second look by officials at what might otherwise pass without notice, and subject Sa'ad-16 to strict American, and Western, export regulations. The project's Iraqi director, M.B. Namody, tried to allay these fears from the beginning. He sent a letter to Gildemeister on February 27, 1985, declaring that the project was "non-nuclear." He omitted any discussion of the installation's eventual aim—to produce missiles that, technically, could deliver nuclear bombs, and also carry chemical as well as high-explosive warheads. He claimed that the Sa'ad center would be used for "checking of basic materials such as ferrous, non-ferrous metals, plastics, etc., and scientific instruments and apparatuses, development and modernization of scientific instruments and apparatuses."

In March, 1985, the Sa'ad-16 authorities sent Gildemeister Projecta a six-page list of facilities describing each of its laboratories. H.A. Al-Dahan of Sa'ad-16 called the real-time flight shooting range—Lab 0614, a unit that could help Iraq gain target accuracy for its missiles—a "laboratory for measurements in consideration of climatic conditions." Though rockets might need meteorological measurements for accurate firing, that particular official explanation was a bit far-fetched. Still, it was not noticed at the time by Western officials.[4]

Sa'ad and MBB got their high-powered computers from the United States. The American supply rolled in with export approvals provided by the U.S. Commerce Department. Among the items were "instruments for measuring or testing combinations of electrical, radio, and communications circuits and parts thereof," that could be applied to activities such as flight simulation. Among the companies from which permission was sought: Hewlett-Packard, Scientific Atlanta, I.B.M., D.E.C., Wiltron, and others. Some items, such as Wiltron's (10 MHz-40 GHz) scalar network analyster system were shipped to Iraq via Reim Airport in Munich, MBB's home base.[5]

Perhaps the most important part of the Sa'ad-16 project didn't involve missile hardware or testing equipment at all but simply the act of teaching the Iraqis how to do it themselves. That is what is called "technology transfer." MBB helped supervise an extensive training program, some of it conducted on-site in Iraq, much of it held on home ground in company facilities in the Munich area. Each lab had its special courses. The Iraqis worked with zest and skill and progressed rapidly. By the end of the Iran-Iraq war, Sa'ad-16 was on the verge of becoming fully operational and had already served to train Iraqi experts in missile-making. Everything except a few final screws had been delivered to the project.

The project was a German-Iraqi dream, a technological achievement of the first order. As British engineer Christopher Cowley acclaimed it in an extraordinary BBC-TV interview, the laboratories at Mosul were by 1989 on their way to becoming an ideal missile-making research and development center. "It was absolutely brilliant. I'd never seen anything in Europe that compared with that particular research facility," the British engineer enthused. "I'd never seen any university in Europe and specifically in England that had such superb equipment.

"At the time I was there they didn't have the manpower to utilize what was available but the various departments were being set up and again there'd been no restriction on the amount of money that had been used. The building was absolutely ideal. There was a whole atmosphere about that place, [so that] when you walked in, you thought, 'this is impressive.' "

•   •   •

The ingenuity of the MBB-G.I.P.R.O. contract lay in its anticipating the very restrictions that Richard Speier and other authors of the Missile Technology Control Regime were then in the midst of devising in Washington. The authors of the artfully-drawn contract between MBB and Gildemeister had two apparent aims. They sought to avoid confrontation with German law. Simultaneously, they foresaw ways to avoid cumbersome arms control regulations that might inhibit profits. The key to this concept was that, officially, MBB was only a sub-contractor. Gildemeister, which had a direct contract with Iraq, fronted the deal and assumed legal responsibility for export licenses—including those involving specialized aspects of missile technology.

This posed a technical problem. Gildemeister lacked the technical and legal expertise to submit a license application to the government about missile goods. The way out? MBB assumed contractual responsibility for examining the sensitive equipment requirements for all licenses. Still, MBB was not responsible for the license itself. The actual export application had to be made by Gildemeister.

The contract found the loopholes in M.T.C.R. even before the M.T.C.R. agreement was fully conceptualized. Categories One and Two of the agreement, then in its initial stages of drafting, distinguished between overall systems and sub-systems for missile production, and individual items of manufacture. How would the manufacturer fudge the distinctions? If, according to the law—the law referred to in the contract was that of the German Federal Republic—an individual piece of equipment didn't need a special license, but did require one as part of an overall system, then MBB committed itself through the contract to pack and ship this piece to the client separately.

With the spirit—though not the letter—of German law effectively evaded, the contract's authors moved on to other hypothetical situations. What would happen, for example, between Gildemeister Projecta and MBB when an "outlawed" item somehow arrived in Iraq from a third country? Who was responsible for making this outlawed item part of the project? The answer was spelled out contractually in black and white. That responsibility was MBB's. The German arms manufacturer maintained overall responsibility on-site for installation and maintenance of all equipment wherever it might come from. In fact, whether that piece of equipment came from Germany or another country was irrelevant; only the shipper of "illegal exports" from Germany could be charged with a violation of export law. Since MBB wasn't responsible for shipping it from Germany, but only for on-site installation, the industrial giant would escape legal responsibility or punishment for its evasion of the intent of the law.

Sa'ad-16 contracts, including MBB-TT's contract with Gildemeister, provided a commercial answer to M.T.C.R. regulations even before the treaty was fully formulated. Through the contracts, MBB could effectively evade the intent of German law while not violating a single letter of content. The contracts laid the basis for Iraq's long-range missile programs and would—among other factors—enable the Iraqis to significantly modify the Russian SCUD-Bs and to attempt to develop a solid-state rocket like Condor-2.

•   •   •

As sophisticated as the MBB-G.I.P.R.O. contract was, it was hardly necessary. MBB and Gildemeister got export licenses from the German government as a matter of routine. They didn't have to plead their case or make any special appeals, even if illegal missile items were included in the export. They just had to fill out the application.

Gildemeister officials gave the German government its first application forms early, even before the deal was completed—by June, 1983— in order to sense out the obstacles and enter the contract with Iraq in good conscience. One license application involved "the export of machinery, electronic equipment, regulations, measurement instruments for an institute of research and development, and training with 8 main sections." The governmental licensing office at Eschborn promptly stamped the application "approved." A government letter dated June 3, 1983, was typical. Signed by Dr. G. Welzien, it stated, "Here is the requested confirmation. Our conclusion is that the merchandise can now be exported without further correspondence."

Other export permissions followed just as easily. A "free rein for deal makers," pronounced a Green party Bundestag representative, Maria Luise Teubner, in 1989 after some publicity had first emerged in the German press about German weapons-related exports.

"We simply have an open door," added Hermann Bachmaier of the opposition SPD, eager to exploit a chance to criticize Chancellor Helmut Kohl's ruling CDU.

The magazine *Der Spiegel* insinuated that more than bureaucratic incompetence was involved. Licensing authorities had adopted "the so-calling splitting procedure," the magazine wrote. This meant that orders for systems or sub-systems "were divided up into individual shipments and therefore could be considered legal—'close your eyes and let them through.' " The magazine spotlighted the role of the licensing bureau's Dr. Guenter Welzien—by then retired—the man who had signed the permissions. Customs inspectors wondered if Welzien's seemingly automatic approval of MBB applications didn't make him liable to penalty. They obtained a warrant and searched his home.

I never met Dr. Welzien. But from what I came to know of Germany's business-friendly atmosphere, no lone clerk would or could oppose an export application from any of Germany's corporate estab-lishment, much less the partially state-owned MBB, which was the country's largest aviation and aerospace manufacturer. German civil servants operated strictly according to the letter of the law and exer-cised little individual initiative in interpreting it. MBB's batteries of lawyers and specialists made sure both that export applications were legal, according to the literal wording of the regulations, and that the company could freely trade its missile products. After the first press revelations, German prosecutors looked into the possibility of charg-ing the retired Dr. Welzien with neglect or malfeasance. They decided they didn't have a case and let the matter drop.

Officals such as Richard Speier and his colleagues in the Pentagon had operated on at least one false assumption: that Western govern-ments would get detailed and accurate reporting from their own nation's major industrial firms, and would have access to the details of missile deals. Thus Western governments could maintain overall responsibility for missile supplies to countries outside the NATO orbit. This was not the case in Germany. MBB deliberately created a business structure aimed at warding off governmental interference and purposely deceiving both the government and the public. The German B.N.D., the country's overseas intelligence service, did have knowledge of some basic facts. But MBB executives proved extremely stingy in providing German officials with essential technical details that might have provided the basis for halting the project at an early stage.

The government, in any case, had little power to stop the deal. They didn't even have the legal power to find out about it. As Dr. Joachim Jahnke, the man who later headed the export section in the Economics Ministry told me in 1991, "Most of our information comes from foreign intelligence services, like the Americans or Israelis. We don't have the power to conduct an independent investigation in Germany.

"Then, if we do believe the law has been violated, it's our obligation to turn the information over to a public prosecutor as soon as we have a basis for suspicion."

There could be no suspicion without information. But German officials lacked a mechanism to get the facts. The Foreign Trade Act of 1961 mandated that any restrictions on trade were "to be stated such that freedom of economic activity is interfered with as little as possible." German officials lacked even the tools to conduct an informal investigation unless they already had substantive evidence of criminal illegality. The export-hungry Germans wanted to leave their companies with the right to sell goods unhampered.

Just as MBB's job was to sell its products, the primary goal of the German Economics Ministry was to encourage German exports, not prevent them. Dr. Lorenz Schomerus, head of foreign economic policy at the Economics Ministry, admitted to me in a telephone interview that most German politicians just wanted to see "the quickest and smoothest possible handling" of German exports.

MBB, so far as could be determined, stayed within the letter of the law. But because of its slippery dealing and long-range ambitions, the company, and more indirectly Germany, assumed a primary responsibility for Iraq's burgeoning missile capability. A German economics official, Hans Rummer, summed up the system best. He told a German reporter that his office was the "Federal Office *for* Trade and Industry"— not *against*.

CHAPTER NINE

The German Question

> "Look, our company was charged with helping a foreign government develop chemical warfare. We reject this totally, and as Germans we are sensitive to this charge. This is why we took the government to court."
>
> ***Helmut Maier, Director General,***
> ***the Karl Kolb Company***

IN THE 1980s, Germany was a triple miracle: economically, politically, and legally. Beneath the surface, though, there were stirrings of a long-suppressed dream, one that few Germans dared to discuss openly: that of German unity. Many Germans felt that re-unification between the country's eastern and western halves might take a generation or two to achieve but was inevitable. Few suspected that the drive towards unification would surge irresistably and in 1990 Germany would officially become one.

Germany was once again Europe's strongest country, measured only economically, and still an ascending power, transformed from a basket case into a land of bounty. German goods, with a reputation for quality—both for sturdiness and advanced engineering—sold everywhere. Germany reeked of wealth as individual Germans experienced a prosperity never previously known. The vanquished of World War II became victors in a way Hitler could never have imagined.

Politically, Germans were rightly proud of their social democracy, stable electoral system, and a legal code that offered protection to individuals and corporations. The new framework had been carefully designed to shield Germany against a resurgence of Nazi-style dictatorship.

The transportation system was superb. The German autobahns were like American superhighways except better-built, cleaner and unencumbered by speed limits or bothersome tolls. The national airline, Lufthansa, was profitable, and German airports modern and efficient. Trains belonging to the national German rail system ran up and down the country connecting Hamburg to the south, Berlin to the East, Frankfurt to the north, and Munich to the west and, as in times past, they were invariably on time.

Militarily, the country was still "betwixt and between." Strong feelings of pacifism and a determination not to get involved in "foreign adventures," as twice before in the century, inhibited the country from assuming the political role that its economic power might have warranted. Germany, allied with the West, was actually trapped at the center of the Superpower conflict. The Federal Republic experienced street demonstrations from anti-militarist and pro-peace youths each time the Americans tried to station major new weapons such as Pershing missiles or binary chemicals on German soil. Germany still had foreign troops—Russian on one side, American, British and French on the other—stationed in the country as a legacy of defeat and occupation. Germans purposefully kept their own army modest. The country became a member of NATO but didn't dispatch soldiers to foreign lands.

German history—when it included poison gas and nerve agents—was anathema to most Germans, particularly the political leadership and intelligentsia. The chemical warfare plants at Dyhernfurth and Falkenhagen, where Germany had begun nerve agent production during World War II, stood unused and abandoned. Few if any modern Germans knew anything about chemical warfare and even fewer wanted to learn. The stigma in German society was too great. The idea that

German citizens would provide the equipment and expertise to "crazy" nations like Syria, Libya, or Iraq was not accepted, or seen as believable, by responsible Germans from the political right all the way to the far left. Germans didn't conceive of themselves as falling into that World War II trap again or dirtying their name in the world community. The Holocaust was confined to the collective psychic closet, seeming to many Germans part of an abnormal world from a barely-believable past. The less said about it, the better. Germans didn't want to know about history—or, at least, certain parts of it.

Then the suppressed reality began to re-emerge as German companies were implicated in sales of equipment and know-how that could produce poison gas and nerve agent for some of the world's most erratic dictatorial states, including Iraq and Libya. On the face of it, this surfacing reality had nothing to do with the average German. It had to do with a few small firms which could be looked on as bad guys—and which, in any case, provided equipment that might not have been specifically designed for chemical weaponry. The sales were part of fierce world-wide competition in which Germany's powerful chemical industry played a leading role. An industry pamphlet published in Frankfurt in early 1985 viewed the coming year "with realistic optimism." Turnover in the chemical industry had risen by eleven percent in 1984, with domestic turnover accounting for seven percent of that growth and foreign turnover sixteen percent. This new balance resulted in a startling situation in Germany, the pamphlet pointed out. The share of foreign business "for the first time in the history of the Federal Republic's chemical industry...[reached] "a share of over 50 percent." This meant "that practically every second job in the chemical industry depends on foreign trade."

Almost all that trade was civilian. But by 1984, Western governmental intelligence services had gathered what they regarded as convincing evidence that identified German companies as being primarily responsible for chemical warfare production in the Iran-Iraq War. The American government brought the attention of the German government to the activities of the Karl Kolb Company. This firm had its offices in a suburban enclave in Dreieich, not far from Frankfurt Airport.

American officials confided to Chancellor Helmut Kohl and his aides that the company and its affiliate, Pilot Plant, had supplied the Iraqis with a number of installations capable of manufacturing mustard gas and the fatal nerve agents tabun and sarin. *Der Spiegel* reported that agents from the C.I.A. "put on a sound and light show" for Kohl and a few top aides, with the benefit of slides, photos, graphs and charts.

With the information surfacing about German companies selling equipment that could produce poison gas and nerve agent to some of the world's "crazies," it appeared as if Helmut Kohl got the message. Like other good Germans, he did not want Germany to be tainted with scandals like poison gas or nerve agent production. That could be damaging not only to Germany's reputation but also its political standing and even its trade. Kohl's political intuition told him the odor of scandal could raise ghosts buried forty years before, touching sensitivities better left dormant. It could create the kind of controversy where his own leadership would be questioned. Kohl ordered his Economic Affairs Ministry to bring the German involvement in chemical weaponry to a halt.

German officials immediately took what they thought would be decisive steps. For one, they expanded the list of chemical raw materials that had to be monitored by law. Additionally, the German government took a radical step that no European country had taken before. Since almost all chemical industry equipment is dual use and can be used for civilian or military purposes, the Germans banned the export without a license of any plant capable of manufacturing phospho-organic materials—the kind of highly toxic equipment that could produce nerve agent. This became "Section D" of the German governmental regulations concerning illegal weaponry. "No one else has regulated the sale of chemical industry equipment," an official proudly proclaimed. "Frankly, we've done more than anybody else."

For a brief time, top officials in Washington and Bonn thought that stopping commercial misconduct by several small German firms would be easy. Once governmental pressure was applied, the errant companies would swiftly desist from further trade. Government officials told the Karl Kolb Company that its traffic with Iraq should stop.

Then came a surprise. Instead of lying down and taking it, Karl Kolb and its associated companies fought back, saying the equipment they provided could not possibly produce poison gas and that they were shocked by the allegations. Company chairman Helmut Maier claimed the equipment his company had sold was "off the shelf." What had been sent to Baghdad were standard items for the chemical industry, laboratory-scale equipment that was not at all specially designed for making toxic chemical weapons. They contended they had a right, if not a duty, to sell, to export, to profit, so long as they were in conformity with the law and the ideals underlying the triple miracle—which they said they were.

Some very tentative back-room negotiations followed, in which probed the possibility of the state compensating the Karl Kolb Company or its affiliate Pilot Plant for loss of income. But there was no budget for such compensation under the law. The German government response fell far short of what Karl Kolb officials thought attractive or fair. Karl Kolb officials swiftly concluded the bureaucrats were asking them to be the fall guys for selling the type of equipment that, they argued, many other German firms sold all over the world.

As experts legitimately point out, much chemical industry equipment is dual use, good for both civilian and military application. Kolb's chairman Maier told me later, both contentiously and with some bitterness, "If we had followed governmental regulations we wouldn't have been able to export a tin can."

The company challenged the government to prove its case. A series of court cases began in the financial court in Kassel in 1985. Few could dispute the admirable principle followed rigidly by the German courts: a man or company is innocent until proven guilty. A strong bias existed for free trade unless it could be specifically and definitively proven that the facility was not only dangerous but "specially constructed" for chemical weaponry.

The court's verdict was a shocker. The Karl Kolb Company affiliate, Pilot Plant—and not the German government—came out on top. This was partly on technical grounds. The judge scolded the government for not having made its administrative decisions strictly according to German law. Not a quorum of the government, but only a few ministers, had decided on changes in the raw materials and technical sales proscribed by law and the way these were to be applied. The court ruled that the lack of a quorum meant that the government had acted arbitrarily and improperly—and its regulations were illegal. Strangely, the judge also ruled that the German government could make regulatory decisions concerning chemical exports only in the context of international agreements and not on its own.[1]

The implied basis of the decision, as elaborated by the judge in a detailed ruling, was more radical: in the event of an individual or company conflict with government, the German court favored the rights of individual Germans and/or German companies. The burden of proof lay with the government. The court required hard evidence that the particular pieces of equipment contracted by Kolb to S.E.P.P. were specially and specifically designed to actually produce nerve agents and mustard gas. Business contracts, in brief, were sacred. And government officials could not interfere in them at their whim simply because they suspected the equipment provided might be misused by the buyer.

Over the next few years the government kept losing in a dizzying round of appeals in German courts. In January, 1992, the government finally got a decision in its favor: the court ruled that the government ministers could decide on a regulation on poison gas even though they were not sitting together in a single room in a governmental session in Bonn. This time, Pilot Plant appealed to Germany's Supreme Court.

Pilot Plant capitalized on legal victories throughout the mid-and late-1980's. It continued to fulfill "commercial" obligations to Iraq, both by supplying spare parts for the chemical plants and partly by finding alternative routings via Austrian and French firms to service the clients.[2] At the same time, other companies, some of which had been associated with Karl Kolb in Iraq, were supplying Baghdad with additional equipment, as well as chemicals, that could be used for military purposes.

While the governmental appeals and counter-appeals sallied back and forth, Western intelligence experts dealing with the problem estimated that the Iraqis were hard at work using Karl Kolb's and other German equipment to make mustard gas and the nerve agents tabun and sarin.

Bonn and its environs became familiar territory for researching chemical weaponry and the spread of missile capability in the Third World. The hills spread upward on the other side of the Rhine, to the east, their nestling green cover punctuated by fortress-like stone castles springing out of the river. This is the country of Ludwig von Beethoven and German high culture. A small ferry line carries both cars and passengers across the river. Beethoven's Fifth seems to spiritually crescendo over Germany's crack express trains speeding up and down the Rhine Valley, as well as resound over commercial ferries plying the river North and South. Cruise boats dock in suburban Bad Godesberg to disgorge passengers. At times, walking around the tree-lined streets of elegant Bad Godesburg or traipsing through the mall areas in Bonn, or even strolling lazily along the Rhine itself, the legacy of World War II seems to lack relevance.

The U.S. Government used several diplomatic levels to transmit information to Bonn. If the matter were extremely sensitive or required a policy decision, the American ambassador would himself convey the information to the Chancellor's office, one of his top associates, or a high Foreign Office official. One popular line for urgent matters went from then-U.S. Ambassador Richard Burt through Chancellor Helmut Kohl's top security advisor, Horst Teltschik. More routine diplomatic exchanges were carried out between the State Department and the German Foreign Ministry. But within the cumbersome German bureaucracy, it sometimes took weeks before a document with a "secret" classification could be properly catalogued or attended to.

There developed another level of transmission that was official but not really so. It consisted of "non-papers"—a term that gained great popularity among government officials—containing sensitive or classified information that could be easily accessed by officials whether or not they had high-security clearance. This was used with good effect when it came to non-conventional weaponry: chemical, biological, nuclear, missiles. These written memos and briefing documents, intended to communicate vital information, officially did not exist because otherwise handling them would have been too cumbersome. They were of unknown or non-certifiable origin. They were not attributable. They never bore a letterhead or carried a signature. But they were universally known by German officialdom to have originated somewhere deep in the belly of the sprawling American Embassy complex, in Bonn's exclusive Bad Godesburg suburb.

Non-papers had their advantages. They were "deniable." At their best, they facilitated communication between the Americans and Germans, and then between different sections of the German government, on the details of commercial relations between German firms and countries such as Iraq or Libya. Since they officially did not exist, they did not have to be stamped "secret" or "confidential." More formal confidential documents made it incumbent upon German officials to pass the papers over to security officials for a rigorous review, a process that could take weeks or months. If that weren't bad enough, the chances were odds-on that the document might never arrive at the desk of the official who should be handling it in, for example, the Economics Ministry, since that official might lack a proper security classification.

But non-papers could also be a detriment once an investigation got serious. Non-papers were usually too vague to be of any significant help to police. They did not constitute proof. They could not be used in court. As one of the German investigators, a man later responsible for the prosecution of one of the German companies, told me disgustedly: "What good are they? I don't need intelligence. I need a piece of paper that somebody has signed. What I need is evidence, not rumors and suspicions."

The gigantic Economic Affairs Ministry is on the outskirts of Bonn. Dr. Lorenz Schomerus, the man in charge of the section dealing with weapons exports and very used to non-papers and their use, authorized me to meet a number of people in his ministry. They were all knowledgable gentlemen whose attitude bore the stamp of a uniformity imposed by ministry policy. A few themes lay outside the realm of their conventional wisdom. One was that German experts knew enough to provide technical expertise about chemical warfare to anybody. "And what German would help foreigners, especially those not inside NATO, to make chemical weapons?" one German official responded as I sat in his office. "I don't find it acceptable."

By "acceptable" he meant not only acceptable but also "believable." The idea that Germans were, once again, willingly participating in the manufacture of poison gas and nerve agent was simply beyond the realm of the official imagination, and at odds with the dominant force of public opinion in the country.

A second idea about which German officials were skeptical was that a Third World country such as Iraq could successfully produce nerve agents like sarin or tabun in industrial quantities. After all, the ancestors of modern Germans were themselves world-class industrialists. They had experienced enormous technical difficulties in constructing their nerve agent factories some 50 years previously. Hundreds, perhaps thousands, mostly slave laborers, died in the effort, mainly from wayward toxic fumes. German officials believed that the technical complexity of plant construction for nerve agents would forbid Third World countries like Iraq from doing it. If Germans couldn't do it (though that was half a century before), German officials assured themselves, how could Iraq gain enough expertise from Germans, men with no practical experience, to master the complex management and technical problems?

Even while proclaiming their sensitivity to the problem, the German bureaucrats were scrupulous about not accusing one of their own firms of illegality: "We can't be sure that particular plant is the one producing chemical weapons," one of the German officials told me at the time. "Maybe it's another plant... How do we know?"

Since German officials believed their own arguments, stopping the entire process of chemical weaponry proliferation proved far more difficult than originally anticipated. The ministerial aides often got annoyed by probing inquiries. Either they wanted to be left alone to do their job, or it was a job they didn't particularly enjoy doing.

Beneath every conversation simmered the horrifying reality of the Holocaust some 40 years before, and Germany's principal role in poison gas and nerve agent development. The German reputation for technical wizardry in the use of chemical weaponry during the Holocaust was exaggerated. Their real talent was in management. Even at its most advanced, the use of poison gas in the concentration camps was technically as simple as running a car engine, which was the way it had been done, for the most part, at places like Treblinka and Auschwitz.

•   •   •

In 1984, the German government arranged with Karl Kolb and the Iraqi government to send a mission to Iraq. Its job: to determine if the Iraqis had used Karl Kolb's equipment to make poison gas or nerve agent. Though German bureaucrats in Bonn refused to tell me who were the two experts who had gone to Iraq, their names appeared in court records. One was a government employee at the German government export licensing center at Eschborn. His name was Mannfred Ruck. His broad responsibilities included overseeing exports of the German chemical industry.

Ruck, later to be ridiculed by a few of his colleagues for what they thought was his investigative ineptitude, was quite friendly and welcoming by phone. He promptly gave me an appointment. The suburban Sud-Eschborn rail station just outside Frankfurt turned out to be smack in the middle of a field. To get to the offices where Ruck worked, you had to follow a well-trodden dirt path, circle a building, swing left down a surburban lane, cross over a street, finally arriving at a government office building that looked more like a residential apartment.

Ruck's office worked hand-in-glove with the Economics Ministry in Bonn. By the time I got to him, on a cold winter's day with a touch of snow swirling outside, he had been ordered by his bureaucratic superiors not to speak to me. "You see, they're concerned, there's a court case pending," he explained to me apologetically, after I had reached his office on the seventh floor. "Also, they were surprised you found out my name and that I'd been to Iraq. It isn't exactly public knowledge."

While I gave myself points for enterprise and initiative, I calculated that no German could appear too uncooperative when discussing chemical weaponry: the national consciousness wouldn't allow it. I asked him if we could just sit and chat for a few minutes, even if we didn't discuss the case directly. That couldn't hurt, so long as we didn't explore details of his trip to Iraq. His room was sparse: a square window with a view of a sprawling residential area, a few files, a number of books. Though thousands of applications poured into his office and those of his subordinates, there was no sign of a computer.

The export licensing bureau filled a curious function. What its officials did was to assess—based on the manufacturer's description—

whether the product's export was in violation of German regulations. If it was, clerks would review the item or pass it on to their superiors, like Mannfred Ruck, for a ruling. If the application did not on the face of it conflict with the provisions of law, the office with rare exceptions automatically approved it. The exporter's word, through his written application, was accepted at face value. The office did not open shipments for inspection and could only do so on special authority.

Ruck spoke briefly about Germany and chemical arms. "You know," he said, "we really don't have too much experience with chemical weaponry. What we had in the world wars, those factories are just broken down, there's nothing there. No one wanted to go back to them. We really don't have many people in our society who know anything about it. Not really."

The German expert's trip to Iraq took place in October, 1984, he said, trying unsuccessfully to stick to generalities. It had all been quite difficult to arrange. There had been considerable negotiation with the Iraqis on the ground rules. The Iraqis were a sensitive people and very touchy about insult, feigned or real. "You didn't want to insult their honor," he explained, warming up a bit, "or you'd get nowhere in meetings with them. The people in the Middle East are like that."

Finally, the German and Iraqi governments agreed that the equipment provided by Karl Kolb could be inspected. He and a colleague flew to Iraq for a few days. He performed his inspection and promptly returned to Germany. I asked him if he felt he had free access at S.E.P.P. He said he got access to what it had been agreed he could see. A later press report indicated he had seen two buildings of the nine then either in operation or construction, but Ruck would not describe to me in detail what he had seen at S.E.P.P. or how many of the factory installations he had actually been in.

What he saw, he said, in his view did not have chemical weapons potential. He didn't want to go into the details on how his report was used, or not used, in the court case. That case was still pending. The government had appealed the verdict to a higher court. He didn't use the word, but it was all 'sub-judice.' Whatever he said might prejudice the case.

Did he have any experience with an assessment of chemical weapons capability before this case? "No, I haven't, but I'm in charge of checking chemical industry applications for export. And if you know chemistry, you can do the job," he contended.

Mannfred Ruck struck me as decent enough, like most German bureaucrats, but ineffective. He pointed out that until German experts saw those plants actually producing chemical nerve agents, or could prove positively that they did, and could additionally prove that the plants were "specially constructed" to do the job, firms weren't liable. The law, not intelligence or diplomacy, governed German governmental policy. American and Israeli diplomats—and others—could complain all they want. They could yell and shout and gesticulate. From the German standpoint it was a matter of black and white, what was printed in the regulations. There wasn't room for interpretation.

The law that governed in 1984 was straightforward enough. If chemical weaponry couldn't be found on-site at a given facility, it could not be presumed to exist. If there was only a bit of it, and the plant had other uses as well, that wasn't enough. The burden of proof lay with the government. If there were no pudding there could be no proof.

•   •   •

The chemical industry is difficult to regulate and excruciating to investigate. The same basic equipment can be used to produce either regular pesticides or chemical weaponry. There are some differences though, mainly in the kinds of safety and protection devices that are necessary for the workers, and in the anti-corrosive metallic elements that must withstand the deadly chemical combinations run through the plant. The rest is just chemistry.

I got a tip that one company producing some of the most anti-corrosive items for S.E.P.P. was Quast GmbH. Quast's home base was a village called Inden-Pier some 65 miles from Bonn. I telephoned and told a secretary I was researching the German chemical industry. She gave me an appointment with Willie Gallman, the operational boss of the company under co-owners Martin and Engelbert Quast.

"Please come at 11. We shall be happy to provide you with information on our company," the woman's voice replied cheerfully.

Inden-Pier had a few quaint houses, a store, a corner junction and, down a side road, Quast GmbH & Co. The company spread out over one or two acres of ground including a transportation shack. The offices filled a low, squat building that looked like temporary army headquarters or an enlarged Quonset hut. Quast produced stirrers, mixers and reactors for the chemical industry—big, sturdy-looking vessels and pipes for the most sophisticated chemical plants. "We build according to our own and according to your design..." proclaims a company brochure. The company specialized in fabricating equipment lined by hastelloy, which is one of the world's best, strongest and most anti-corrosive of alloy metals. It is an expensive item compared to less resistant metals, the kind of equipment that would be ideal for making nerve agent.

Willie Gallman greeted me after ten minutes. He was about six foot two, his angular face framed by German-style silver steel spectacles. He led me to a comfortable office situated at the back of the building. Gallman explained through his secretary that he didn't speak English (which I didn't believe). His secretary translated for us.

We sat at a lengthy office table at one end of the room, away from the desk, and refreshments were brought in for the conversation. Thanking him for seeing me, I immediately told him why I was there. "My research into the German chemical industry concentrates on chemical weapons deliveries to Iraq," I announced. There was a brief pause while I waited for his reaction. He twisted briefly, then he just sat there poker-faced.

I pointed out that a U.N. report had confirmed the use of chemical weaponry by Iraq and I now understood that his equipment had been used to help make this weaponry. His equipment in Iraq was quite a serious matter, I suggested, and I wanted to know why and how it had come about.

This shook him. His face fell—in fact, he didn't look very happy. Gallman declined to answer in detail. He said (through his secretary) that he could not, and would not, talk about commercial orders to or from any client or supplier. That would be strictly against policy.

After a moment's pause, he denied he had ever been in Iraq or fulfilled any order for Iraq or S.E.P.P. He had nothing to do with Iraq at all. Almost all of their product went to Germany or other European countries, and nothing more.

"What about orders supplied to the Karl Kolb company in Frankfurt?" I finally asked.

He waived his rule banning him from talking about orders. He confirmed that he had supplied hastelloy columns, stirrers and reactors to the Kolb company. But, he said, as far as he knew about it, "the order went from Quast's factory in Inden-Pier to Kolb's offices in the Frankfurt area."

"Had there been export of these goods?" I questioned, knowing that it was only at the point of export that German law might be broken.

Not at all, he stressed. "We supplied to another German company." He pointed out that I knew the name of this company and should speak with its people. As for further routing of the equipment beyond Frankfurt, he had no idea. He had personally operated within the law.

I thanked him after a half hour and left. I had learned that Quast was not responsible—at least in its own eyes—for export of chemical warfare equipment to Iraq. Quast had done nothing illegal. They had not even sent one iota of their equipment overseas to Baghdad. They were only sub-contractors. They were only part of the system. Resonances of an earlier day crossed my mind. I took a train back to Bonn. It ran precisely on time.

•   •   •

Between appointments in Bonn, I telephoned the Karl Kolb firm in Dreieich. Managing director Helmut Maier was not in. I wound up speaking to his technical manager, Dieter Backfisch, who said he was familiar with the case and felt authorized to speak.

Backfisch told me Pilot Plant, a sub-company put up by Karl Kolb, went into liquidation in October, 1985, due to the actions of the German government, which put a near-complete block on the exportation of chemical industry equipment to Iraq that could handle toxic materials. The fuss was "ridiculous," Backfisch contended, since the plants in Iraq were laboratory size and very small.

Pilot Plant employed about five people, and sold to everybody, "but on a very small scale." Pilot Plant's principal business was Iraq. As for "our equipment," it was not custom-made for Iraq, Backfish contended, and much of it was off the shelf. When it was put into existing buildings "we always had problems in fitting into them."

Backfisch said that two German governmental experts went down to Iraq to check out whether the Kolb-Pilot Plant equipment was being used for chemical warfare. The first was a chemical industries expert, the second an expert on safety. They came to no conclusions. As a result of the court verdict, Backfisch claimed, it was clear that no units supplied by Pilot Plant could result in the production of chemical weaponry.

"You see, the Pilot Plant equipment was not a production plant. It has no capacity," he explained to me. "It is a pilot plant, something a bit larger than a laboratory but not for production."

He estimated that small amounts of toxic materials could indeed be fed into it, but what was supplied was "a research type unit. You put in 50 kilos [110 pounds] or so, make a run, distill and extract, try it at different temperatures, and you see what comes out." More specifically, the pilot plant "could use a twenty to eighty kilo capacity for a batch, depending on the material, and a run could take three to four, or even five to eight days, depending on materials."

Kolb and Pilot Plant had no responsibility whatsoever for the kinds of raw materials and chemicals run through the plant. "Any kinds of chemicals can be put in. We don't know what kinds of chemicals," he said.

•   •   •

Helmut Maier, Karl Kolb's company manager, was waiting for me. He was extremely tense. About five foot eight, balding, dressed in a dark business suit. A typical businessman, nothing more. "The whole matter is entirely ridiculous," he told me. "There's nothing toxic—nothing that could make chemical weapons. The German government knows everything. They looked at all the plans."

Maier identified himself as general manager of both Karl Kolb and of the now non-active subsidiary company, Pilot Plant. He said right off he would not discuss specifics. The German government had all the details.

The company's Iraqi business started in the 1970s. The Pilot Plant subsidiary was created in 1977. Said Maier: "Iraq has many universities and research institutes, and people are trained everywhere. They needed to do research in agro-chemicals. That's when they turned to us."

"There are open vessels at the place [in Iraq]," he continued. "Hundreds of pipes, connections, gaskets, normal equipment. The facility isn't designed for high toxic materials—there aren't even any safety procedures. I repeat, the whole thing is ridiculous.

"For our defense in court, we called the German government experts. They should have been witnesses for the government. Their testimony would have completely supported our argument. The German government wouldn't let them appear before the judge.

"We wanted to go to court against the government because we're caught in the middle of a political issue, which doesn't relate at all to our equipment. We have business in dozens of countries and our name and reputation are at stake."

Maier fiercely disputed German export regulations, which he claimed were "specifically" directed against his company. He corrected himself: "They were directed against all exports of chemical plants, but they were made because of us. These regulations are so vague—no one could export a cooking pot without permission."

Maier argued that the Germans were submissive to American pressure and that the C.I.A. was the source of the trouble. The agency was ready to cast unfounded allegations against innocent German businessmen such as himself. "We know American officials visited the German government. But where did they get their information from? Even some of the basics, like location, it is wrong, from what we know. I'd like to know where the C.I.A. got their experts. In Iraq, it's all open, there are no secrets, we gave every information and have been fully open."

Maier had the boldness to use German history to defend himself and his company. "Look, our company was charged with helping a foreign government develop chemical warfare. We reject this totally, and as Germans we are sensitive to this charge. This is why we took the government to court."

"Additionally, we asked that somebody go there to verify on the spot. But then their report was kept secret. This was of considerable worry to us. I was in a terrific fix. For us, it was a question not only of proving lack of intent, but showing that our pilot plant was small and could not make chemical weaponry. We had to prove our innocence—not only as regards intent. And we did."

Maier claimed that Karl Kolb and Pilot Plant had competition in Iraq, and now the Iraqis were turning to others to meet their commercial needs. Karl Kolb and Pilot Plant stopped supplying Iraq in 1984 after German export regulations changed. Then the Iraqis began buying worldwide. "We have indications that the Americans are supplying what the Iraqis couldn't get from us," Maier contended. But when pressed, he offered no specifics.

When pushed for some detail on technical specifications, he said he wouldn't discuss them. "The German government has all the plans, all the specifics. Get it from them."

I said that estimates differ on the capacity of the plant provided. The most reliable, I said, was in the order of an input of 10,000 liters, or about 10,000 gallons.

Maier: "Absolutely impossible."

In speaking about the location of S.E.P.P., Maier commented: "It was written that it was set far off in the desert. That's bullshit."

"The facility provided by Pilot Plant was located next to a main highway. Every day thousands of trucks pass by." Why, questioned Maier, would the Iraqis put such a facility for chemical warfare right next to a main road where everybody could see it?

If Maier were to be believed, I could relax in my inquiry and rest somewhat assured: even if Kolb had supplied Iraq with equipment, it wasn't lethal. Also, it had nothing to do with chemical warfare. If the Iraqis wanted to run toxic chemicals through the installation, and come out with some mustard or nerve agent, that was the Iraqis' business. What did it have to do with Karl Kolb?

If those chemical warfare facilities could be found, if they could be identified as of German origin, and finally if they could be identified as being Karl Kolb's and proved to be not only used for but specially designed for making chemical weaponry—then future chemical equipment sales would perhaps cease.

In these years of sparring between Karl Kolb and the German government, one war was won, one lost. The German nation and German citizens triumphed in their continuing battle for the rights of the individual and the corporate entity against the intervening power of the state. The West in general, Germany included, lost its war to prevent the spread of chemical weaponry to errant Third World countries.

Halabja:
A Foretaste of Future War

**"Like figures unearthed in Pompeii, the victims of
Halabja were killed so quickly that their corpses
remained in suspended animation."**

Nicholas Beeston of the **London Times**

SPRING, 1988. The eighth year of the Iran-Iraq War. As winter drew to
its end, the missile terror that became known as "The War of the
Cities" began. It was Februry 29th, a leap year, but this leap year was
one which those who lived in Teheran will never forget. Missiles
plunged into neighborhoods, killing randomly and causing panic. The
Iraqis made no pretense that they were aiming for anything but civilian targets.

Iran hit back. Given the sprawling nature of both capital cities,
Baghdad and Teheran, the generals on both sides couldn't miss hitting
something. They launched their missiles, sent them screaming through
the stratosphere over a distance of several hundred kilometers, and
prayed for enemy deaths. "The War of the Cities," the orgy in death-

dealing missile warfare that marked the last stage of that forlorn and tragic war, reached its climactic apogee in March and April, 1988. In most cases the generals got more deaths per launch than they could have reasonably wished. The missiles slammed haphazardly into vast residential areas to kill tens and sometimes hundreds of women, children, and old men. Once launched, no defense in the hands of any Middle Eastern nation could stop a ballistic missile from arriving at a target, any target, so long as it was not too precisely defined.

The vicious, eight-year-old Gulf conflict became a laboratory for murder. Civilians evacuated major cities, especially Teheran, where Western intelligence analysts estimated that some one third of the ten million people resident in the city fled to calmer climes. Still, the missile was only a vehicle, a deliverer, it was not the message in and of itself. The message lay in the missile's warhead, and particularly its explosive and destructive capacity, which it carried in its tip. The warhead could contain conventional weapons. It could also store the "nonconventional": the nuclear or chemical or biological. These last were all "terror weapons" or "weapons of mass destruction." They were all, to some extent, illegal by virtue of dictates developed over the course of decades in the world community.

With the winter rainy season coming to an end, both Iran and Iraq girded themselves for the offensives that each hoped would be decisive in turning the tide of war in its favor. Two weeks after Iraq launched the War of the Cities, the Iranians retaliated with ground offensives deep in Iraqi territory. The main attacks were in northern Iraq, in Kurdistan. On March 14th, Iranian soldiers approached the Iraqi provincial capital of Suleymaniyah, also a center for the country's Kurdish population. Spokesmen announced this was in retaliation for the firing of SCUD-B missiles at Iranian civilians in Teheran and the holy city of Qom.

Soon, Iranian announcers triumphantly broadcast the news that their army had destroyed most of an Iraqi brigade brought in as reinforcement. As the battle progressed, Iranian advances continued. Nearby was the city of Halabja. The Kurdish underground and its more overt guerrilla combat units, friendly to Iranian forces, joined the advance. In the eyes of the Iraqis, they were a subversive element that could tie down Iraqi forces and keep them immobilized at a time when every available man was required to fight the more numerous Iranians; and they were particularly despicable because they were Iraqi citizens. The battle for Halabja was part of the Iraqi counter-attack against the Iranian offensive. The lesson: to demonstrate that those who cooperated with the Iranians would pay a fierce price. The immediate players at Halabja were the Kurds, the Iraqi Air Force, the Iranian Army, a scattering of Kurdish rebels, and Halabja's residents.[1] Less directly, the Iraqis had a supporting cast of dozens from European companies that contributed the supplies of poison gas warfare at considerable profit.

•   •   •

In 1973, the simmering Kurdish rebellion had forced Iraqi leaders, Saddam Hussein among them, to maintain forces in the country's north near Mosul. The Kurds thus inhibited the Iraqis from sending more than a single division to fight the Israelis, who had been attacked by Egypt from the west and Syria to the northeast in what became known as the Yom Kippur war. Two years later, the Shah abandoned— an appropriate term, according to the Kurds, is "sold out"—the Kurds in the 1975 Algiers agreement. The armed revolt fizzled out.

Iraq's 1980 attack on Iran came as the Kurds were outwardly quiescent. Beneath the surface though, there was a new revolt brewing. Iraq's Kurds sought, if not independence, then at least the kind of political identity through autonomy that would provide them with the right to run their own internal affairs. The Kurds compared themselves—not unjustly or unreasonably—to Hitler's Jewish victims. Thousands of Kurds had been murdered by the Iraqis. Yet the Iraqis continued to expel Kurds from their villages and "de-Kurdize" Kurdistan. The Kurds were and are a people—but they are a people alone, their "homeland" located inside the borders of modern nation-states that have no interest in vacating the territory: Iraq, Iran, Turkey and Syria. Kurdistan was and is and probably will remain only an idea.

As the Gulf War between Iraq and Iran went on year after year, the Middle East dictum that "the enemy of my enemy is my friend" pinpointed the quandary. Tragedies occurred without external political consequence for either the victims or the perpetrators. The Kurds had a natural sympathy for Iraq's enemies and entered into a loose alliance with the Iranians. For the Iraqis, the nagging Kurdish rebellion was not only an annoyance. It was a dangerous diversion. And it got some Iraqi Army people and Saddam Hussein very angry.

The townspeople of Halabja looked on with curiosity— certainly, without fear—as the Iranian troops marched by that March 16th. A still little-known Iranian-made film describes the battle in detail. The video is an almost unedited forty minute documentary made by Iranian army camera teams about the events at Halabja. Except for some 45 seconds released by the Iranians in the days after the attack, it was never seen in its entirety on Western television. The footage constitutes a unique historical record of what became modern history's seminal chemical warfare battle.

The film follows Iran's victory march through northern Iraq. The Iranian army cameramen/reporters paused to interview a number of villagers. The villagers used the occasion to welcome the Iranians and cast aspersions on the manhood of the Iraqis. One interviewer spoke with an Iraqi officer from a group of what appeared to be at least two hundred Iraqi prisoners squatting in the dust. The Iraqi officers and soldiers showed no fear, but identified themselves and succinctly told the story of their capture.

Then the film panned past mud adobe huts and paved and unpaved city streets. The cameraman paused at a shop near the *suq*, the market area. He walked up and down the stalls with its paltry produce, his shadow preceding him to market.

The camera next filmed the Iranian troops, accompanied by Kurdish rebels, making their way through the town. Some of the Iranian soldiers carried bazookas, others rifles. One civilian, probably a Kurd, drove up in a sporty new car.

The next seconds in the barely-edited documentary took place on the outskirts of the city in the hills above Halabja. One of the video crews, parked in the safety of the surrounding hills, began recording the Iraqi Air Force initiating an attack. Suddenly, there was the sound of explosions. And though you couldn't see the planes actually unloading their deadly ordnance, you could hear the swoosh of the jets, the bombs dropping, and catch glimpses of the white clouds of nerve agent and mustard gently settling onto a suddenly surreal and extremely still earth. You could almost feel the knife-like effect that created numbing silence on the streets of Halabja city.

The car carrying the camera crew began to move swiftly. The camera continued to roll. Civilians began to scurry out of their houses, trying to escape the crowded downtown area and move into the surrounding high ground around Halabja.

The Iraqi planes came from the south. Though their engines could be heard, the planes could not be seen in the footage. According to some of the eyewitness reports quoted later by Iranian newspapers, the Iraqis hit Halabja first with high-explosive munitions. The noise was deafening. The residents tried to escape from their poorly-constructed adobes and scatter either into shelters or to places outside the city. It was then that a second sortie of Iraqi MIGs swept in. The Iraqi pilots, their warplanes loaded with cannisters of mustard gas and nerve agent, knew their attack would be more effective—i.e., it would kill more Kurdish civilians—if Halabja's residents were outdoors. The Iraqis unloaded their chemical bombs onto the valley floor below.

The early afternoon time turned out to be well-suited for the chemical attack. Sun peeked out from intermittent clouds flecking Halabja Valley. The wind was low, almost non-existent, allowing the bursts of chemical weaponry to settle downward like mist. White clouds of toxic chemical liquids, clearly visible in the film, swaddled Halabja valley and the city.

The chemical bombs caught the residents of Halabja out of doors on low ground. The camera captured fat Kurdish women wearing ghalabiyas moving into the hills along foot paths. Others scrambled over rocky ground to the safer heights. Some Kurdish women wept. Children held hands with their mothers. A few infants were carried.

Those who had escaped from Halabja city, and the low points at valley center, reacted instinctively but they acted correctly. Their safety lay in reaching high ground. It was their best and only option, their sole escape from the confines of Halabja as the descending clouds of toxic poisons floated downward. High ground was the one area where the chemical rain didn't fall.

As the cameras rolled, the clouds, barely a kilometer or two distant, hung over the city, dispersing their poison. Beyond the eyes of the cameras there was silence. No one at that distance could yet tell what suffering lay at the heart of Halabja. The only sound was that of the bombs and the occasional blast of high explosives. No human cries could be heard.

A few seconds later, the film unveiled the awful story. What was surprising was the foolhardiness, some might call it bravery, of the Iranian video cameramen.[2] Directly after the bombing they came down into the city streets, unafraid of pockets of chemical weapons liquids. The camera caught their shadows preceding them. Shortly, there was a cut in the film. One couldn't be sure how much time elapsed. It could have been only a few minutes. The sounds changed. One heard the sound of footsteps as the camera crew approached the city. The film itself became like a frozen still frame. There was quiet. The film showed a barren city. Where once there had been life and activity, now the streets were empty. The silence was interrupted only by the wailing of a few survivors.

The dead were everywhere, Kafkaesque mannequins on street after street within the Kurdish city. Most of the victims lay outside. Their faces gleamed—as if a dab of reflector cream had been rubbed on them. Many of the dead had a froth of saliva frozen on their lips, dripping down like icicles. This was a telltale sign of nerve gas.[3] What happened to the human body at the point of death was an involuntary release of saliva as the nervous system "jammed" and failed to function.

Many of the villagers on the street met their end instantly. Many had what appeared to be, in the light of the sometimes distorted video colors, blue or black lips. The Iranian cameras wandered the streets of Halabja, finding victim after victim of the Iraqi nerve gas attack. They encountered young face and old faces—all frozen like still-lifes in a museum. People sitting in cars, or lying in doorways, a young woman, a family.

Yet the nerve gas casualties were the "fortunates" among the victims because of the speedy manner in which they met their fate. From the moment of exposure to death lasted only a few seconds. There were also the less lucky, those who were hit by a second wave of poison gas of a more primitive type, mustard gas. They suffered from burns and blisters, the kinds seen four and five years earlier when the Iranians sent chemical warfare victims to Western European hospitals for treatment and photo opportunities. Many survived, but others experienced an excruciatingly slow and painful death.

The most shattering image in the film was that of one old man, still healthy though disheveled, staring wildly and disbelievingly at the victims lying on the street. They were his own family. He wandered from body to body. He wailed, crying to Allah. His own life, too, I felt, was over.

• • •

The Iranians treated the tragedy as a public relations festival. They left corpses rotting in the streets and arranged for a group of Western journalists to visit Halabja to film the dead and "prove" to the world that the Iraqis had used dreaded chemical weapons. Several days after the attack, a low-flying helicopter, carrying an assortment of the world press, brushed the tops of trees and landed at Lake Dar Bandi Kham, itself a strategic target for the Iranian forces since it provided hydroelectric power for northern Iraq and Baghdad. The Iranians transported the journalists to Halabja, eight kilometers away, by bus.

A series of Picasso-like still-lifes, both grotesque and horrifyingly real, confronted the assorted representatives of the world press. Nicholas Beeston of *The London Times* wrote, "Like figures unearthed in Pompeii, the victims of Halabja were killed so quickly that their corpses remained in suspended animation. There was the plump baby whose face, frozen in a scream, stuck out from under the protective arm of a man, away from the open door of a house that he never reached.

"Nearby, a family of five who had been sitting in their garden eating lunch were cut down—the killer gas not even sparing the family cat or the birds in the tree, which littered the well-kept lawn."

Patrick E. Tyler of *The Washington Post* painted a verbal portrait of a moment that through his words became frozen in history. "Some victims hugged children in silent embraces, others sprawled in doorways. One family lay near a table set for lunch."

A French journalist quoted one of the surviving wounded as saying: "The Iranians arrived. We gave them a welcome. Then around noon— that was the bombardment. Everybody's been killed. I saw the cloud. I saw the gas."

One boy, Soman Mohammed, a 14 year old hit by mustard gas, told *The Toronto Globe and Mail's* Paul Koring "how black jet fighters dropped bombs which spewed clouds that smelled 'like weed killer.'" Soman's mother and sister, both wheezing and themselves the victims of mustard gas, lay across the room "huddled in a single bed."

Koring described how a blistered baby suckled at its mother's breasts and how men lay on beds with their "horribly burned genitals exposed." A U.S.-trained respiratory specialist, Dr. Hamid Sonrabpour, interviewed later while caring for the wounded at Teheran's Lebafi-Negaed Hospital, related how this "pathetic group of burned and coughing figures, especially the children, had 'really touched my heart because they were helpless civilians.'"

If there had been doubt before as to whether the Iraqis really used chemical weaponry in the Iran-Iraq war, that skepticism faded. But establishing the facts didn't mean anyone really cared about the Kurds or the murderous consequences of a weapon of war that the world had outlawed for over 50 years. The Kurds had no Picasso to paint their plight, no Hemingway to write of it, no leaders ready to bomb or mangle civilians in far-off lands to get their cause splashed onto the headlines of newspapers throughout the world.

The battlefield was too far away from Western capitals to be relevant. Halabja made a brief impact, then became just another battle in the ongoing war between the two crazy states, Iran and Iraq. It quickly turned into back page stuff and was then swiftly forgotten.

•   •   •

Halabja was part of the Iraqi campaign of dispersion and genocide against the Kurds. From spring to summer, 1988, the Iraqis launched an all-out attempt to either forcibly remove the Kurds from Iraqi Kurdistan or, by gassing and terrorizing them, to get them to flee themselves, according to information that I received from Kurdish sources. Shortly after the massacre at Halabja, beginning on March 22nd, a series of poison gas and nerve agent attacks on the Kurds relentlessly unfolded. The Iraqis dropped chemical bombs on the villages of Siwsinan, Dokan, Balakajar, and Jafaran, and then on Walean near Qaradagh on the 23rd. Some 75 Kurds were killed, 47 of them women and children, and 300 wounded. As a new day dawned on March 24th, there were reports of more Kurds killed at the villages of Senan and Seyo. As the wounded and homeless were fleeing from Qaradah to Suleymaniyah on March 27th, some 412 persons were reported massacred as Iraqi planes dropped cannisters of nerve agent and mustard gas. In late April there were chemical attacks in the region of Garmian in Kurdistan.

On the 3rd of May there were extensive bombardments of villages in the Koya region, including Goptapa, Askar, Garchinan, Galnagaj, Sotka, Kalasherea, Zarzy, and Chaimrezan. Some 112 were killed, another 844 wounded in these attacks. And on the 15th of May, 51 were killed and hundreds wounded in the villages of Nazaneen, Hiran, Doli, Simakloy, and Wari.

Iraq wanted to solve the "Kurdish problem"—and "de-Kurdize Kurdistan." This would achieve two ends: remove the possibility of a Kurdish uprising against the central governmental authority, and disperse this Kurdish "Fifth Column" in its ranks. Massive deployment of chemical nerve agents and mustard gas led to Kurdish deaths in the thousands and legions of walking wounded.[4]

By June, the Gulf War wound down. Iran and Iraq desisted from further military action. Saddam Hussein drew up a new shopping list for more weaponry justifiably confident he would find Western vendors to supply his lethal needs. His target for poison gas: the Kurds. A people small in number, lacking fixed territory and without significant arms for defense, the Kurds were at the mercy of the nations.

The Iraqis conclusively demonstrated that using chemical weapons was a good, if not the best way to solve the nagging Kurdish problem. Blasting unprotected enemy villages with it could be devastating, at little cost. The Iraqis showed the way for other countries like Libya and Syria to gather together a chemical weapons arsenal. They proved chemical warfare was a superb terror weapon, ideal for use against a defenseless civilian population.

The Iraqis went unpunished—as they had through all those years of poison gas and nerve agent use during the 1980s. Practically speaking, chemical weaponry became just another weapon in a fierce and bitter war.[5] The attacks on the Kurdish cities amounted to mass murder. Not only did the Kurds and Iranians lose. The West and free people were defeated, too. By failing to wage war against the spread of a scourge—chemical weaponry—its future use became probable. In the words of one Western military officer involved in stopping chemical weapons proliferation: "We tried to close the barn door, but by the time we did the horses were already out to pasture."

Unfortunately, the war of the 1980s against chemical weapons was one that few knew they were waging. The lesson of the Iran-Iraq war as regards chemical warfare was crystalline in its clarity. The weapons worked. They spread fear and destruction. They won battles and terrified civilian populations. Launched from airplanes, they could be effective. If delivered by missiles with a proper chemical warhead, they could potentially be devastating. These lessons could still have brutal consequences in the future.

CHAPTER ELEVEN

Condor Flight!

"Look. You cannot have an effective missile system operating in two or three years. Ekkehard Schrotz sold it that way, but that was his business, not mine."

Wolfgang Brunner, MBB design engineer, Condor project

THE NAME, "CONDOR," calls up grandiose visions of lonely, dramatic flights high above the confines of earth. The bird is a predator of the skies, of South American origin, one that glides above the craggy peaks and hills of California seeking out its prey. The Condor is also renowned in modern aviation. Hitler used the Condor Legion, comprised of Messerschmitts, Junkers, and other top-of-the-line aircraft, to attack Spanish republicans during that country's civil war in 1936. The planes did their work so remarkably that Pablo Picasso memorialized their effectiveness in his heart-felt anti-war masterpiece, "Guernica."

More recently, the Condor is a medium range ballistic missile. "Medium range" means that it can travel from 350 to 650 miles in flight. "Ballistic" indicates that its journey is self-propelled in space but that it can be "steered" by ground control. It re-enters the earth's atmosphere protected by a heat-resistant shield, and cruises towards a designated target using its inertial guidance navigation system. The last stage of its attack is swift, under half a minute as, aided by gravity, it dives to destroy its target. Assuming its designers have done their job right, the Condor's fairly light warhead should explode within 2500 feet of the target zone. The Condor missile conspiracy involved many nations. The missile's origin was German, it saw development in South America, and it was designed to fire up primarily in remote desert locations in the Middle East. For Iraq, Egypt, and Argentina, the Condor missile represented a super-delivery system that could, with reasonable accuracy, devastate targets in the Falklands, Teheran, the Gulf, Israel—and beyond. The Condor conspiracy spurred a billion-dollar conglomerate. It involved dozens of companies in six or more European countries. It included bizarre associations between Arab leaders, Swiss-based organizers, and giant international armament and aircraft firms founded more than half a century ago in Nazi Germany.

•   •   •

Everything about the Condor was sleek: its name, its appearance, its state-of-the-art innards. The missile incorporated some of the world's most advanced guidance, propulsion, and warhead technology systems. Condor's technological concepts brimmed with German know-how—some of it borrowed from America's Pershing-2, after which the missile was ostensibly patterned. At its inception, Condor was a program run by German missile-makers working for a state-owned German company testing and developing missile systems for foreign clients. That program could make the company a world-class competitor. It could conceivably make Germany, and not just the company and its client states, a missile power in its own right.

In the early 1980s, the Condor missile was just a dream. By 1984 contracts were signed, money exchanged, work begun, and the dream began to take shape. Four years later, in 1988, factories had been prepared, design plans and specifications provided, and real-time simulation laboratories, with militarily-designed Dopler curve facilities to measure a missile's flight, had become operational. Work was in process in secret locations in at least three different countries in remote corners of the globe.

The contracts for Condor-2 were worth several billions to those who would provide the technology and hardware. Only large aerospace companies have the technical expertise and industrial resources to develop major rocket projects. MBB played the central role in Condor-2's design and formation. Though the company was contractually more limited than in the impressive Sa'ad-16 project, its role was not less important. The head of the original Condor design team at MBB was Wolfgang Brunner. Dr. Brunner is a solid six-footer with dark hair and a flashing smile. A natural athlete who enjoys outdoor sports, he was in his early forties when the Condor-2 project began. He is also a first-class design engineer, one of the best of his generation in Germany, a country where engineers get reputations like athletes in the States and where big bucks, or Deutschmarks, can grace genius. In 1984 and '85, Brunner was a rising star at MBB. His brief was to develop a military rocket, about twenty feet long, with a $500,000 unit price.

The scene of my talk with Brunner was the Traub Restaurant in Fischbach, a tiny lakeside village nestled by the shores of scenic Lake Konstanz in southern Germany. "Our job was responsibility for the whole missile lay-out and design, including the fin activators and the (fuel) nozzle," he explained.

Across the lake were the twinkling lights of Switzerland. The area was a holiday favorite. Brunner, based in the area when I met him, loved it for its access to sport and its wholesome way of life. Brunner's days at MBB were behind him; he had resigned because of policy differences over Condor and other matters.

To the din of waitresses carrying platters of beer and fish, Brunner offered me his personal perspective on the early days of the Condor deal, the problems he had, how an intermediary series of companies called the Consen Group and its personnel related to MBB, how Western intelligence services got confused on Condor's technical specs, and how Condor-2 had really gotten off to a less-than-flying start.

Brunner said that getting Condor going in 1984 and 1985 was anything but a sure bet. "Look. You cannot have an effective missile system operating in two or three years," Brunner recalled in our long conversation. "Ekkehard Schrotz"—the head of the Consen group with whom he worked intensively at the time—"sold it that way, but that was his business, not mine.

"My job was to head up the concept or definition phase of this new missile—what would be known as Condor-2," Brunner told me. "It was derived from Condor-1. The existing motor was solid state. Frankly, I don't know if Condor-1 ever flew at all."

Condor had an internal code-name at MBB that was used by the Consen group and the Argentinians as well. That designation was "Alfa." As time passed, Alfa also got referred to as "Vector." It was all one and the same thing.

The sponsoring countries—Argentina in particular, but later (when Brunner was no longer associated with the project) Egypt, and more indirectly, Iraq—provided a list of goals for the missile: a warhead of 750 to 1,100 pounds, a C.E.P., or Circular Error Probability, of .001, which would bring the missile to within two-thirds of a mile of enemy targets in the Middle East or South America. While this was not an exceptionally accurate weapon by Superpower standards, short of what military experts refer to as tactical, it was still far more accurate than any missile up to then in use in the Third World.

Rumors spread in 1985 about Argentina getting or producing a missile that resembled the American nuclear-tipped Pershing, and sharing its expertise with the Egyptians and Iraqis. These stories made a number of Western intelligence services—especially the British and the Israelis, the most likely targets—nervous. The American-made rocket was on the way to becoming a bulwark of NATO defense and was top-of-the-line Western missile technology. The British feared that the rocket might be able to hit the Falklands from convenient sites within range. There was concern that the Condor not only looked like but could also function with the efficiency of the Pershing. When I asked him about this, Brunner downplayed the possibility. He said he regarded the comparison as rather amusing and his attitude implied it somehow lacked weight. "It's not serious about Condor being like the Pershing. This whole thing is ridiculous."

He related his view of how it happened. "We were all sitting around, the MBB aerodynamics people and me. There was a big discussion on flight mechanics. They wanted to convince me that a re-entry vehicle can not fly stably. I told them, look at the Pershing. It's flying. You put in these fins. You make it like this." He then went to the blackboard and chalked out a missile in front of the MBB team. Recalling the experience, he claimed that he had made the missile look like the Pershing. "I drew it that way—but it was just a sketch. You start with a shape and then you make your flight dynamics.

"After two or three months the aerodynamics people came to me and said, we can fly without the fins. I said we leave them in. That's it. That's why the Condor had fixed fins and looked like the Pershing."

I got a totally different view of the fins—and by implication Brunner's role in the Condor affair—when I consulted a missile expert with comparable experience to Brunner's. In fact, he knew of Brunner. This engineer has to remain nameless and stateless (at his request, as disclosure of his identity could affect his livelihood). He pointed out that the extraordinary secrecy in which MBB worked on Condor and its related projects came, not just from normal commercial discretion, but because the Germans feared alienating their British and other European partners in Airbus, the Tornado jet fighter and similar projects. In his view, the real job of the fins was to permit what the experts refer to as terminal guidance, meaning directioning during the final stage of descent to provide pinpoint accuracy in hitting the target. A successful Condor would make MBB, and more indirectly Germany, a player on the world missile market able to compete with the Americans or Russians, just as Kraftwerk Union's Brazilian and Iranian nuclear deals had boosted Germany's nuclear industry.

This engineer also contended that Condor's design input was based on American experience in manufacturing the Pershing missile, the details of which were borrowed, copied, illegally obtained or simply used by MBB. Since both early American and Soviet rocket and missile designs were, originally, either borrowed from the V-2 rocket, or from German engineers such as Werner von Braun who had designed the

V-2, that would mean, in the engineer's words, that "the wheel was turning full circle."

If true, this would cast Brunner's explanation in a somewhat harsher light.

•   •   •

The Condor-2 project included multi-layered labyrinths of complexities. The three main partners in the venture, those countries that would get missile production capability, were Argentina, Egypt, and Iraq—a mixture of the impoverished, the calculating and the lunatic. Each wanted advanced missilery and each was on its way to seeing its dream realized. The South American partner, Argentina, had lost a military gamble by taking on Britain in the 1982 Falklands War. The chief Middle East partner was Egypt, a state that had long sought advanced missile capability. It cut its deal first with Argentina and then with a European front, part of the Consen Group, based in Switzerland. The third country, Iraq, was still in the midst of hostilities against Iran and kept a low profile. It was a partner with Egypt, but not with Argentina, and at first had no direct connection with European suppliers. The parties to the conspiracy felt that Western countries might be politically sensitive about providing missile expertise to a country that was in the midst of a hot war in the Gulf and using poison gas to kill its enemies.

Argentina developed Condor-1 to launch weather satellites into orbit. Condor-2 veered the program in a decidedly military direction in 1983 and '84. Condor-2 was to be a multi-stage rocket powered first by liquid and then solid state fuel.

Argentina had been through tumultuous years. In 1982, Argentina's leadership attempted to make a reality of the country's long-standing historical claim to the Malvinas, or Falkland Islands, which were under British control. The Argentinian attack on the lightly-defended islands surprised and shocked the world. As Britain responded and quickly gained the initiative, Argentinian military weaknesses became glaring, but there was one major exception. In May, in the midst of war, several British cruisers were patrolling the South Atlantic. Suddenly, a French-made Exocet rocket belonging to Argentina whizzed across the waves. A

British destroyer, the H.M.S. Sheffield, was severely damaged and twenty British sailors killed.

Argentina lost the war. But the success of the Exocet rocket convinced the Argentinian generals that missile power was a key to their country's future. The Argentinians' neighbors and rivals, the populous and powerful Brazilians, had developed a missile program called "Sonda." The Argentinians felt they had to stay abreast of the latest technology. Not only that, but they decided that there was potential profit in missile-making if they could sell the product and technology to other Third World nations who had difficulties—usually political—in making missiles on their own.

The Argentians chose a site for Condor not far from their observatory and satellite ground station in Cordoba. The military dug out a series of reinforced bunkers deep in the Sierra Chica Mountains. Inside were laboratories for testing missiles. Foreigners flooded into the nearby vacation town of Alta Gracia. Many were Germans. Some hailed from France or Italy. They were the Condor project's engineers and scientists, imported to give the project their technical expertise and provide logistical back-up. Pascal Suez, a worker on the site, told an inquisitive NBC-TV interviewer, Robert Windrem, that most locals suspected early on that the top-secret installations near Faldo del Carmen were a missile factory.

A number of the foreigners stayed in Alta Gracia's modest Sierras Hotel. One of the hotel employees, Rosendo Zacharias, said the Europeans kept pretty much to themselves. "We didn't have any contact with them," he said. "We just saw them around. They used to leave at seven in the morning by coach to work at Faldo del Carmen... We knew they were scientists because they wore identity cards." He added that his understanding was "...the order to put them up in the hotel came from the Presidential Palace in Buenos Aires."

Suez identified the head of the project as a German. "The building works started with moving earth, then laying the foundations. There were at least eight or ten buildings, and it took three years to build, finishing in 1986."

•   •   •

Egypt was the second country in the Condor deal. Though poor and overpopulated, Egypt had access to huge reserves of Arab money and its own first class corps of engineers. Egypt, when agreeing to a peace treaty with Israel at Camp David, had extracted from the United States a commitment for two billion dollars of military aid annually, roughly equivalent to the amount given to Israel. Egypt's bloated bureaucracy and teeming millions seemed to swallow up aid money without any effect on daily life. To finance Condor, the Egyptians turned eastward, to the one seemingly bottomless source of funds for military projects in the Arab world, the Saudis. Saudi Arabia was always ready to back Arab-originated projects.

This was during an early stage of the Iran-Iraq War. It was at least six years before the Iraqi invasion of Kuwait and Desert Storm. Egypt, like the Saudis, feared Iranian-style Islamic fundamentalism. As the Iran-Iraq War dragged on, Iraq and Egypt became military partners. Egypt supplied arms and Egyptian military officers occasionally travelled to Baghdad. The Egyptians also permitted soldiers to be recruited from among the Egyptian nationals working in Iraq. Some 600 were later reported to have died there. Like the Iraqis, the Egyptians had few compunctions about poison gas, had developed indigenous chemical warfare production units and had shown themselves willing to use it, as when they bombarded fellow Arabs with mustard gas in Yemen in the early 1960s.

Mohamed Abdel Halim Ghazala, Egypt's wily, capable defense minister under President Mubarek, took the Condor project under his wing. Formerly a loyal associate of Anwar Sadat, he had stood close to the former Egyptian president when he was assassinated, but had miraculously survived. A proud Egyptian, pro-Western and pro-American in his orientation, he believed that Egypt's acquisition of independent missile capacity would put it at the top rank of Arab military power and make it a dominant power in the region. He was also a wheeler-dealer unafraid to bypass the Americans when he thought it advantageous for himself or his country. Egypt brought Iraq into the deal through the backdoor. Technical know-how obtained by the Egyptians would be shared with their Iraqi colleagues. Materials would be cross-shipped from Cairo to Baghdad. Iraq, with Saudi help, would pay the bills.

Of the three partners among the client countries, the last one in the deal, Iraq, was the only one then in the midst of battle and the one that most craved missiles. Iraq was a "back-door" partner and had no direct relationship with Argentina. Saddam Hussein had his spanking-new facility at Mosul under development. His missile men had inaugurated a number of projects to upgrade the Russian-designed SCUD-B. The Iraqi leader was devoted to the buildup of Iraqi power. He had the funds to invest. The Condor represented a new stage of missile development, a post-SCUD weapon that would help assure Iraq's place on the stage of the region and the world.

• • •

Condor had a lot going for it: money, German scientists and engineers from MBB, and an intermediary group led by resourceful managers. This was the Consen group. Its network of companies spread throughout Europe and included engineers from many countries including Italy, France and Holland, but especially from German-speaking territories such as Germany, Austria and Switzerland.

The network of Consen companies behind the Condor missile project—the group that did the deals between MBB and customers in Argentina, Egypt, and more indirectly, Iraq— exhibited brilliance in business conception and the mind and outlook of super-spooks. It would take Western intelligence agents and journalists years to figure out how the Condor project was set up. Some of the companies to be used in the project were already in existence by 1983. Others had to be incorporated.

For much of the time the companies in the Consen family went under a "Consen Group" label. But that was for simplicity's sake. The relationships between Consen and its different arms were stuff made for financial detectives or novelists. Different companies were formed, changed address, disappeared. New ones emerged. Headquarters was in Zug, a swanky suburb not far from Zürich that has been called "the Scarsdale of Switzerland."[1] Among others, Marc Rich, the fabulously wealthy financier and spot market oil dealer wanted on charges of fraud in the United States, makes his home there. The Consen headquarters at 7 Imrotel, with a commanding mountaintop view of the Swiss lake below, was a modest-sized residence in a swish area and a well-protected bastion of privacy, one much in accord with Swiss tradition. It was the nub of the Consen operation.

Other offices were in Salzburg and Monaco. Monaco was where Ekkehard Schrotz, the German businessman and technical expert, employed a small staff to help grease the wheels of commerce. Salzburg was a city known more for its music than its missiles. Consen offices dotted side streets of the city—including one extremely private complex up a winding road heading into the mountains.

The Consen Group constituted what one Western official called "a Fourth Reich." Behind the façade, Consen personnel were engaged in one of the major technology transfers of the post-World War II world with the prospect of hundreds of millions of dollars in profits. With that kind of money at stake. Discretion was the key to success. Though its branches were scattered throughout Europe, South America and the Middle East, Consen's roots lay in a company called Bohlen Industries, in and of itself a part of a unique German industrial legacy. The Krupp and Bohlen und Hahlbach families are one and the same, the result of a complicated merger of two families nearly a century ago. While the industrial entity retained the name Krupp, individual family members are called Bohlen und Hahlbach Krupp. Krupp companies had been the backbone of the Kaiser's military production before and during the World War I. They then formed the industrial underpinning of the Third Reich during World War II. Located mainly in the Ruhr Valley, but with firms dotted throughout Germany, the Essen-based enterprise once had the power to shake the world. The family's private wealth ran into the millions. As quoted by William Manchester (in his study *The Arms of Krupp, 1587-1968*, a German popular saying goes "Wenn Deutschland blüht, blüht Krupp." When Germany prospers, Krupp prospers. Another saying went: "The Ruhr is Essen....and Essen is Krupp."

The Krupp firm's chief executive, Alfried Krupp, had supported Hitler during World War II. He later claimed to be non-political, but he consented to use almost 200,000 human beings, including 4,978 prisoners from Auschwitz and other concentration camps, virtually all of them

Jews, in his factories, "employing" slave labor for German military production. The Allies arrested Alfried Krupp and tried him as a war criminal at Nuremberg in 1947. The judges' guilty verdict affected both Krupp personally and his family company. Alfried Krupp got a life sentence and the court also ordered the liquidation of all Krupp family property including the crown jewel of the family's treasure, Krupp Enterprises.

The court decision got reversed speedily. With the rise of the Cold War and with Germany divided and powerless, U.S. authorities decided they needed a strong and productive Germany, one that would utilize the best industrial hands and brains in what was once Europe's most powerful country. In 1951, the U.S. High Commissioner in Germany, John J. McCloy, in a controversial and much-debated action, decided to restore to the family much of its fortune and the firm. He also released Alfried.

The decision meant divvying-up of the family fortune among Krupp descendants. A significant amount, over several million dollars, devolved upon Alfried's half-brothers, Berthold and Harald. Berthold was an Oxford-educated scientist who had researched penicillin in Munich during part of World War II. Harald, tall and thin, had been captured in Bucharest in 1944 by the Soviet Red Army. Both survived the war. Neither of these brothers were directly involved in running Krupp Enterprises during the war nor shared in responsibility for employing slave labor.

With their new-found fortune, the two brothers targeted the booming German chemical industry for investment. They set up Bohlen Industries. Bohlen established offices throughout the world, including Bohlen Industries of North America and at least three other related firms in Canada and the United States, as well as subsidiaries in Luxembourg and elsewhere. The firm acted as financiers and investment partners in a network of small chemical companies. The brothers acquired Wasag Chemie, a German firm. Using it as a base, its tentacles spread throughout Europe—especially, but not exclusively, in the German-speaking parts. They formed or bought into several firms in Germany proper, including W.N.C. Nitrochemie in the Munich area. They acquired an ownership position in companies in Austria,

Switzerland, and even one in Egypt, called Wasaabaal. Many of these firms produced war materials, especially propellants for rocket motors and explosives. Bohlen Industries' base was, like Krupp's, in Essen, in the German industrial heartland of the Ruhr Company offices were at Rolandstrasse allee, a modest street a few hundred yards from the main railroad station.

In the mid-1970s, Bohlen Industries brought in an ambitious middle-aged manager, Helmut Raiser, to add energy to Bohlen activities and to spark company profitability. Raiser, a Bavarian by origin, worked as managing director of Wasag Chemie. Well-connected in several German exile communities abroad, and a Spanish speaker who knew Argentina well, he pushed expansion and export wherever possible. Shortly, Helmut Raiser exploited his old associations in South America to seek out lucrative commercial opportunities.

Helmut Raiser amicably left the company in 1982 to set up a series of interlocking companies that could service missile and other armaments projects. This is the group that became known as "Consen." (I tried to contact Raiser a number of times, but he refused to speak to me except to tell me once that he wouldn't speak with anyone from the press.) Bowas InduPlan, the Bohlen company based in Salzburg, was the contractual father of the Condor deal. As of January 1st, 1983, Bowas InduPlan had six investors. All were either members of the von Bohlen und Hahlbach family or associated with them. One of these investors was Raiser himself. He had the largest single share.

Raiser based himself in Zug. There, Raiser and the Bohlens, acting through Bohlen Industries, set up Bowas A.G. Feur Industrievertrieb, with offices at Im Rotel 7. Among those on the board of the Zug firm was Horst Gade, a German national who helped run Bowas InduPlan in Salzburg. So, curiously, was Alexis Von Goldschmidt-Rothschild from Basel, one of the Swiss Rothschilds, who had gotten involved with the Bohlen crowd.

Consen owners used a Bohlen-linked proxy figure to set up the Monaco subsidiary. He was Jürgen Spaethe, a German, one of three children, himself the father of two boys, Nicholas and Anthony. He had done his degree in economics in Munich and gotten an MBA in France. Spaethe had first come to Monaco in 1981 to become managing director of a company called von Bohlen Investment and Management Services. In 1983 and '84 he helped the fledgling S.A.M. Consen get going. Berthold von Bohlen und Hahlbach came to Monaco on numerous occasions in the early '80s and served on the Consen board. The tentacles of Consen, formed initially as an off-shoot of Bohlen Industries, spread throughout Europe. The modest-sized residence high in the hills above Zug served as headquarters for operations. Swiss economic records listed the company as specializing in engineering and industrial installations, with Helmut Raiser as president. Raiser and his backers formed the Institute for Advanced Technology, or I.F.A.T. in 1983, also based at the Zug address. I.F.A.T. managed the Egyptian part of the Condor project. A company set up specially by the Argentinians to service the Condor project also had an office in Zug. This was Integradora Aeroespacial Sociedad Anonima, known as I.N.T.E.S.A., a company in which the Argentinian Air Force had a key interest. I.N.T.E.S.A., in turn, became a partner in one of the two Consen-related companies in West Germany servicing Condor. That was G.P.A., officially Gesellschaft gur Prozess-Automatisierung GmbH, based in an office complex in Poing, a tiny village not too far from Munich Airport.[2] Numerous items of equipment for the real-time simulation laboratory bought by Egypt were shipped through G.P.A.

Consen's managing director—a young man specially chosen by Raiser—was Ekkehard Schrotz, the engineer who ran the Monaco office. He was considered a guiding financial and technical light behind the wide-flung Condor project. Schrotz was not universally popular. Brunner had referred to him as "a cold guy, very standoffish, and not someone you could really trust." Schrotz became extraordinarily secretive and elusive after the car bomb destroyed his Peugeot in Southern France in 1988, shortly before I found out about him.

Consen's Swiss branch was a tightly-knit outfit with only eight employees, according to a 1988 financial report. Ninety five percent of its product was imported from Germany. The same financial report, designed mainly to provide information on the firm's creditworthiness for potential clients, noted, "official information regarding collections is available against proof of interest only." Listed as affiliates or belonging to the same interest group as Consen SA were a stunning assembly of Bohlen-related firms: Bohlen International SA, from Luxembourg, Bohlen Finanz AG from Zug, Condor Project AG from Zug, and BOWAS in various incarnations in Paris, Munich, Salzburg and Zug.[3] This report additionally noted that Consen Switzerland had a 100 percent interest in Consen S.A.M. in Monaco.

Conchem, whose parent company was listed as Bohlen International SA of Luxembourg, according to the financial report, had been set up in 1975 with Dr. Josef Schwerzmann as sole member of the board. It became an operational company in the group playing a key design and planning role. The company had a permanent office in Baghdad.

Consen links also extended to Argentina. An additional company tied in with the Argentinian Condor project was Desintech. This firm had offices in Zug as well as Austria and Argentina.

A financial report on Bohlen Industries listed Alfred Jeck as one of the company's managers, with the von Bohlen und Halbach brothers as shareholders of the company. Those associated with the enterprise were noted as having "positive reputations." Jeck, an old-timer helping to run Wasag Chemie and WNC Nitrochemie, was an associate of Rolf Engel, one of those who ran Egypt's rocket programs in the 1950s and '60s. Jeck built WNC Nitrochemie into one of Europe's primary propellant companies with a specialty in rocket-filling. WNC Nitrochemie's clients included the German and American defense establishments, and the firm provided propellant fuel for the U.S. Air Forces' Hawk missile.

Other companies less directly related to Bohlen also figured in the Condor deal. One Vienna company, Consultco, played a leading role in construction and planning in Iraq. Consen companies based in Salzburg included Delta System and Delta Consult. When these companies got some unwelcome publicity from the Austrian press, another Consen-related firm, Taurus, suddenly sprang up in Salzburg. A fire destroyed much of the Taurus building just days after an Austrian police team raided its premises and seized vital papers. An official investigator told me the arsonists had arrived too late—company papers were already in police hands. In all, several hundred European and American companies provided equipment or service for Condor, ranging from bolts and screws to full-scale assembly lines or machine tools. The orders were highly specialized, their ultimate destination in doubt.

Some of these companies didn't know the final uses of what they were supplying—or, for that matter, exactly where it was going beyond a designated local address.

Untangling the Consen web took years. The link to Bohlen Industries was its most surprising aspect. A family spokesman, Eckbert von Bohlen und Halbach, told the *Financial Times* in 1989 that the Consen companies had been established by someone "who used me and my father as good will shields." He said he knew nothing of missile components. He contended that Bohlen had no links with Consen. "The only thing we were aware of was that there was some rocket propellant and chemicals involved."

• • •

Consen's base was that wide area of Central Europe that includes southern Germany, Austria and northern Switzerland. Its personnel consisted of German-speaking engineers. Consen records I obtained showed that it played a key role both in Egypt and Iraq. Companies on-site, such as Condor Project AG and Conchem Project AG, had organizational charts, what they called "organigrams," detailing the assignment of engineers in civil, mechanical and electrical areas. A chart for Iraq was titled "Project Management for DOT" and "CAT," the code names for Condor in Baghdad. Condor had an additional code name: "Project 395."

The Condor project in Iraq and Egypt functioned under a joint command. Rudolf Trummer was the head engineer in both Iraq and Egypt. (Monaco police, after the bombing of Schrotz's Peugeot, had mistakenly transcribed his first name as Robert.) Trummer, a civil engineer, first worked for Consen in Argentina. As Consen's work shifted from Argentina to Egypt and Iraq, Trummer shifted with it. He later went to work for the Feneberg Engineering and Planning Group in Graz, a company that did civil engineering work on the Condor project in Iraq and Egypt. He was a discreet type who had a residence in Denia, Spain, a resort community on the Costa Blanca coast near Valencia, a family in Austria, and an aversion to speaking to journalists. I undertook one abortive trip to his remote mountain-top home in southern Austria, in a tiny village near Hoch, below Graz and above the Yugoslav border. He wasn't home.

Though I never got to meet Trummer personally, I did manage several telephone conversations over the next few months that were unfortunately brief and not particularly informative. Trummer claimed that I was infringing upon his "freedom" when I called him and on two occasions he ended up shouting at me. "You are not giffing me liberty," he yelled in heavily accented English over the phone.

I wondered what liberty he thought I, or other journalists, were depriving him of—except possibly his unquestioned "right" to build medium-range ballistic missiles for Third World dictators.

•   •   •

In 1985, the Argentinians demonstrated the Condor 1-A—the rocket they had developed for civilian uses, including meteorological research—at the Paris Air Show. Condor 1-A, however, was by now a ploy, a cover for the Third World military rocket project believed to be comparable to the Pershing, Condor-2.

Consen managers saw that Argentina was cash-poor but ambitious. With the idea of making a bundle, Consen principals such as Ekkehard Schrotz and Helmut Raiser helped find Argentina a partner for its missile project. That partner, the Arab Republic of Egypt, had no resource itself. The plan was to gain access to Egypt's big money patrons in the Arab world, while offering them secure production facilities in South America. Egypt was a friend of the United States, had close relations with wealthy Saudi Arabia, and increasingly sought to extend its own aid to the beleaguered Iraqis in the on-going war against Iran.

Those heading Consen skillfully played the elements to weave together a three billion dollar deal. The Consen group made contact with the right Egyptians—those in Defense Minister Abu Ghazzala's office and those surrounding him. A formal contract between the Egyptian Ministry of Defense and I.F.A.T., a Consen company in the Consen group, was signed on February 15, 1984.

Next, the Consen partners wanted to assure financing for the project and solidify the Argentinian-Egyptian connection. Discussions and negotiations went on for a number of months throughout 1984. A high-level Egyptian delegation visited Argentina in October. The two countries struck a deal. The Argentinians confirmed this contract in two letters to the Egyptians. The first, in December, 1984, was from Raul A. Tomás, of the Argentinian Ministry of Defense's Production Section, to Field Marshall Mohamed Abdel Halim Ghazala, the Egyptian Deputy Prime Minister and Minister of Defense. Titled "BME-Program Arab Republic of Egypt,"—the "BME" stood for Ballistic Missile Egypt—the letter noted the participation of Argentina with Egypt in the project, which could now move ahead at full speed, and expressed "the satisfaction of our Minister of Defense about the materialization of this cooperation, which hopefully can be extended into other fields for the mutual benefit of our two countries."

A second communiqué came from Argentinian Air Force Brigadier General Hugo Enrique Ventura, and was addressed to the Egyptian Armament Organization in the Ministry of Defense in Cairo. It was short and to the point. "I have the pleasure to inform you that we have signed today the contracts directed to accomplish, like subcontractors of I.F.A.T., with the export from Argentina to your country, of the goods and services included in the contract subscribed by you, in the context of the BME program."

The agreement itself included serial production of missiles planned initially to be built in Argentina. Intelligence sources estimated that two hundred Condor missiles would roll off the assembly lines in Argentina alone.[4] Meanwhile, Egypt would begin its own factory construction and serial production of the missile at a secret site in Heliopolis, not far from Cairo. Another two hundred missiles would be built in the first stage in Egypt. "I am sure," General Ventura summed up in his letter to the Egyptian Ministry of Defence, "that this important step will reinforce the relationship and cooperation betweeen our countries."

The stage was set for a confluence of interests that could bring the fruits of Western technology to both Argentina and Arab production centers in Egypt and Iraq. The Arabs called their version of Condor "Badr 2000" after a famous military battle waged by the greatest of Arab military generals, Salah Al Din, when he resisted the Crusader incursion into the holy lands.

The Condor deal was harbinger of a proliferation of Third World missile capability. It could even encourage weapons makers in Iraq and Egypt, at a later stage, to enter the lucrative missile export business on their own as independent producers. It threatened to change the strategic face of the globe.

CHAPTER TWELVE

Stopping Condor

"Schrotz told me he must fly the missile soon. I said to him, there was no chance."

Wolfgang Brunner, Condor design engineer.

IN EARLY 1985, Wolfgang Brunner, the MBB design engineer at the heart of the Condor project, headed off to Rome. He was to meet with engineers and high officials of another of Europe's giant engineering and armament firms, S.N.I.A.-B.P.D., based in Colliaferro. What he remembered most about that meeting was the biting cold in the tiny meeting room at S.N.I.A. and how unprepared Rome was for a brisk winter day.

The U.S. Government had expressed its concern about the Condor project to both Italy and Germany as early as the spring of 1985. German officials took their lead from Washington and never wanted to offend their American friends. German Foreign Office people asked their counterparts in the Economics Ministry to inquire of MBB where the project stood and if it could be stopped, a particularly delicate matter because of MBB's central role in the country's economy.

To the surprise and delight of German officials, after a few meetings, by the end of 1985, MBB seemingly agreed to halt Condor or slow it down—an expression, as it turned out, of the vagueness of the federal government request, the clubby atmosphere between corporate executives and government bureaucrats, and MBB management's basic contempt of the lower level of federal officialdom. A German Foreign Office bureaucrat told me that his department of government thought "the problem was solved." Except it wasn't. The project that Wolfgang Brunner had come to Rome to discuss was "FK-120." This was a cover for Condor. "FK" was short for the German term 'flugkorper,' meaning a missile or flying object. The "120" meant that the missile had a range of 120 kilometers, or about 80 miles. The client for the FK-120 was the Arab Republic of Egypt. "We had a small study group—we met for a few days at S.N.I.A. in Colliaferro," Brunner recalled. "We sat in this cold room, just a few of us. I remember that room was real cold, there was no heating and I was freezing."

In its initial stages, as Brunner told it, the FK-120 was technically somewhat different from Condor. "We prepared a lay-out for the FK-120. FK-120 was a single stage missile. There was no separation of the booster. It was steered with rear fins until the end." Additionally, the FK-120 had a high-explosive payload of about 400 kilograms, or some 900 pounds. It carried what the professionals call a sub-munitions warhead, a kind of cluster-bomb technology. But its target accuracy wasn't precise enough—around .001—to make it a tactical weapon. "For sub-munitions you really need very good hitting accuracy," Brunner noted.

None of the FK-120's particulars initially exceeded what was legal, according to the Missile Technology Control Regime. But the project's sub-systems—without Brunner being involved—soon matched those of the Condor. S.N.I.A. was later contracted to provide specialized propellant knowledge for the FK-120/Condor project, and was prepared to enter into a joint venture with MBB to develop it. Consen separately recruited some of S.N.I.A.'s, and MBB's, best missile engineers. Even though Egyptian hopes for an intermediate range missile could not be fulfilled in the Americas, the job could still be done. Egypt aimed to get a state-of-the-art missile, and build it in Egypt itself.

•   •   •

By mid-1985, Condor-2 had run into problems on three fronts: political, technical, and legal.

Technically, the project at first appeared to be feasible. "Looking back," Brunner said about Condor, "by the end of 1985 we were technically in good shape. If we'd had a go-ahead we could have done it— over a number of years."

To get the Condor missile (as Condor) flying within a few years, Brunner felt he needed continuity on the team, access to MBB's already existing functional departments, and a proven test range. A good range did not exist in Germany. That was one of the reason German engineers wanted to develop expertise outside the country and access to technical facilities where experimentation could be carried out.

Brunner contended that "Vector," or Condor, from MBB's vantage point, never reached the point where any advanced work really happened. "We came to the conclusion that to correct and to improve upon Condor-1, and to get more accuracy, we needed a second stage liquid motor. This was because the efficiency of the motor was poor, we had no access to the thermo pumps, and the fuel was injected by pressure. The payload was 300 kg at this stage. This was in 1985 and 1986. This was my first job like it. We made good progress. We were very proud of our work. The Argentinians were pleased."

The work on Condor trickled down throughout MBB. Since the second stage motor for Condor-2 was now to be planned as a liquid propellant, the MBB design team called on the resources of MBB's Space Division based at Lampoldshausen. This division had responsibility for the preparation of a liquid propellant motor for the all-European Ariane-4 satellite. Even so, Brunner had his doubts about a liquid propellant second stage motor. He would have preferred it to be solid state, which was the long-range plan. "Schrotz (the functioning head of Consen for the job) didn't like the liquid propellant motor," Brunner added. "Personally, I didn't like it, either."

Why not? For one, the fuel source for the European space project, Ariane, was the same Soviet-originated fuel that powered the SCUD-B, known as U.D.M.H. This fuel was available only from Japan or the Soviet Union. Neither MBB nor their Condor clients were happy about so severely limiting the missile's fuel sources when supply might become an issue. Brunner also recalled the parallel pressures on the company: on the one hand, "the Americans were eager for us to get

Ariane into orbit." On the other hand, MBB engineers working on both Ariane and Condor still didn't know how additional contracts would spread the cost load in the design of a good liquid propellant motor.

Brunner felt that, generally, "we were short on people," especially for some of the specialized missile-making tasks. He had to apply to MBB TransTechnica, the division set up to service the Sa'ad-16 missile research and development center in Mosul, Iraq, for help, but didn't get much. In any case, he didn't think very highly of the quality of their work. His opinion about MBB-TT engineers was succinct: "they were idiots."

Brunner was also dissatisfied with what he considered to be the lack of facilities in Germany for making the rocket engine itself and fuelling it. "You can't make a propellant motor from point zero. Bayern Chemie [another MBB company] can handle several hundred kilograms but not tons. You must have mixers, machines.... They don't exist in Germany. We don't yet have mixtures for solid propellants."

Brunner lacked confidence in the ability of Consen engineers to follow up with competent technical work at the production bases in Argentina and later Egypt. "Their people—the Consen people—weren't good people. I taught them, but I was never impressed." He stressed that Consen technicians needed the kind of backup that could only come from a large company such as MBB, where ideas could be played with and put into practice. "You need an operations department. And aside from us, Consen and Schrotz didn't have anybody."

Other problems nudged in, too. Consen's top people had a lot of money riding on Condor-2's success. Not only was the continuation of the Condor project at stake, but so was Consen's name, and possibly one or two other massive missile programs on which Consen might have wanted to bid. Consen's ability to close a deal on these projects and get them into contractual form, which would free up additional cash, depended on making Condor fly.

Consen's Schrotz applied pressure on Brunner to work harder and faster, but Brunner was resistant. "Schrotz told me he must fly the missile soon. I said to him, there was no chance.

"Somewhere into 1986 there was a final no-go," reported Brunner. "We were permitted to do the definition phase. Finally the project was cancelled. This was done by Kuhlo [one of MBB's top officials]."

By early 1986, Brunner left the Condor project and moved on within MBB to head up the company's involvement in a new warhead project being developed for NATO and the German government called "Technex." He developed relations with people from the American company cooperating on the project, Martin Marietta, headquartered in Orlando, Florida. Within two years he had left the company altogether. Later, MBB officials went to great lengths to smear Brunner, an honest man. Udo Philipp, who didn't know Brunner, tried to use him as a scapegoat for the company's difficulties with the German government and Consen. He claimed that Brunner was the only company man to have served as a link between all MBB's missile projects and, if anyone had siphoned off company technology to Third World nations, it had to be Brunner. This laughable claim was probably made, I later concluded, to shield top management from an official inquiry into the project—an inquiry that came later but failed to prove malfeasance.

Brunner told people inside MBB in 1986 that if anybody wanted to continue working with Schrotz, they wouldn't be working with him on his new project. For a short time it looked as if Condor were dead. Brunner told me he regarded that as good riddance. But unknown to Brunner, Condor refused to die. Consen and MBB continued to work in concert, though discretely. MBB and Consen executives resurrected Condor through devious means and with the active help of Egypt, Argentina, and possibly Iraq.[1]

• • •

Politically, MBB had to perform a juggling act that a Tammany Hall-trained politico would have found difficult. Dangers and problems lurked at every corner. The U.S. pressure to stop Condor, applied through the German government, had its effect. As good a business as Condor was, MBB executives had other, equally lucrative relationships that they did not want to jeopardize. Some of these were on a strategic level. MBB's relationship with Argentina, for example, violated the interests of Germany's NATO and industrial ally, Great Britain. MBB was a partner with British companies developing such projects as the enormously successful commercial airliner, Airbus, and the Tornado fighter jet, Europe's answer to the American F-15. Seen from an MBB standpoint, the Condor project could be exposed to political pressure if the British were to make a fuss; the going could get tough.[2]

The Germans also had to consider Israel. MBB did business with Israel and a few in MBB's top management claimed they had close relationships with Israeli leaders. Top German political leaders were always sensitive to the possibility of negative reaction from the Jewish state and accusations that they were behaving in an anti-Semitic or anti-Israel way. Word spread inside MBB that vice-chairman Sepp Hort had approached and spoken with the Israelis about the Condor project—at least, about the Argentinian part of it—and the Israelis had not evinced particular opposition. Officials in the Israel Ministry of Defense told me they had no idea what the MBB official who told me this was talking about. They told me it was unconfirmed speculation and untrue.

For more hard-headed Germans, the Israeli card was seen as necessary for public relations, but no more, and basically hypocritical. Germany's interests were really with the Arab states, which formed a huge potential market. Historically, Egypt was Israel's most challenging military rival. Ludwig Boelkow, the first "B" in MBB, was a long-time friend of Egypt, the country where his passion for solar energy got born. A top-grade engineer and businessman, he knew full well that the Israelis had a favored place in the American arms orbit and a special relationship with the Martin Marietta Company, the American missile manufacturer that was both MBB's competitor and occasional partner. German engineers invariably expressed great admiration for the military prowess of the Jewish state. Those I spoke to had enormous faith in the ability of Israel's Air Force to bomb to smithereens whatever they themselves had built, and even greater faith, mingled with a bit of prayer, that this would happen only after they had finished their work and been paid for it.

An MBB official actually said to me that if Iraqi missile prowess ever got really dangerous to the Israelis, they could always bomb the sites, as they had done with Iraq's nuclear reactor, Osirak, and knock it out.

In mid-1985, those working directly on the Condor project—and not just high level management types—began to feel outside pressure. "The Americans had interfered in the process," said Brunner. "We realized that political circumstances were developing that might stop us from continuing."

The Americans embarked on their diplomatic offensive with caution. Richard Speier and his Pentagon colleagues were wrapping up final details on the missile treaty that would restrict and regulate most sales, and could only work if there were cooperation between the the the governments of the large industrial nations. Pentagon officials briefed State and the export control people at State approached the Germans. In Germany, the Foreign Office passed the matter over to the Economics Affairs Ministry and officials there, in turn, discreetly inquired what was going on directly with MBB. The Bonn government told MBB that there was American and other international concern about Condor and indicated that anything that violated the terms of M.T.C.R. should be stopped.

Bonn's initial sounding-out of MBB had its effect. An internal memo noted that "pursuit of business against the will of the Bonn government" could put the company into trouble with its principal client— the German government—and also with partners in the Western alliance, meaning NATO countries. A hurry-up atmosphere developed. This meant finishing as much work as possible in the shortest order so that MBB could get paid before there was the danger of a cut-off. "After about half a year we were urged to get the export licenses into place," Brunner said, indicating that this was extremely early to even begin to think about actual shipments of hardware.

MBB decided to either phase out its direct involvement with Argentina, while continuing the project with Egypt under the code-name FK-120, or attempt to transfer as much specific systems work as possible to indirect but capable linking intermediaries such as the Consen group. Internal memos outlined the choices. The company first considered making an end-run through France while still holding a profit share on the job. As one executive noted in a memo, "there are no obstacles for cooperation with large, well-known French companies for the development and construction of rockets." He cautioned, however, that MBB couldn't enter into subcontracts with French companies "if it were apparent that such works were related to the Vector program. [Vector meant Condor]" In such a case, MBB had to assign the work to intermediary companies without itself getting in the middle. "You should arrange for corresponding agreements with Consen as fast as possible," he urged.

As a result of the mounting governmental pressure, a number of meetings took place between MBB and Argentina during 1985. One held on June 11th included Ekkehart Schrotz of Consen, two executives from Consen's Argentinian subsidiary, Desintec, and both Argentinian and MBB representatives. MBB's team was headed by Karl Adolf Hammer, director of the company's military research department. An MBB participant suggested to the Argentinians that the work might be continued by routing it through the French giant, Aerospatiale, an MBB shareholder. Aerospatiale and MBB worked together on a number of projects, and even had a representive on MBB's board of supervisors. The Argentinians opposed MBB's suggestion to switch the project from German to French hands, and said they expected MBB to fulfill its responsibilities, as agreed contractually. One of them indicated surprise about the political dimension of the new problems, especially "additional limitations which went beyond" the scope of German arms control laws. The Argentinians noted with considerable displeasure that Raul Tomás, the Secretary of State of the Argentinian Ministry of Defence, had visited Germany just a few months before, in March, 1985, but nothing had been said to him about potential problems.

MBB executives explored their choices. In a memo, Karl Adolf Hammer of MBB cautioned that: "In principle, the possibility of supporting a transfer of the current project to the customer through a group of MBB specialists working in the customer's country was broached, but there could be personnel problems in such a solution."

As a result, MBB promised to initiate a "new decision-making process" that would take into account the altered political environment. For the time being, MBB would contact firms outside the Federal Republic to sound out the possibilities of their continuing the program. MBB proposed that Argentina contact the German government directly to try to get the situation remedied at the political level. In the longer run, MBB would work out proposals for a transfer of the program to secondary firms or individuals.

MBB executives assured German government officials who questioned them that the company would cease working on Condor-2. German officials I spoke with in the Foreign Office and the Economics Ministry took this to mean that MBB ceased working with Argentina on Condor-2 in 1985. What the executives really meant, as demonstrated by the course of events, was that Condor, as Condor, would cease. Existing contracts with Argentina would be completed and then phased out, not to be renewed. Contrary to the understanding of the German officials, various parts of its program would proceed. Anything falling outside of M.T.C.R. guidelines for illegal activity—this could be research, designs, individual components and even sub-systems— would continue.

Among MBB's considerations, according to a company source with whom I spoke: MBB did not want insinuations in the industry that MBB had failed to finish a job, nor did MBB seek out messy court cases initiated by its customers against it. Argentina was biding its time nervously, but could bring legal action, while Consen actually threatened to sue MBB if the giant aerospace firm failed to live up to its commitments. The Condor work got systematically transferred into the FK-120 program. Rudiger Kuhlo pointed the way in a company document in which he emphasized that he understood Argentina's desire "to assure a transfer of tasks which would allow for a continuation of the program based on the results already obtained." This could be done either by the customer or by a qualified company operating outside the Federal Republic. In an obvious but devious solution, the job might might be transferred intact to an intermediary company in which MBB specialists would be paid directly by the client.

The overall design functions initially handled by Wolfgang Brunner's team wound down. At least two projects continued with Argentina, both of which, it could be argued, lay outside M.T.C.R. guidelines: one, research and development in the missile; the other, the design, building and testing of warheads that could be delivered by missile or, alternatively, by airplane, including state-of-the-art cluster bomb technology, fuel-air explosives, and attack warheads against enemy runways. An MBB official told me the deals with Argentina, after the supposed cutoff, came to some 50 million Deutschmark worth of "research," over $30 million at the time. In his words: "That's more than a little bit of research."[3]

But MBB was unlucky. The Condor venture started just as President Reagan concentrated U.S. efforts on stopping the spread of missile technology. At every step MBB executives, engaged in a murky, multi-sided venture, approached a thin, barely distinguishable line separating the legal and the newly-or shortly-to-be outlawed.

•   •   •

Brunner left the Condor/FK-120 projects by early 1986. Within months, the FK-120 got re-designed. Badr-2000 (as the Egyptians called it), Ballistic Missile Egypt (as designated by the Argentinians) and FK-120, Vector or Alpha (as code-named by MBB), were, for all intents and purposes, one and the same program. An MBB source suggested that MBB management maintained the separate designations to weave a defensible camouflage in case of a later inquiry, and informed me that a lot of the equipment designed for Argentina would be transferred instead to Egyptian facilities.

Even as the Argentinian aspect of Condor slowed, the Egyptian program got stepped up. The design changes made on the FK-120—officially admitted years later by MBB—brought the project beyond the permissible limits outlined in the M.T.C.R. To keep its own profile low, MBB, with Consen as intermediary, gathered together a second level of support companies, each to undertake a particular aspect of the actual production work. Surprisingly, the names of a number of these companies, which constituted a bluechip list of some of Europe's top armaments manufacturers, were published by the Consen group in a 1987 public relations brochure. A number of them were sub-suppliers for the Pershing-2 missile.

From Italy came S.N.I.A.-.B.P.D., owned by Fiat, which was in turn owned partially by Libya's Muammar Gaddaffi. S.N.I.A.-B.P.D. provided missile expertise. When the Italian government, also under pressure from the Americans, made inquiries of S.N.I.A., a group of engineers split off from S.N.I.A. to attempt to handle the engineering consultancies on their own.

From Germany, the Wegmann company was responsible for the control systems. Wegmann admitted only to selling MBB "a small number of components for a tractor rocket launch system, around DM one million worth," but looked upon the transaction as being between two German companies and thus not subject to export regulation. "We were subsequently investigated by judicial authorities and cleared, although we were told that the equipment MBB bought from us was originally ordered by the Consen group," a Wegmann spokesman said.

M.A.N., manufacturers of trucks and other heavy vehicles, prepared the missile launch units. One of the American diplomats who carried the formal protests about Condor to the German government told me his embarrassment about the M.A.N. aspect of the protest. "I mean, let's face it, we're talking about big trucks," he exclaimed, indicating that he preferred to concentrate U.S. efforts on more blatant violations of missile control.

MBB asked S.A.G.E.M. from Paris to manufacture the inertial navigation systems. I tried to contact S.A.G.E.M. in 1989. The company's elegantly-situated offices in Paris ironically stands right next to the Iranian Embassy in one of Paris' most fashionable residential areas. S.A.G.E.M.'s aggressive bids for Iraqi-Egyptian contracts could have made them the object of a terrorist attack from their next-door neighbor. S.A.G.E.M. refused to comment when asked about its role in the project.

Another company named in the Consen brochure was Bofors, the major Swedish arms manufacturer with a history of relationship with German clients and co-production partners that goes back to the first part of the century. The Consen document said all six companies were "most important in Cooperation and as Subcontractors."

Consen coordinated the activities. The man in charge was Ekkehard Schrotz. "Schrotz build up castles in the heaven," Brunner contended, arguing that Condor-2 was itself an unrealizable dream designed mainly to fill up Consen's bank accounts but little else. "Where did Schrotz get the missile men to get it to the stage of a good operational system?" he questioned. "I don't believe Schrotz on his own was ever capable of delivering a missile that could fly. By the time I left Condor, no one in MBB wanted to work with Schrotz because we didn't trust him," Brunner related. "We were just about to follow him," Brunner contended, "but fortunately we didn't."

• • •

M.T.C.R. came into force in April, 1987. About that time the American State Department fired off a lengthy note to the Germans— what diplomats refer to as a démarche—asking whether Condor was continuing.

This letter wound up on the desk of the German Foreign Office's missile expert, Dr. Gerd von Wagner. Von Wagner transferred a copy of the American letter to German Economic Ministry officials. Officials there proceeded to check out the substance of the interrogatory directly with MBB. The company's top executives offered bland assurances that "nothing wrong was being done." German officials were in no mood to tackle the industrial giant, one of the country's largest employers, which would be much like the U.S. Department of Commerce taking on General Motors. Foreign Office officials felt frustrated, though, by what they considered to be the slow-moving and unhelpful bureaucracy in the Economics Ministry.

The American as well as German side of the exchange was bothered. The State Department team, headed by veteran diplomat John Zimmerman, had the usual conflicts with the Pentagon and Department of Commerce concerning nuances of the inquiry. Those few U.S. officials dealing with the Condor case felt they were walking on commercial eggshells: a bad word, a leak to the press, and MBB's business reputation could be damaged. Not just that—German-American governmental relations could be soured.

Sometime after the U.S. note, an American deputy assistant secretary of state in charge of arms export controls, G. Philip Hughes, paid a visit to MBB. The American inquiries were discreet and even gentle. In order to prevent a leak, the visit bypassed all normal diplomatic circles, including responsible officials within the American Embassy in Bonn such as the capable U.S. scientific attache, Ed Malloy. Part of the American concern was that some of the West's top-secret technology, both for missiles and warhead design, might have been leaked to the Argentinians and Egyptians and made part of the Condor project. An MBB management official—Dr. R. Mecklinger, who headed the Apparate, or works division in charge of military projects—assured the American government that top-secret technology had not been leaked from MBB. MBB would not violate its NATO commitments. Too much was at stake for the firm: both its commercial name and lucrative SDI, or "Star Wars," development contracts, for which it was being considered by the Americans.

The Americans in charge believed the MBB official. Certain design materials and technology might have been delivered to the Third World countries, they concluded—but not top-secret NATO technology, neither from the super-sensitive Pershing nuclear warhead, in which MBB had a role, nor from the less sensitive but highly advanced "Technex" project for a conventional warhead, in which MBB was slated to be the central producer.

A few weeks later, an American official received a telephone call from Germany. One of MBB's top management officials got on the line. "There is something to the story," he confided, in an obvious effort to protect his posterior and future projects. But he managed to downplay it enough to keep American interest at a minimum.

In the summer of 1988, a second American diplomatic missive arrived in Bonn. It included extremely detailed questions concerning MBB. Its tone—and the precision of the questions—ruffled a few Germanic feelings. "We're not a colony, you know," Jürgen Chrobog, an assistant to Hans Dietrich Genscher and a spokesman for Germany's Foreign Office, told me unabashedly. "We're an independent country." In a foretaste of later negotiations between the two governments in a number of areas, he added: "Independent countries don't always take orders from the United States government."

He also commented sarcastically on Great Britain's role in attempting to stop German sales to Argentina. The British, he suggested, were behind a lot of the rumors and shop talk concerning the Condor project—because of their interest in keeping Argentina defenseless. "Our hands are cleaner than that of the English," he said, referring to Britain's multi-billion sterling arms sales to the Gulf states. "We haven't made our exports dependent on arms sales to Saudi Arabia and the Gulf states."

In one of those slow diplomatic shuffles, the American inquiry wandered from the German Foreign Office to the Economic Affairs Ministry. Built on precise intelligence information, it deserved precise answers after proper investigation. Weeks passed. Then more weeks. And then months.

The German response, or lack of it, seemed to some officials in Washington desultory at best and typical of the German attitude on proliferation questions. Between 1985 and 1989, more than 150 U.S. governmental inquiries had been submitted to Germany on forbidden weapons equipment, much of them concerning dual-use kinds of technology that could be used by an errant nation to build either civilian industry or the instruments of war. An American diplomat, tired of German passivity and appalled by the lack of results, remarked, "We demarched them and we demarched them—and we got nothing."

German bureaucrats, first in the Ministry of Foreign Affairs and then in the Economics Affairs Ministry, didn't have the power to arbitrarily halt sales and, moreover, had only severely limited powers of inquiry to check the truth of a situation. Because of its peculiar history, Germany had strict regulations on when its intelligence and police services could act against German nationals or companies. "We're dependent on our B.N.D., our foreign intelligence service, and their relationships with other intelligence services, like the American C.I.A. and the Israeli Mossad," one official, Joachim Jahnke, in charge of export matters in the Economics Ministry, noted. "But the B.N.D. doesn't have the power to do an internal investigation here in Germany."

"We are a democracy," another official noted. "And since World War II we've acted like one."

"Our secret police can act only on two conditions," Jahnke explained to me. "Either it's a possible case of espionage, or a threat to the security of the constitution." The best that a federal agency could do was to intensively screen the companies believed to be selling their goods illegally. If there was genuine suspicion that a law had been broken, officials hastened to turn over the information to public prosecutors to determine whether those guilty could be prosected.

•   •   •

As German governmental pressure applied itself to MBB, top management looked for a way to reduce their exposure in the project without incurring losses. Consen took over MBB's engineering role, coordinating dozens of firms in Germany, Austria, Switzerland, Italy—and elsewhere—throughout 1987 and '88. When the project made real headway, Ekkehard Schrotz got his warning bomb in Speracedes, France.

Consen, led by Schrotz, had to get the Condor missile—referred to by engineers as "the bird"—up into the air and flying not only for prestige but for business reasons. "Without the bird in the air there would be no big payday," Brunner told me.

But designing, manufacturing and then testing a state-of-the-art missile took time. To keep the cash flowing and new contracts on the table, what Schrotz needed was help. Initially, he tried to hire away top MBB engineers at good salaries. He got some. He also chased a group from S.N.I.A.-B.P.D. in Italy and founded a breakaway team. But he required a big name, one that had star quality in the missile field and could help keep his clients in line.

He zeroed in on Karl Adolf Hammer. Hammer had been dissatisfied with the prospects of an internal shake-up at MBB. He had been offered the chance to take overall charge of the Schrobenhausen production facility, which would be made an independent profit center. For a number of reasons, among them that he didn't want to move his family out of Munich, he refused the job.

Schrotz prevailed. He enticed Hammer to jump to Consen in the fall of 1987. Colleagues said the man with the golden touch for missiles got a "golden bonus" of around one million Deutschmarks, well over half a million dollars, to make the jump. Brunner offered a dissenting opinion about Hammer's otherwise vaunted skills: "Schrotz needed somebody like Hammer for show," Condor's first design engineer told me. "But from this Hammer alone, you don't get a working missile."

Hammer's move, at a time when MBB was trying to get out of Condor while preserving its profit position, led to some conflict between him and MBB managing director Hans Arndt Vogels. Company spokesman Udo Philipp got right in the middle of it. He told me and several German journalists that MBB chairman Vogels had made an edict: Karl Adolf Hammer wasn't allowed inside the gates of MBB and was banned from any contact with his former employer. "Consen isn't an honorable company," said Philipp in 1989, clearly reflecting what his boss, MBB chief executive Vogels, had instructed him to say. "We won't deal with them." Vogels feared bad publicity and was fighting at the time both for his managerial future and the fruition of his company's pending merger with Daimler Benz.

Philipp said that a German official asked him to intervene with his boss and persuade him to come clean. Vogels wouldn't. Even as MBB continued actively in certain aspects of the project, MBB claimed that Consen and Hammer were dealing in "piratical action" by pursuing the Condor project's realization.

Vogels unexpectedly opened up on MBB's situation at a meeting of the board of supervisors of the company in early 1989. Klaus Mehrens, a trade union executive from I.G. Metall, the giant labor group that dominates metal workers' affairs throughout Germany—he represented the group on the MBB board—told me that a second board member asked the chairman an innocent question about on-going work. Vogels launched into a complicated explanation relating to Condor, which he indicated was a key to company profitability. The members of the board of supervisors had never heard of the project and knew nothing about the details. Vogels mumbled how contracts worth at least 200 million DM—or about 140 million dollars—were at stake. He said that MBB was trying to extricate itself from a complex, difficult and sensitive situation.

In later conversations, I spoke with other MBB executives and members of the board of supervisors, including Aloic Schwarz, the astute, kindly, bearded gentleman who served as vice-chairman of the board of supervisors. His regular job at an office inside the compound at Ottobrunn included overseeing all workers' matters. He expressed shock at MBB's complicity in an arms affair. His face actually turned red. "They wouldn't dare do that," he said, expressing shock and disbelief. He said he couldn't believe he was hearing inside details from a journalist (and a foreigner at that) and being asked to confirm them. He felt his personal relationship with MBB's top executive had been violated. He told me that the company management had made a commitment to refer all non-NATO arms work to the board of supervisors for approval or comment, and he knew nothing about MBB's dealing with Consen or with Iraq, Egypt or Argentina. Vogels wouldn't dare lie to him, he said, and he expressed anger and bewilderment as to why there was possible obfuscation of the truth.

MBB management had provided that delicately-balanced board of supervisors, the company's overseers, what information MBB management thought they needed. But nothing more.

•   •   •

Hammer kept a low profile and wouldn't talk with the press, possibly because he was afraid of terrorist action after the bombing of Schrotz' car in southern France. My own attempts to have a face-to-face chat with him failed. But I did manage to engage him once or twice by telephone. I told Hammer that MBB claimed his actions while he had been an MBB employee were unauthorized and not part of company policy.

His reply to this: "That's not true." There was an awkward moment of silence. He wouldn't take it further, nor would he meet me personally to tell his side. Instead, he called MBB to speak with the man who he thought was vilifying him, Udo Philipp, the head of public relations for the giant firm. According to Philipp, Hammer told him bluntly that the story about his undertaking "piratical action" was nonsense. MBB management knew at every step of the way what contracts it had entered into and what was happening. Hammer didn't want to be the fall guy.

Still, Hammer tried to leave no traces. To track him became a game. He was elusive and careful. Not a single photo of him seemed to exist. We checked MBB spokesmen, trade magazines, and even got indirect access to the archives at MBB's military center at Schrobenhausen. Nothing worked. Finally, BBC-TV cameraman Mike Spooner and I laid in wait at Hammer's home on the outskirts of Munich near Ottobrunn.

As we waited for him to appear, police surrounded us and detained us. The police then connived with Hammer to deprive us of our photo opportunity and send him scooting off to points unknown.

A short time later I met engineer Hans Grundner at the Gasthaus Stangl in Neufahrn, outside Munich. Grundner was one of those who had worked on the Condor project inside MBB but ran into trouble by making a side investment in G.P.A., one of the German companies linked to Consen. The Condor project and FK-120 were hardly "renegade actions," he said, but lucrative ventures by a company intent on profit. MBB company management tried to make him a scapegoat and fire him. He swore that he had acted just like everybody else, and that each MBB work project had been fully authorized by management. He tried to protest by taking his case to labor representatives who could conceivably protect him. These officials wouldn't take up his case. In the European manner, he wanted to find out how much his story was worth, which was not very much, though I said I'd check with my editor.

After that first meeting, Grundner wouldn't see me again. Perhaps he felt he had been too frank, or sensed there was too little in it for him. My impression is that his wife, who answered the phone several times, didn't want to see him get into any more trouble.

CHAPTER THIRTEEN

Warhead

"It's not your garden-variety weapon,"

Henry Sokolski, deputy for proliferation,
the Pentagon, 1990

SCHROBENHAUSEN, the town where MBB's military production center is based, lies in a wooded part of Germany northwest of Munich. Its quaint village has a central square lined by small shops that includes a single restaurant. MBB is about five minutes by car outside the town. To get to it you have to turn off the country road and drive several hundred yards down a forest lane. At the entrance gate is a guardhouse which surveys the road and all incoming cars. Visitors to this high-security complex are infrequent—foreign visitors even more so.

Marked off by electronic fences and security gates, the MBB plant at Schrobenhausen is Germany's leading military production facility. It houses the development, testing and production facilities of some of the West's most advanced missile technology. This is the place where the Roland, HOT, and MILAN short-range rockets got produced. The test shooting ranges spread eastward from the main road, out of sight of prying cameras or other ground-based electronic surveillance, over hundreds of acres. Even so, Schrobenhausen is not large enough an area for MBB or the German government to engage in full-scale missile testing. As an MBB engineeer plaintively commented, "For that, you need a 500 or 1,000 kilometers. We just don't have this in Germany."

During 1986 and 1987, MBB personnel at Schrobenhausen, working within the framework of the FK-120 contract—alias Badr-2000 and Condor—produced three warheads for the Condor missile project. One of the warheads, called MUSCO, included two types of units. The first was a conventional high explosive warhead. A second was a kind of fragmentation device encased in a modular dispenser unit that could be used to hit and destroy enemy airfields. Word got out in 1988 that MBB had supplied this type of unit to Argentina, Egypt and more indirectly Iraq, upsetting British defense officials who contended that such a weapon could be useful to the Argentinians in attacking British forces in the Falklands.

According to Wolfgang Brunner, who had a responsibility for designing the Condor missile, the MUSCO was a small-scale derivative of the company's MW-1 module dispenser bomb units, which included the MUSA and MUSPA warheads already in production for NATO, the German army and the European fighter bomber, the Tornado. (Brunner carefully pointed out that he himself had no responsibility for the FK-120 warhead and was involved in other MBB projects when work on it was undertaken at Schrobenhausen.) The "MUS" in the MBB bomb designations meant "multi-splitter," German for a multi-fragmentation bomb. The "A" in MUSA stood for "Active." The "PA" in MUSPA meant "Passive." The "CO" in MUSCO was short for "Condor." The use of the term MUSCO within the FK-120 project belied the MBB pretense that FK-120 and Condor were separate projects.

A third type of warhead filled out the Condor package. This was potentially the most dangerous: the fuel-air explosive. The F.A.E.'s deadly blast had a killing potential some five to ten times more potent than conventional high explosives. The F.A.E. is one of the West's most advanced technologies, sometimes compared in its blast effect to the power of a small atomic bomb. "It's not your garden-variety weapon," said Henry Sokolski, the deputy at the Pentagon's unit on non-proliferation. "These are blast effect weapons and what you can't see can kill you."

The F.A.E.'s dual technologies—first dispersing the fuel into an evenly spread-out cloud, then igniting it—are a complicated business. The Americans first experimented with the technology in Vietnam, the Soviets in Afghanistan. The Americans experienced considerable technical problems and for a time in the late 1970s did not pursue widescale research or production. The technology works like this: a bomb is released by either a plane or missile. An initial explosion spreads the fuel in the air—say, in an area up to 300 feet in circumference. Then an igniter strikes the cloud, and creates a tremendous blast that could be as much as several miles wide. The bomb or missile warhead usually contains either propane or ethylene oxide. The blast can be some ten times the impact of a normal high explosive of the same weight.

The military advantages of an F.A.E. are numerous. Most natural obstacles are no defense against it. The vapors stick like glue to the shape of a terrain and spread out like an enveloping mist. They can penetrate caves, houses or cellars. An installation would have to be fully sealed to stop the engulfing flow. With the charges vaporized in air, a mixture of combustible gases results in what the experts call an "aerosol." Then an igniter gets inserted into its center. One expert told me it's just like throwing a match into a gas-filled room. A monster blast follows.

The deadly killing power of the F.A.E. caused concern from as early as the mid-1970s when a U.N. committee concluded that fuel-air ammunition is "an inhumane resource of warfare eliciting excessive suffering in people." At a 1976 meeting in Geneva, the U.N.'s Extraordinary Committee for Conventional Weapons adopted a document qualifying fuel-air ammunition as "a form of weapon requiring international prohibition."

The F.A.E.—a military specialty item totally unknown to the general public until the fall of 1990 when it was reported that Iraq had it in its arsenal—got famous during the 1991 Gulf War. Intelligence analysts were concerned about its relationship to chemical weaponry, which experts believed to be a crucial factor in both Iraqi and Egyptian attempts to get their hands on the technology. The F.A.E. constitutes an ideal vehicle for chemical weapons bombing because of its dispersion capabilities. The bomb would be released and the first stage of the process would let loose a uniform cloud of nerve agent or poison gas. This would float down to earth. If used to spread nerve gas, the second phase of the F.A.E. process, the ignition of the cloud, becomes extraneous.

The F.A.E.'s development represented a higher level in the Middle East arms competition and an advance in the kinds of technology to be used by Arab states in the Middle East. Although the Iraqis also got cluster bomb and F.A.E. technology elsewhere, especially from Cardoens Industries of Chile, the F.A.E. dimension and its inclusion in a ballistic missile warhead formed one of the most dangerous aspects of the ongoing Condor project.

•   •   •

As MBB increasingly became a player in the booming business of Third World missile sales, MBB executives capitalized on their close ties with Egypt that went back several decades. Though retired from active management, Ludwig Boelko was an honored member of the company's board of supervisors. Against competition from the Americans who sought to become Egypt's exclusive arms suppliers, he helped MBB secure Egypt's lucrative missile work. MBB knew it was treading a fine line in obtaining missile contracts that violated M.T.C.R. guidelines. The Condor project offered Egypt and its partner, Iraq, an opportunity to use German scientific and engineering expertise.

The man in charge of the Condor project inside MBB was Karl Adolf Hammer, the company's military research and development director. Many considered him one of Germany's most expert engineers—someone in the tradition of German missile-makers and aviation engineers like Ludwig Boelko and Willie Messerschmitt. Hammer had a good reputation both inside and outside MBB, and was one of Boelko's protegés. The two men had been associated together since at least the late 1950s and 1960s, when Hammer had gone with Boelko to Egypt to help build missiles. Hammer continued his association with both Boelko and Egypt during the 1980s. One MBB employee described their relationship as in some ways that of "a father to a son."

Hammer was not only MBB's military research man but the figure most closely identified with the Condor project. As MBB and the Condor project ran into pressure from diplomatic and other sources,

Hammer remained faithful to his clients and the lethal technology they sought. He got impatient with MBB bending and shaking in the wind. He pushed for the project's continuation.

•   •   •

Both Egypt and Iraq had been seeking F.A.E. technology since the early 1980s. In the midst of Iraq's war against Iran, the two Arab states were close allies and sought to add to their weapons arsenal. As part of their long-range interest in acquiring F.A.E. technology, the Egyptians decided to meet the problem head-on and acquire this technology from the world leaders in it—their ally, the United States of America.

The Egyptians tried both to acquire ready-made bombs and the means to make F.A.E.s themselves. The routing was roundabout. The Egyptians had done their homework about what the U.S. had and where the Americans had it. They knew that the U.S. stored 9,000 surplus CBU 72/B F.A.E. bombs at Hawthorne Depot, Nevada. The Egyptians made inquiries on the possibility of purchasing some ready-made F.A.E.s, explaining that these bombs were to be used for clearing mines in the Egyptian desert.

Two American companies had combined their efforts to share manufacturing responsibility for these bombs. Minneapolis Honeywell designed the weapon. Day & Zimmerman, Inc., of Philadelphia produced the fuel components for the bomb.

The head of the Condor project in Egypt, Yousef Khairat, asked the help of an Egyptian/American engineer working in the U.S., Abdel Kader Helmy, to clear the ground to purchase the bombs. Helmy, a U.S. citizen, agreed to obtain copies of U.S. patents on the F.A.E.s for Khairat and investigate the possibilities of Egypt manufacturing an F.A.E. on its own. To purchase the surplus bombs, Helmy suggested that Khairat enlist the aid of another American associate, Samuel Hazelrig. The circle widened. Hazelrig in turn got in contact with James Huffman, who had worked with him in the early 1980s at Redstone Arsenal in a project to analyze foreign-made missiles.

Huffman put the Egyptians in touch with Day & Zimmerman. Since the F.A.E. was classified "Significant Military Equipment," special export controls applied. At the same time, the Egyptians requested that a small weapons consultancy firm, Madison Technical Services, Inc., "devise a strategy to approach the U.S. Department of State." On May 31, 1985, Day & Zimmerman informally sought State Department approval for the Egyptian purchase, initiating a request for an "advisory opinion" to determine "whether the Office of Munitions Control would be likely to grant a license or approval for the export of CBU-72/B F.A.E. bombs to the Arab Republic of Egypt."

To Egyptian displeasure, in September, 1985, officials ruled that the U.S. would not grant an export license for the bombs. The Egyptians then asked Hazelrig to prepare a report on how to best get the technology, including what could be done to get the State Department to reconsider its negative assessment. Shortly, according to U.S. federal court records, Hazelrig flew to Monte Carlo, home base of the Consen office headed by Ekkehard Schrotz, where he personally delivered a copy of the report to Egyptian liaison officer Youssef Khairat.

From Monaco, Hazelrig proceeded to Cairo, where he met a number of senior Egyptian military officials, including General Abdel Elgohary, one of the supervisors of the Condor project. Hazelrig later told U.S. investigators that it was clear to him that the F.A.E.s were for a ballistic missile project and not mine-clearing. Meanwhile, the Consen-owned I.F.A.T. Company, based in Zug, the contractor for the FK-120 project whose personnel also worked for the Consen companies serving Iraq, got into contact with the F.A.E.s' designers, the Honeywell Corporation, based in Minneapolis, Minnesota. I.F.A.T. succeeded in purchasing a 300 page Honeywell confidential report on the highly complex F.A.E. technology. A *Los Angeles Times* story in December, 1990, reflected the conviction of U.S. intelligence officials that I.F.A.T. was acting on behalf of both Iraq and Egypt. The sale of the document violated Honeywell's own internal regulations.

Later, in 1987 and '88, within the general context of their acquisition of missile technology for the Condor project, the Egyptians attempted to smuggle certain kinds of sub-systems and ready-made components out of the United States. This included "carbon-carbon" technology for the missile's nose, a high strength metal to shield the missile from burn-up as it re-entered the earth's atmosphere. Several Egyptian agents got staked out and caught. U.S. customs investigators taped telephone conversations between the Ministry of Defense in Cairo and their undercover agents scattered across the States. Just as the goods were about to be shipped in the spring of 1988, U.S. Customs closed the trap, arresting several Egyptians and Americans and seizing the goods. U.S. agents interrogated the suspects and within months brought them to a Federal court in Sacramento to face charges. Their testimony and government-supplied evidence— including taped transcripts, testimony from an expert at the Defense Intelligence Agency in the State Department and bank documents—provided significant clues to the Condor project and its warhead. The case proved enormously embarassing to the Egyptians and provided the United States with the political ammunition to clamp down.

When the Egyptians saw they couldn't easily get an F.A.E. bomb supply from the United States in 1985—though they could get information on the technology at a price—they turned elsewhere. More specifically, they approached an old friend, the company that had been with them in Egypt in the 1960s building experimental warplanes, and was in daily contact with them because of Condor—namely, MBB.

•   •   •

The MBB warhead team at Schrobenhausen worked hard on the FK-120 Condor missile and its F.A.E. and MUSCO warheads. The missile itself had pressure, heat transfer and structural works tests through the fall of 1986 and into 1987. Additionally, MBB undertook wind tunnel and interference tests. The MUSCO and F.A.E. warheads had parachute tests in the fall of 1986.

By the spring of 1987, progress on the various FK-120 warheads had proceeded to a point where more general testing could begin. A team of Egyptian officers made an official visit to Schrobenhausen on April 7th to watch a demonstration. MBB exhibited both the MUSCO and F.A.E., according to MBB documents that came into my possession. Both warheads "got put through their paces."

Later, both U.S. officials and MBB downplayed the German firm's provision of the F.A.E. as well as other missile technology to the Middle East. MBB, the company's spokesman said, never delivered a complete weapons system to Egypt and, more indirectly, its ally Iraq. The Pentagon's Henry Sokolski, one of the men in charge of missile proliferation matters, told me, "There not as much there as meets the eye," and leaned to the theory that Chile's Cardoens Industries, a principal supplier of Iraq's cluster bombs, also made substantive contributions to Iraq's F.A.E. development.

An American threat against MBB for violating NATO and M.T.C.R. guidelines on missile sales hung in the air, and the firm faced an outside possibility of not being able to export its product to the United States. MBB had managed to successfully de-emphasize its involvement. But important components of the F.A.E. and MUSCO warheads and their technological plans did make their way to MBB's clients.

· · ·

MBB's ostensible client was Egypt, but Egypt brought Iraq in through the back door. MBB created an elaborate subterfuge in order to deliver its goods. Like other MBB deals, this one was carefully structured. MBB's relationship went through a second German company, the Consen-linked P.B.G., which was the official exporter of the goods and technology to Egypt. In turn, P.B.G.'s client was the Swiss-based Consen company, I.F.A.T., general manager for Egypt on the Condor project. And Egypt's client was Iraq.[1]

Located in Freising to the north of Munich, not too far from remnants of the death camp Dachau, P.B.G.'s offices on Wippenhauser-strasse were in the middle of the village, down a small alley behind a group of stores. A neighbor's shop sold traditional Bavarian postcards, colorful pictures featuring lederhosen worn by tall, handsome men, and swirling peasant skirts and embroidered lace shirts worn by fair women.

Werner Schoffel headed P.B.G., the same Schoffel who had once been a buyer for the Bohlen-owned Bowas InduPlan in Salzburg, the contractual father of the Condor project. P.B.G. was part of the Consen group. An upstanding burgher of his small community, Schoffel was highly secretive. He employed three or four secretaries but used them only for the simplest clerical tasks. They typed invoices and answered telephones. He carefully locked up or hid all sensitive company papers.

Those close to him never knew, they could only suspect, the true nature of his activities. He kept the real company business—what could eventually turn out to be incriminating documents—under lock and key.

Schoffel was often away from his office travelling either to Salzburg, where his primary relations were with Ludwig Aumayr of the Consen-owned Delta-Consult office, or to Zug, Switzerland, where a primary contact was P. Maier of the I.F.A.T./Consen office. When he was in Freising, he spoke to both of these men frequently by telephone.

Still, the actual transfer of equipment and technology probably never went through Switzerland at all, only the paper work and payments. A shipping company in Bremen served as P.B.G.'s exporter. At least five or six shipments went from P.B.G. to Egypt, through Frankfurt Airport. They were designated as "a thermal plastics plant," an official of the Bremen company told me. There were some additional shipments to Argentina, but these were far less frequent than those to Egypt. The shippers did the consolidation on their own or through representatives at Frankfurt Airport, and then dispatched the goods to the Ministry of Defense in Cairo.[2]

What did the Egyptian Ministry of Defense need with a thermal plastics plant, I asked the manager of the shipping company. He laughed at this very funny and, to him, naive question. He said he wasn't sure.

P.B.G., not the shippers, had the responsibility for filling out the details of each shipment. Most of the items came from Germany. But some goods came from other countries: among them, Italy and the United States. The shipments contained all sizes of cartons.

At P.B.G.'s request, an employee of the Bremen firm personally accompanied the shipments to Egypt on five or six separate occasions. What was particularly important to P.B.G. was getting a receipt signed by an authorized representative of the Egyptian Ministry of Defense. As a highly-paid messenger, the employee didn't get any time for sightseeing and returned to Germany on the next available flight. The manager of the firm confidently declared total ignorance about the whole matter. "Whatever has happened, we had no knowledge," he summed up.

Evidence on what happened to the shipments after they got to Cairo came from a former Consen employee, who offered his story for money to at least three news organizations. He confirmed what Western intelligence organizations knew all along. This man, who was a project manager for the Consen company in both Egypt and Iraq, described the Middle East weapons pipeline between Cairo and Baghdad. He said that many of the shipments "went to Egypt, and it was just an open secret that they were trans-shipped to Baghdad. Sometimes these shipments didn't even leave the airport to go to depots in Cairo."

CHAPTER FOURTEEN

Raid in Munich

"This investigation is one that we have to do. Not for anybody else. For ourselves. For Germany."

Hans Jurgen Bachmann,
German customs investigator, Bavaria office.

CIGARETTE-PUFFING Claus Tiedtke, in his mid-50s, the chief German customs inspector for Bavaria, could have been type-cast as the classic detective in a vintage Hollywood film from the thirties. He wore a 1950s checkered suit with red suspenders. He had gray hair and a handsome, square-jawed face. He peppered his English with a lilting but still gutteral German accent. He liked an occasional shot and kept a bottle of blended whisky in his office cabinet.

The view outside his cramped fourth floor quarters looked down onto a tree-filled courtyard. Located in a quiet corner between Markstrasse and Sophienstrasse in central Munich, the five story, rust-colored building oozed Old World flavor, turn-of-the-century seediness and a German burgermeister past. Antique elevators tucked away in quaint corners ran creakily. Most of the time office workers preferred the greater efficiency of using their own two feet. They tramped up and down a wide, bannistered stairwell to get to their offices. Munich's main train station was just five minutes' walk away.

Tiedtke and and his associate, Hans Jürgen Bachmann, had been investigating illegal exports on the Condor missile and its related armaments projects for almost a year. Though the main target was MBB, the investigators also looked into a series of satellite companies related to the Consen group that dealt with MBB and other German companies.

Bachmann, in charge of high-tech investigations for customs, had the job of trying to simplify complex technical subjects and defining where the law had been violated. A native of the Bavarian capital, he got into customs service after graduation from university and two years of special training. He was in his mid-40s but looked 35. Handsome, dressed casually in a red sweater and slacks, with a shirt open at the collar and without a tie, he parted his hair on the left; it remained uncombed most of the day with careless strands flopping on his forehead.

Usually taciturn, Bachmann was generally unwilling to speak to outsiders without the direct permission of his superiors. He at first mistook me by telephone not for a journalist but for a liaison man from U.S. customs. From that unlikely start, he later welcomed the idea of talking (though in generalities and under Tiedtke's watchful eye) to an outsider who seemed to know something. The German investigators' preliminary inquiries into Condor, Consen and MBB lasted some nine months. In March, 1989, the Munich prosecutor decided the government had enough evidence to justify a full-scale raid on the suspects. That would enable investigators to check all relevant documents to determine whether there was illegal activity.

"Right now this is the biggest and the most complicated investigation we've ever had here," Bachmann explained in idiomatic English about the inquiry. "This investigation is one that we have to do. Not for anybody else. For ourselves." After a pause: "...For Germany."

In his view, Germany had caused suffering in the past but should no longer do so. Bachmann would fight those responsible for breaking the law and personally take on the techno-mercenaries. His country's honor and the core of its character had been sullied by illegal arms deals and the Condor project.

•   •   •

Initially, the German customs team in Munich attempted to link up its investigation with police in neighboring Austria and Switzerland. Officials even broached the possibilities of a simultaneous raid on Consen offices in the three countries. The Austrian and Swiss governments delayed their answers to specific German police inquiries over a period of months — whether by design, bureaucracy or lack of interest. "It's difficult to work with those guys," Bachmann commented about the touchy and fiercely independent Swiss. "Everything with them just takes too long.

"And do you know what they did when the French sent some people down there last year without full permission?" he added as if in an after-thought, shaking his head sadly, then touching his forehead as if his secret desire were to bang it against a wall until it hurt. "They arrested the French policemen...."

The proposal got bogged down in bureaucracy. Bachmann lost first his patience, then his temper, and finally he gave up. The process of coordination with the Swiss and the Austrians was too cumbersome. Even with permission, the results could be meager. The German authorities—meaning Bachmann at the working level—scrapped the idea of intra-European fraternity among different German-speaking police forces and pursued the investigation on their own. "It's just not worth it the way those guys work," he said.

The final go-ahead for the raids on German companies and individuals stemmed from the highest political level in Germany. But as the lions of March departed Bavaria and the lambs of April arrived, approvals got stalled somewhere in the Federal Republic's bureaucratic pipeline. Spring was on the way and members of the tightly knit Munich investigating team grew increasingly impatient. They got concerned about possible political interference, not in Bavaria, but at the federal level.

Then they were reassured. Information filtered down to the investigating team from the Finance Ministry in Bonn—acting possibly in coordination with the office of the Chancellor himself—that the raid would take place. However, that would "not be before Easter," or so went the rumor, both because of time considerations and because, in predominantly Roman Catholic Bavaria, Easter was an extremely important holiday.

The light finally turned green after the holiday on a Wednesday, the fifth of April. Investigators learned that top officials targeted the raid for two days hence—on a Friday. That didn't leave much time. But investigators breathed a sigh of relief that action was imminent. They got ready.

German bureaucracy is immense, log-jammed and often excruciatingly cumbersome. The logistics of coordinating a raid required extensive paper work. The Bavarian team had to "borrow" agents from other German regions. Unmarked cars had to be requisitioned and communications checked. Court-backed enabling documents had to be in the possession of each raiding party for each location. And it all had to be done discreetly enough to pull off a surprise.

Friday in Munich is a day ordinarily marked by crowded roads and a high rate of absenteeism from work. Though it's supposed to be a normal working day, the overwhelming majority of Bavarians eat fish, as good Roman Catholics, or seek time for stolen holidays. Prosecutors and customs police did not consider a Friday an ideal day for a raiding party. In a better world, one more suited to their convenience and regional tastes, habits and inclinations, they would have preferred a Thursday. But marching orders had been issued. The customs team got ready. They gathered agents together from various parts of Germany and tied down the details.

Bachmann and Tiedtke shared Tiedtke's small office for the duration of the operation. A secretary sat outside. Considering that Tiedtke and Bachmann led a "high-tech" customs unit, the equipment in raid headquarters was astonishingly primitive, more reminiscent of a World War I front-line bunker than a customs police command center in a thriving city in Europe's most prosperous country. There was only one telephone line and one radio transmitter. Not a single computer was in sight, only a manual typewriter. The secretary plucked away key-by-key preparing documents. Somehow, the prepararations for the raid all came together by late Thursday.

On Friday at 7 A.M., the raiding party gathered in the downstairs conference room at customs headquarters. It consisted of 50 agents.

Tiedtke sat in the front row. Bachmann stood in front. The group got rolls, coffee and final instructions, not in any particular order. Bachmann said that each of eight locations in Bavaria, and one outside it, would be hit simultaneously. He said that documents would have to be seized and brought back to customs for sorting. He provided his agents with the legal papers[1] to authorize entry to places that were not expected to be particularly welcoming. He wished them luck.

Two hours later, the raiding parties moved out in a series of unmarked cars. Tiedtke and Bachmann were confident. "We've called in people from all over Germany. If something was done wrong, we will find it out," Tiedtke remarked.

•   •   •

At 9:30, over a dozen customs agents wearing plainclothes entered the guarded Security Gate Two of the MBB complex in suburban Ottobrunn. A light drizzle dampened the sidewalks. One of the investigators' briefs was to avoid public exposure for the company, at least until it could be determined if the charges would lead to prosecution. The customs agents went to work quietly and efficiently.

Shortly, the sun peeked out, glistening the mat of thick green grass around headquarters. The temperature climbed to around 72 degrees. The pavements dried while the grass still sparkled with occasional drops of rain. At lunchtime, MBB employees ventured out of their myriad tinted-glass buildings and strolled through the grounds, on their way to the corporate cafeteria, unaware of the police presence.

The customs agents sealed files and confiscated documents in the offices of MBB's missile division, including an MBB daughter company called Trans Technica, a special object of the investigators' interest. "A designer of missile systems," (as the company's brochure proudly announced), MBB-TT offices were located near the heart of the compound.

The investigators raided a second MBB location as well on Friday, April 7th. That was at Schrobenhausen, 150 kilometers to the north of Ottobrunn, site of the firm's military production center.

Though MBB was a key target, the giant conglomerate was only part of the day's work. The two Consen-linked companies in the Munich area also got hit. Both either employed former MBB staff workers or were managed by them. P.B.G. was one of them. P.B.G.'s principal was its managing director, Werner Schoffel, whose home as well as office was in the Munich suburb of Freising. Schoffel's neighbors knew him as a good, middle-class German. Schoffel was away for the day visiting a Consen company in Salzburg. German customs agents seized documents from both his office and, to his great embarrassment, his home. His wife returned from a shopping expedition at the neighborhood supermarket to find the investigators in her house. She was shocked and humiliated when they asked her to hand over her shopping bags and searched them piece by piece. Her husband was furious when he returned to Freising.

Another firm raided on that temperamental spring day was G.P.A., or Gessellschaft für Prozess Automatisierung, located in a small commercial and industrial center about 15 minutes drive from Munich's airport. G.P.A.'s financial papers showed that its managing director was Guenter A. Bittner, the firm had been founded in 1986, and its tax adviser and a second partner was Otto Boese, whose home was in Freising. He also served as a financial adviser to P.B.G. A third partner in G.P.A. was the Argentinian Air Force firm, Integeradora Aerospacial Sociedad Anonima, or I.N.T.E.S.A., registered in Luxemborg, related to a company of the same name partly owned—and set up—by the Argentinian Air Force in Falco del Carmen, Argentina.

• • •

On that morning of April 7th I "lucked out". I received a tip-off from a German friend that a raid on MBB was about to happen. I spent the morning circling MBB but seeing nothing. Coincidentally, I had pre-arranged an appointment at 2 P.M. with chief investigators Tiedtke and Bachmann, having no idea when I made the appointment that the raid would take place that specific day. Possibly neither had they, but if they had wanted to cancel the meeting, they didn't know where to reach me.

By the time I entered the investigators' office, the raid was on. "We are going after what you were interested in," Bachmann announced to me. For the rest of the afternoon I sat in raid headquarters. Coffee arrived with regularity. Tiedtke occasionally offered me a drink. I noted that

Tiedtke's secretary departed at her regular time—3 P.M. She had her own priorities in life that did not include raids on errant companies. I told Bachmann I had known about the raid beforehand and had been waiting for his men at MBB. He got furious. He couldn't understand how I knew about it. He pressed me about where the leak had come from. "Was it someone here?" I assured him no. I pointed a finger upwards. "It was from up there." It could have been God or a higher authority. He didn't think I was funny. When I assured him the tip-off wasn't divine and had nothing to do with him or his staff, he relaxed. I didn't volunteer that the information came from someone within the federal bureaucracy, a person who had an interest in the case being reported.

That Friday, the German investigators were less communicative than usual. Late that afternoon, cars and vans straggled into the courtyard at Karlstrasse, the first at 5:30. The second came a half-hour later. Agents logged the papers in under the supervision of investigator Bachmann and other officials. Night falls late in Munich in April. Chief inspector Claus Tiedtke occasionally looked out the fourth-floor window to check the arrivals of the assorted raiding team. As the dark descended and Munich streetlights winked on around 8, the seized papers were moved under guard to the main Munich customs house across town.

No one knew then to what extent MBB or other companies had violated German law covering arms sales to foreign countries and, if so, whether adequate evidence could be found to prosecute those responsible. I suspected—and rightly so, as it turned out—that MBB's lawyers were too smart to leave traces of illegalities lying around corporate headquarters, and had been scrupulous about insulating the company from an attack from customs or any other agency. The letter of the law was not always its spirit. One of the members of the investigating team, whom I cannot name, told me later that for the first time in memory an investigation had been intensively watched by the higher politicians in Germany, people who, he said, "want the investigation but not, in my opinion, any real results from it."

MBB was a public company. It had obligations under German law. Whether an actual law had been broken or not, the fact of an investigation into missile and armament sales to Third World countries would cause company officials to re-examine their policies and inhibit them from future shady dealings. This would be one factor that would help break the back of the Condor conspiracy. But actual prosecution could lead to unexpected consequences: political scandals that would trace back directly to the government of Bavaria, its coterie of officials and hangers-on, even the Chancellor of the country and his cabinet.

Bachmann's earlier words about German responsibility for German malfeasance stayed with me for a long time. "This investigation is one that we have to do. Not for anybody else. For ourselves. For Germany."

A few people inside Germany had awakened. To Tiedtke and Bachmann, it really mattered whether Germany sent dangerous technology to unstable Third World countries. It took only several months for the public prosecutor to exonerate MBB from any wrong-doing. P.B.G. got charged but Schoffel was still free and walking around, with no known conclusion to the proceedings against him, some four years after the event. Someone associated with the raids remarked that the topic was politically-charged. Federal officials wanted to have an investigation in order to ward off American pressure, but were not too enthusiastic about getting results, which could have political consequences at home. The middle way had a Solomonic quality. Corporate profits did not significantly suffer and neither did the good names of those involved. Yet without harming Germany's political leadership, or American-German relations, or causing arrests or dismissals at MBB, or even affecting the conglomerate's pending merger with Daimler-Benz, a warning signal had been sounded and the Condor conspiracy had been slowed.

CHAPTER FIFTEEN

Turning the Tables

"I have no doubt that in the future, among the Third
World countries and its peoples, Iran will be one of the
centers for weapons, armaments and military industries. In the past, this was a monopoly of Eastern and
Western arrogance."

Hashemi Rafsanjani, Speaker of Parliament,
Iran, 1988

"What is of concern is the Iranians' determination to
pursue weapons of mass destruction in all of the categories. Biological weapons. Chemical weapons. Nuclear
weapons and also the missiles to deliver them."

Robert Gates, Director of Central Intelligence Agency,
1991-1993

IN EARLY 1985, Iraqi MIGs searched out their target: a group of buildings at Bushehr-al Bandahr along the Persian Gulf, recognizable from
the air as a half-constructed nuclear power plant. The buildings were
lightly defended. The MIGs swarmed and then they hit. Not once or
twice, but again and again. Not just in one bombing raid but in as
many as half a dozen or more.

The bombing of the Bushehr site was no drop of opportunity. Rather,
the Iraqi MIGs bore a message: A specific warning to the Iranians to

desist from completing the multi-billion dollar nuclear power plant that was once a showpiece-in-the-works of the Shah's regime, and a more general warning not to embark on a high-tech weapons campaign against them. Paradoxically, it may have been the Iraqi strikes against the Bushehr plant—work contracted with the German firm Kraftwerk Union a decade earlier, but then abandoned—that spurred Iran's decision to re-evaluate what sophisticated modern technology could accomplish for the country, and re-examine chemical, biological and nuclear weapons options.

Initially, after the Ayatollah Khomeini had swept into power, the ideological militants of the new Islamic regime dismantled or abandoned much of the Shah's expensively acquired nuclear projects. Spiritual, not practical values, the Ayatollah and his followers contended, must take primacy in the affairs of the nation. Soon, though, Iran was in the midst of its cruel war with Iraq. By the mid-1980s, Iran had, practically speaking, lost a generation, with literally tens of thousands of the country's young men killed. Almost every family saw a son or a relative fall. With each passing day, Iranian cemeteries stretched out further throughout the countryside. Mothers grieved at gravesides. Families visited the tombs, washing the stones and leaving flowers. They put up pictures to remind them and others of the deceased and their own losses.

Iranian generals required far more than Islamic fervor to fight the better-equipped Iraqis. Their soldiers on the ground desperately needed supplies and ammunition. With their American equipment lacking spare parts, Iranian generals demanded the nuts and bolts of practical weaponry from anyone who could give it to them. Lacking missile capability, they sought to beef up their missile forces. Lacking fire power with their artillery weapons, they needed more pieces and ones with greater range.

Much of what the Iranians wanted was off the shelf stock, the kind that the quartermaster of any large U.S. base has stored away in abundance. The Iranians felt they had been exploited and even brutalized by the Americans for decades; and so, they did not want to approach the United States, the country that the militants referred to as the "Great Satan." They managed to obtain spare parts and some major U.S.-made items through a country that had once been Iran's secret partner in a number of strategic projects, but with which they had broken off relations and roundly condemned, the country they referred to as "the Little Satan": Israel. In a series of deals, some of which were secretly approved by the American administration, some arms and a great quantity of replacement parts flowed into Iran. Some of these deals formed the core of the later Iran contra scandal that sullied the Bush Administration.

In 1985, the speaker of the Iranian Parliament, or Majlis, Hashemi Rafsanjani, assumed increasing power. This turbaned pragmatist with a round, seemingly open face consolidated his position within the still-turbulent revolutionary regime and became its effective leader. Rafsanjani was a different form of religious traditionalist. Though no less militant than the pasdaran, the revolutionary guards, in his ultimate goals, he displayed a determination to make Iran not only a spiritual symbol but a technological and military power. He firmly believed that religious values, modern technology and science were not in conflict but were fully compatible, as in the early days of Islam when Moslem civilization led Christian Europe in science, medicine, and mathematics.

Rafsanjani baldly asserted traditional Iranian interests using modern diplomacy and, when feasible, technology. By the mid-1980s, Iran was pursuing pragmatic alliances that would not only circumvent the Iraqi enemy but reduce its own isolation. From Syria and Lebanon to Libya, from the already emerging Islamic republics in the southern Soviet Union to Pakistan, Afghanistan and North Korea, from Sudan to Chad, the Iranians encouraged contacts with regimes that were not necessarily revolutionary or fundamentally Islamic, but often were. In pursuing interests in the Islamic world, Iran faced competition from Turkey and Saudi Arabia. The Iranians often supported underground, pro-Islamic extremist groups in countries where they thought they could advance their interests, such as Lebanon, Sudan, Egypt, and Algeria.

During these years, the Iranians carefully reviewed tactics. Earlier, the Ayatollah Khomeini had derided the Shah's nuclear program as "the work of the devil." This stance justified the abandonment of the Shah's expensive nuclear program. Rafsanjani, on the other hand, though also an Islamic militant, was determined to use modern technology to fight the war and build up Iranian defenses. In 1985 and '86, in a dramatic reversal of policy—which the authorities took care not to signal too loudly—the Iranians tried to draw the nation's administrative and scientific elite, many of whom had left the country after the Islamic revolution, back to Iran. Scientific and engineering talent, not Islamic fervor, would become the criterion for job placement and advancement. Advertisements appeared in Iranian expatriate publications trying to persuade engineers and scientists to return. There would be no retribution for political dissent or opposition to Khomeiniism. Skilled Iranian scientists and engineers, encouraged by the authorities, filtered back to the country. Most of them were singularly lacking in Islamic revolutionary fervor.

Over the next years, Iran sought to attain military self-sufficiency. The most significant advance was the push to gain missile independence. In 1985, Iran signed its missile deal with North Korea, part of a $500 million armaments agreement with that country. Iran both received finished product from the North Koreans and got help in building its own home-grown industries. Through what the intelligence experts call "cratology," satellite photos identified secret shipments of missiles from North Korea crossing the Indian Ocean to Iran. Some of the missiles got trans-shipped to Syria, Iran's strategic ally against Iran. Iranian engineers made significant advances in developing their own missiles.

Even while camouflaging some of the specifics, there was increasing public candor about Iran's goals. Speaking in 1988, Speaker Rafsanjani told his people that self-sufficiency in military production was one aim of the regime, and that advances in Iran's military industries had been significant: "I have no doubt that in the future, among the Third World countries and its peoples, Iran will be one of the centers for weapons, armaments and military industries. In the past, this was a monopoly of Eastern and Western arrogance."[1]

The then-president of Iran, Khamenei'i, advanced this line of thought further while visiting North Korea in May, 1989: "What I can say clearly on the basis of the fighting experience of our people for ten years is that we Third World countries must have the capacity to defend ourselves and we cannot depend upon any power for defense.... The Third World countries should not consider their economic, scientific and technical development to be of secondary importance. It is indispensable and essential in defending their independence in the future." For their chemical weapons program, the Iranians varied the Iraqi model. The first Iranian uses of chemical weapons came early in the war, according to a number of sources with whom I spoke, and were a natural reaction to the stresses of battle. The Iranian troops would pick up the Iraqi duds—shells still filled with poison gas and nerve agent— put them into their own artillery pieces, and fire them back at the Iraqis. A bit later, according to official American intelligence sources, the Iranians did manage to produce for themselves relatively small amounts of hydrogen cyanide, a process simple in comparison to manufacturing nerve agent or even mustard gas. These U.S. officials asserted that the Iranians used the cyanide on the battlefield in the closing months of the Iran-Iraq War during the spring of 1988, and possibly before.

The religiously fervent revolutionary guards spearheaded the Iranian buying effort in chemicals. They laid down some of the smokescreen and were active in the buying organizations and creating the companies that fronted the non-conventional weapons projects. This was a group that owed allegiance only to the new Islamic order. They had enough of a technical base to oversee the sensitive purchases, and displayed Rafsanjani-type pragmatism when it came to buying and selling. The pasdaran, not the conventional army, handled many of the supersensitive sales from countries such as Israel to Iran, showing that Rafsanjani-type pragmatism could overcome the rigidity of fundamentalist Moslem cant.

Publicly, the Iranians stuck to their declarations that they wouldn't use the Iraqis own methods against them. In August, 1988—two months after the ceasefire between the two Gulf countries—Akbar Hashemi Rafsanjani, by then the effective leader of his country, made another of his revealing declarations. "Now I must tell you that the Islamic Republic has the power to manufacture all sorts of chemical materials which are customary in the armies of the world," he announced. "The Islamic Republic has the capacity for mass production, but it does not use it against the Iraqi nation. This stems from being committed to principles."

Two months after that, in October, 1988, Rafsanjani spoke again, this time to a gathering of Iranian soldiers: "With regard to chemical, bacteriological and radiological weapons training, it was made very clear during the war that these weapons are very decisive. It was also made clear that the moral teachings of the world are not very effective when war reaches a serious stage and the world does not respect its own resolutions and closes its eyes to the violations and all the aggressions that are committed in the battlefield."

Whether or not these weapons should be used, Rafsanjani continued, "we should fully equip ourselves both in the offensive and defensive use of chemical, bacteriological and radiological weapons. From now on," he told the assembled troops, "you should make use of the opportunity and perform this task."

In the long run, the calculations of Iranian leaders forced their country down the singular path of non-conventional weaponry, if only not to leave the playing field entirely to Iraqi initiatives. Senior Iranian Army officers and the pasdaran concluded that, after eight years of war and suffering, the most potent tool in defending revolutionary Islam against the Iraqi onslaught was the killing power of high-tech weaponry.

The Iranians bought raw materials and equipment wherever and however they could. One of the first tip-offs on their efforts came from their purchases of raw materials for mustard gas from the Baltimore-based chemical firm, Alcolac, which had also dealt with the Iraqis. Initially, like the Iraqis, the Iranians concentrated most of their buying activities in Germany. One Iranian diplomat, Ali Sobhani, was asked to leave the Bonn embassy in 1989 by German authorities for flagrantly shopping for items that could constitute a chemical weapons shopping list, thereby abusing his diplomatic privileges. Sobhani went home, then reappeared in various European countries while undertaking purchasing missions for Iranian organizations. Western intelligence agencies tried to track his footsteps but Sobhani, operating under assumed names, was always a step or two ahead of the surveillance.

With the West increasingly on the alert for chemical warfare sales,[2] the Iranians tried an end run through Eastern Europe. In 1988, Iranian delegations showed up at the Lampart Factory for Chemical Equipment, a state-owned plant in Budapest, Hungary.[3] Known in the industry as a run-of-the-mill firm with decent but modestly-priced stock, Lampart had also sold sensitive chemical equipment to Egypt. Here, the Iranians succeeded in placing a number of orders for the most critical part of the chemical weapons factory, the reactors and vessels that come into direct contact with toxic substances. Iranian orders to Lampart came initially in dribs and drabs. Most of the up-to-2,500 gallon reactors and vessels they needed were ordered at a price averaging about $100,000 per order. Within a few short years, Iran's Hungarian orders mounted to what a U.S. official estimated as three million dollars in all.

The pasdaran placed their equipment orders in the name of a number of Iranian firms that had no commercial relations with the West and, so far as could be determined by Western agents looking into it, very little if any business activity in Iran itself. One of them was Vera Pharmaceuticals. This company, said a Western official in charge of an inquiry into its activities, seemed to produce a limited number of pharmaceuticals, a lot of poison gas and nerve agent, and functioned principally as a buying front for the Iranian Minister of Defense. A second company was Khuk Rangkbar, a company that did not exist in the registry of companies in Teheran and had no physical location or other means of identifying its existence. It, too, seemed to be no more than a buying front for the Iranian revolutionary guards.

A third Iranian company ordering chemical equipment from Lampart was the Sepah Pasdaran company. Sepah Pasdaran had the status of a ministry within the Iranian government and bore considerable responsibility for military purchases, often in competition with the Ministry of Defense. Many pasdaran units were officially integrated into the Iranian Ministry of Defense in 1990 and 1991. This firm was not only "clearly and unequivocally identified with the pasdaran," according to one official American source. It was the pasdaran itself.

Pentagon and other officials in U.S. departments had difficulties analyzing Iranian commercial activities because of the lack of an embassy in the country. A Lampart spokeswoman, A. Fonyodi, while confirming the existence of Iranian orders, refused to comment in any detail about orders or clients, except to assert the company had obeyed all Hungarian export regulations. She referred questioners to the government. An official at the Ministry of Foreign Trade, Dr. Zsolt Kohalmi, conceded that there had been a "problem" about Lampart's sales,[4] but claimed the shipments to Iran fit within the guidelines of what was permissible by international regulation—specifically, the so-called Australia agreement that Hungary subscribed to in 1992—and were not illegal. Chemical experts I contacted, one of whom was a businessman who had dealt with Lampart, disputed this claim. The company's own brochure touted Lampart's chemical equipment, especially a kind of glass enamel coating called UNIVER S-99 that was resistant to "all inorganic and organic acids up to a temperature of 200 degrees centigrade, except for hydrogen fluoride and its salts." It was therefore suitable for the manufacturing of mustard gas, tabun, hydrogen cyanide, and almost all stages of the sarin process except for one.

In a departure from standard policy in the chemical industry, whereby a firm would assume at least partial responsibility for installation and initial operation of its equipment, the Iranian companies did not permit Lampart's engineers to visit the places where the equipment was installed. Since the Hungarian firm did not issue end user certificates, its engineers could have no real idea as to precisely how the equipment was being used. In any case, they probably didn't want to ask too many questions or know too much. As with suppliers of sensitive materials in other industries, excessive questions might result in the kind of knowledge that could unnecessarily complicate an otherwise profitable relationship.

Kohalmi admitted the possibility that the Hungarian goods, at the time they were sold until at least early 1993, could end up in the wrong hands in Iran and be used for military chemical weapons manufacture. "Theoretically, a lot of things could have happened because they [the Lampart goods] were not controlled [by international regulations]," he told the BBC. He noted that Hungarian officials had not been permitted into Iran to discover for what the equipment was really being used. "We haven't had the possibility to follow them up and we didn't have to."

The Iranians dispersed their chemical weapons production facilities throughout the country. Western governmental analysts believed the location of Iranian chemical weapon facilities were at least the following: Kazvin northwest of Teheran, Parchin southeast of Teheran, not far from the town of Arak due west of Qom on the Des River, and in Isfahan.

•   •   •

Along with poison gas and nerve agents, biological weapons research played an important role in Iranian arming. Robert Gates, former director of the C.I.A., summed up the problem: "What is of concern is the Iranians' determination to pursue weapons of mass destruction in all of the categories. Biological weapons. Chemical weapons. Nuclear weapons and also the missiles to deliver them."

To get suitable fermenters, reactors, and other micro-biological equipment, the Iranians proceeded to Switzerland. Rumors circulated in Switzerland's tightly-knit high-tech biological industry about Iranian shopping for the kinds of goods that could be used for biological weapons manufacture. In 1991, the Swiss government issued an informal advisory to some of the firms specializing in the kind of goods—such as fermenters—suitable for biological warfare purposes. One of them was Chemap, a division of the giant Swedish company, Alfa-Loval, situated just to the north of Zürich. I spoke with managing director Meyer Salfati, who said the government had called to alert his and other firms about possible Iranian purchases. Salfati rather shamefacedly related how his firm had originally gotten involved, not with Iran but Iraq, long before his time at the company, and how the firm had delivered both data process lines and a small plant in 1978 and 1979. He had been surprised by revelations at the time of Desert Storm: namely, that the Iraqis had used the firm's equipment to produce biological warfare viruses. He cautioned that, as regards Iraq, Chemap had only partial responsibility, though it took that seriously: "Chemap sells spare parts. We had mechanical responsibility but not process responsibility."

Salfati affirmed that his company "bailed out of a deal in 1989," when Iraq wanted a large fermenter of 4,500 liters (or about 1,100 gallons) capacity, to be located at either Taji or Lottifia.

Now, he confirmed, the Iranians had approached his firm, as they had several others in the micro-biology field. Chemap just "wouldn't

do the business" with Iran, not in the current circumstances, he insisted. But strictly legally, meaning by Swiss law and regulation, the kinds
of orders the Iranians wanted could be fulfilled by individual companies at their own discretion. As regards equipment in micro-biology, he
said, "eventually you can't control fermenter manufacturers. You have
to try to control the live material that's put into the fermenter. This is
just a big yogurt-making machine. What you need is the microbes, not
the equipment, to make biological weapons, and we're not in the business of microbes."

Chemap did not pursue the Iranian business. A second Swiss firm,
M.B.R., also located in the Zürich area, almost got a large contract. This
small firm, started up in the early 1980s, was a sub-division of the Swiss
industrial giant, Sulzer. It had a relationship with Iran over a number of
years, and confirmed that the Iranians had approached them for a large
fermenter, something in the 4,500 liter area. This created some soul-
searching among company managers. The managing director of the
firm told me that, like Chemap, M.B.R. had received an advisory from
the Swiss government about Iranian sales. But he personally knew the
medical doctor ordering the equipment for Iran, and believed the fermenter would be applied to the Iranians' stated purposes, malaria control. Like Chemap, however, though the order was "desperately needed" for commercial reasons, M.B.R. managers decided to heed governmental warnings and not sell fermenters to Iran.

Having spoken with those two firms, I doubted that any Swiss firm
would accept an order to send fermentatation equipment to Iran. A
researcher working with me on a television production for Britain's
Channel 4 checked out the story with yet another Swiss company in
micro-biological equipment sales, Bio-Engineering. Located in the village of Wald, 15 miles from Zürich and several thousand feet high up in
the Swiss mountains, Bio-Engineering denied it was trading with Iran
and in any case refused to discuss its business further. The researcher
accepted the denial at face value.

Secretly, Bio-Engineering was just in the process of receiving and ful-
filling Iranian orders. But not too secretly. Underground bombers,
claiming to be from an anti-Khomeini underground group with a name
somewhat similar to the one that bombed Ekkehard Schrotz nearly four

years before in Monaco, heard about the order and got active. One bomb struck the factory on February 14, 1992. The company persisted with its Iranian trade. Four months later, a second sabotage action damaged equipment in a Munich-based forwarding company that was about to tranship Bio-Engineering's goods to Teheran. Even after the second action, Bio-Engineering readied its orders in secrecy. According to a literal interpretation of Swiss law, the export to Iran was fully legal. Again, advisories came from those responsible in the Ministry of Economics, but to no avail.

February 21, 1993. Early on a mid-winter Sunday morning, saboteurs entered the unguarded factory building.[5] Snow covered the ground and the night was crystalline still. The bombers were scrupulously effective. At 4 A.M., an explosion shattered the quiet. Glass vials, a reactor vessel, and other laboratory items blew up and their shards were scattered throughout the premises. No one was hurt. As in the earlier explosions, not a single employee or manager suffered even a scratch.

This time the bomb attack created enough noise to gain notice. The villagers in Wald were suitably troubled. Company officials tried to keep them calm and expressed the hope that normal work would shortly resume. In a telephone interview a day after the attack, company commercial director Harry Graf told me he had no idea why the bombing action was taken against Bio-Engineering or who was responsible. "This was the third time we were hit. We checked and it was legal to send the equipment. This was not in our opinion equipment that could be used for biological warfare. It was at a very low level."

Graf would not disclose details on where the order was going, or anything about it technically, and persisted in an official company stance of secrecy. Nonetheless, he confirmed that, as in the case of Chemap and M.B.R., the Swiss government had previously spoken with Bio-Engineering about the order but would not specifically say that the government had advised the firm to desist from the order. "What we did we discussed with the government. We did nothing incorrect. We're just normal people. The press is criminalizing us, rather than the criminals," he lamented.

The government was more forthcoming. Peter Lehmann of the federal Attorney General's office said that the government had specifically cautioned Bio-Engineering not to fulfill the Iranian order.[6] Othmar Wyss of the Economics Ministry, speaking by telephone, said the Swiss government had advised the company not to sell and not to ship. But, he cautioned, from a legal standpoint, "they had the right not to take our advice."

Wyss emphasized that Swiss governmental regulations had been tightened by the Federal Council only a few days before. These regulations brought Switzerland into conformity with the so-called Australia List of equipment agreed to by major powers. Henceforth, he noted, such equipment would have to pass a rigorous review process before export. He added that there was no proof that the particular equipment blown up in late February was bound for Iran.

Nor was there proof as to the identity of the bombers. Were they from the Israeli Mossad? Or could they have been secret service agents of some other Middle Eastern or even Western government trying to put pressure on the Swiss? Most suspicion fell on the Israeli organization, if only because of the professionalism of the saboteurs.

The bombers left a vivid one page note. Written in passable German "in the name of Allah the Merciful," they declared that the revolutionary regime in Iran had embarked on a biological weapons program. To do this, it was using Bio-Engineering equipment. "We know with certainty that... the machines of death were already received by revolutionary guards in December, 1992, and they have been used in a secret laboratory to produce lethal bacteria."

A description of the death of two political prisoners—the bombers said they were guinea pigs in biological experiments—was graphic: "Their names were Mustafa Sadaki and Ali Habiballah. Their bellies swelled up and their skin turned blue. They slowly went blind and they brought up almost all their blood in their bodies until they slowly met their death," the note went.

The bombers accused Bio-Engineering of having provided the logistics for biologicial warfare, and called on Bio-Engineering factory workers, company executives, and authorities in Wald and Switzerland to desist from the ugly enterprise in which they were engaged. This involvement could cause "the death and ruin of your wives and children," the bombers threatened. "We will not give up," they concluded. "As long as you continue, the same fate will befall you. We will get anyone who is involved in selling or manufacturing these lethal machines, who are just like the [Iranian] revolutionary guards, these murderers."

CHAPTER SIXTEEN

Of Superguns and A-Bombs

"The customer shipped us the metals, that wasn't our doing....It came from Iraq. In any case, this wasn't nuclear materials."

Ulrich Spiess, General Manager, Schaublin

THE IRAN-IRAQ WAR subsided. The June truce miraculously held. An outsider might have thought that, freed from the constraints of an on-going war, Iran and Iraq would put their stress on civilian reconstruction and that governments would respond to pent-up demands by ordinary citizens for a better life. Instead, the serious business of arming and re-arming began. Both Iran and Iraq tried to lay the groundwork for their competing long-range strategic goals of hegemony in the Gulf and leadership of the Islamic world. The two—and a few dozen other countries watching from the side—absorbed the lessons of the century's longest-running conflict. One of the chief ones was that non-conventional warfare worked and that weapons of mass destruction could tip a war in your favor.

• • •

The Iraqis saw another opportunity, sometime towards the end of 1987, to realize their nuclear dream. Saddam Hussein's men caught

Western intelligence agencies napping without the right supervisory tools to oversee exports on a daily basis in a dozen different countries. Innovative in their approach to each technology, what the Iraqis explored was varied:

• They intended to get a plutonium bomb by re-processing the spent reactor fuels—but only if they could find a suitable reactor.

• They actively sought out an enriched uranium bomb. To do this, they had to separate the fissionable U-235 from the garden-variety U-238. They explored a number of options. These included the gas centrifuge method, building modern factories with cascades of rapidly-swirling centrifuges; or separating the molecules with sophisticated modern lasers. They even turned to the history books of the nuclear age, material that was never classified as secret, to detail a process that had been discarded by American scientists over 40 years before during the Manhattan Project. This was the electro-magnetic method used to separate isotopes.

Baghdad was the Brain. The Iraqis usually gave limited autonomy to their people in Europe or the States. When it came to buying, special organizations responsible to the Ministry for Military Industries planned each order—organizations with names like The Industrial Projects Company, S.O.T.I. or Bader. Saddam Hussein assigned his trusted brother-in-law, Hussein Kamal, to head the Ministry and assume responsibility for all overseas purchases.

The nerve system spread throughout the West. The superbly-planned Iraqi buying campaigns were massive and brilliantly deceptive, at least in the beginning. Like the Pakistanis fifteen years before, the Iraqis gained an intimate knowledge of literally hundreds of firms in the West, an intelligence job that most analysts thought was well beyond the capacity of any Third World country. One veteran staffer of a U.S. Senate sub-committee told me that the information collection was so thorough, so professional, that it was impossible for the Iraqis to have done it themselves. He theorized that they had Soviet help in gathering the information. However they got it, President Saddam Hussein and his underlings provided an object lesson in how to evade Western and international efforts restraining sales of weapons of mass destruction.

The effort to acquire a "Supergun" was both a model for Iraq's own nuclear buyers and a base from which to work.[1] The device was inspired by early German technology initially conceived and developed in the Kaiser's Germany during World War I and referred to then as "Big Bertha." The Brussels-based Space Research Corporation, headed by a brilliant Canadian engineer, Gerald Bull, created an advanced design for a giant, long-range cannon that would fire explosive-laden projectiles hundreds of miles across countries, continents or even into space. As designed by Bull, it had enough thrust to serve as a delivery system for chemical, biological, or atomic weapons.

The Supergun concept appealed to Hussein and his generals. The effort to buy it showed fertile imaginations at work, sustained by a talent for detail. The key was to buy dual-use components in different countries in quantities so minute no one could identify the overall plan or the specific end product. In the case of Supergun, a buying office based in Geneva operated autonomously from Baghdad. It coordinated purchases according to design plans provided from S.R.C.'s Belgium-based head office. Then the buying team placed orders throughout the continent or, if necessary and feasible, in the United States or Japan. A piece of steel manufactured in Britain would be ordered to specifications designed to precisely match another piece, ordered totally separately, in Switzerland. Measurements had to be precise to the millimeter. Firms in Switzerland, England, Scotland, Germany, Holland, France, the United States and elsewhere, sometimes unwittingly, contributed to the Iraqi design. Later, in Iraq, the parts would fit together under the watchful eye of local military engineers and their foreign advisers. There, the Supergun would become whole.

The project had one major problem. This was the personality of the inventor and implementer, Gerald Bull, a Canadian-born genius who had previously attempted to sell "big gun" concepts to the United States, South Africa, Canada, Israel, and probably other governments. He finally scored with the Iraqis. Bull, though his scientific and technical achievements were unique, ranking at the very highest level of Western effort, had run into consistent trouble with those governments who were interested in his services. He was considered not only a loner, but also a renegade of the kind that pursues his technical dream irrespective of the consequences. He had spent time in prison for technology export violations and was the kind of person that intelligence agencies kept an eye on.

Bull's participation led to what insiders referred to as a stern warning from one of those intelligence agencies, or from private individuals, about selling to the Iraqis. Shortly afterward, in 1990, he was shot dead at the door to his apartment in Brussels, his wallet still in his pocket—a pointed reminder to entrepreneurs that Bull had not been done in by common robbers. Most, though not all journalists who looked into it, concluded that the Israeli secret service, the Mossad, was responsible, and the Israelis certainly had the motivation to kill him. No final proof concerning his murder was ever found. After Bull's violent death, the Supergun project unraveled in the unwelcome and glaring light of publicity. If nothing else, the affair proved that some people or some government in the West or Middle East cared deeply about the type of technology and weaponry Iraq was getting.

•   •   •

The Iraqi nuclear program's buying system resembled Supergun's, but it operated with less fanfare, considerably more discretion, and far stricter control from the Baghdad brain. The Iraqis labored assiduously to create the companies and agents that constituted their nuclear buying network—people and firms that could buy efficiently but, if necessary, covertly. The Iraqis built separate networks for each technology, and supplemented them with complementary networks. Pieces bought from one company fit with technology or goods from another. This made it more difficult for sellers and their governments to identify the purpose of the sale. In some cases, the same manufacturers got lucrative, overlapping orders for separate technological processes, such as chemical, conventional arms, or equipment for nuclear projects or for SCUD modifications.

Iraq retained a nuclear springboard from before the Gulf War. The Soviet-supplied I.R.T.-5000 research reactor, upgraded in the 1970's from two to five megawatts, formed the basis for initial Iraqi research into the fuel cycle and the production of radioisotopes. Though the Iraqis lost their 25 megawatt, French-supplied "Osirak" to the Israeli bombing in 1981, a smaller French reactor, the one-megawatt Isis, was on line, and could be used for various kinds of experimentation. It was fuelled by the same 12.5 kilos (28 pounds) of French-supplied uranium heavily enriched to a bomb-grade 93 percent level.

Significantly, the Iraqis also had a small reprocessing capability. Italian "hot cells" provided through a government-to-government contract signed in the mid-1970s with C.N.E.N., the Italian nuclear agency, went into operation during the '80s. The Iraqis now had the ability to separate out and "reprocess" plutonium, though in tiny quantities. It enabled Iraqi scientists to carry out experiments that could be valuable for the future. Reprocessing plutonium, for example, was strictly forbidden according to the Iraqis' commitments to the International Atomic Energy Agency, unless undertaken under strict safeguards. The Iraqis never notified the I.A.E.A. that it would conduct such experiments. Yet, after the war, U.N. inspectors discovered that clandestine activity had actually taken place, with six grams of plutonium having been reprocessed.

Without a massive investment in a reactor, the plutonium route to the atomic bomb made little sense. There was no prospect of a reactor purchase in sight. So, like the Pakistanis more than a decade earlier, the Iraqis invested in a centrifuge program to extract and manufacture bomb-grade enriched uranium. The technology was attractive and, if you had the design plans for the goods, accessible for purchasing—so long as the acquisitions didn't set the alarm bells of foreign intelligence agencies ringing. Though a complex technology, the general principles of centrifuge systems were known. David Kay, the former C.I.A. official and Iraqi inspection team official who left the U.N. to head up the prestigious Uranium Institute in London, called the process "a jewel of late 20th century technology.... It's the most modern way of enriching uranium to weapons grade. In fact, it requires so little electricity that when you go into a centrifuge factory it takes more electricity to turn the lights on in the plant than it does to run the centrifuges themselves."[2]

The Iraqis made a considerable investment in the technology. Along the way, they obtained many of the ultra-secret industrial designs prepared for the Urenco consortium, which joined the efforts of Britain, Holland and Germany. The firm's principal plant was in Almelo, Holland. That was where Pakistani spy A.Q. Khan had stolen many secrets of this technology, including all-important design plans, years before. In the Pakistani case, the Dutch had suffered extreme embarrassment as A.Q. Khan, a Pakistani engineer, evaded lax Dutch security systems and walked away with photocopies and plans of ultra-centrifuge processes. Eventually, Khan's classic piece of industrial espionage led to a bomb for Pakistan.

A tipoff on Iraqi intentions came in late 1989. The West German authorities received warnings—according to a British paper, from the Israeli intelligence service—that Iraqi orders of some 100 ring magnets to a Bonn-based firm, Inwako, were destined for nuclear buyers in Baghdad. Ring magnets are part of the magnetic suspension-bearing assemblies in the ultra-centrifuge system. They can also be used for such civilian items as car speakers. German officials, studying the order, learned that it was for magnets composed of an aluminum-nickel-cobalt alloy. The Inwako parts derived from the simpler and earlier "G-1" Urenco technology for these parts. A more advanced "G-2" design for magnets would have been composed of a subtler combination of metals, a samarian-nickel-cobalt alloy, which would have been far more difficult to manufacture.

"It wasn't magic. They had some pretty good people, who had to evaluate what they were going to do and what their goals were," one government official told me. Judging by their known purchases, Iraqi engineers started with somewhat more advanced designs for their bomb program than did the Pakistanis.

The designs were the key. Not only who had them, and how well the Iraqi engineers understood them, but who handed them over. German companies provided the bulk of the technology and equipment for Iraq, with a number of Swiss companies also involved. Among the German companies, in addition to Inwako, were H&H Metalform, MAN Technologien, and literally a half dozen smaller companies. Sometimes larger companies like Siemens or Thyssen used subsidiaries, affiliates or simply willing firms in Switzerland to provide particular parts and avoid export regulations in Germany or other NATO countries where controls were likely to be stricter.

Two German scientists from MAN Technologien actually made a private, expenses-paid trip to Baghdad to examine what the Iraqis wanted to do. One of them, Bruno Stemmler, spoke later both to reporters for the London *Sunday Times* Insight team and also to scientist David Albright and his partner journalist Mark Hibbs, who together prepared a series of articles for *The Bulletin of Atomic Scientists*. Stemmler told them how he had helped the Iraqis fix some problems in the vacuum pumps, tubing and valves. "I was astonished," he said about his first look at an Iraqi centrifuge. "It seemed perfect."

Both men went through extensive de-briefing by Western intelligence services. Stemmler, who was widely criticized for his trip to Baghdad, said that the Iraqis had asked only a limited number of questions, but that the inquiries had been detailed and knowledgeable— about end caps for centrifuges, for instance. He told reporters with more than a hint of self-justification: "I should have liked to have made a co-operation with the Iraqis, but that was before I discovered that he [Saddam Hussein] had lost his mind. I have got a hatred in my heart of war. Saddam Hussein is another Hitler, another dictator and I am against all dictators."

The Iraqis built up an enormous knowledge of individual firms with nuclear specialties. Following the original Pakistani trail, they approached one of Europe's most successful nuclear salesmen, Friedrich Tinner, a Swiss outdoorsman whose sideline was selling the kind of dual-use technology that many states coveted. Back in the 1970s, Pakistani agents had come to a small town called Buchs, not far from Lichtenstein, in order to purchase vacuum parts and technology for their centrifuge program from Vakuum Apparat Technik (V.A.T.). The Pakistani deals had been arranged through Tinner, who then had a falling-out with V.A.T.'s boss, Friedrich Schoertler, who fired him for getting V.A.T. into trouble.

By 1981, Tinner set up a new company, called C.E.T.E.C., in Sax, a tiny village just across the bridge from Vaduz, the capital of the fairytale principality of Lichtenstein.[3] In this idyllic and pastoral setting, Tinner sold various types of high-tech equipment. These included equipment that could service centrifuge installations, including uranium hexafluoride components and other types of vacuum technology useful in centrifuges. Years later, he remained active in his field. I spoke with his former boss at V.A.T., Friedrich Schoertler, who didn't hide the fact that he had a very low opinion of his former sales chief. Acknowledging that Tinner was "trying to be a competitor," Schoertler asserted he would not be surprised by any activity Tinner would choose to undertake so long as there was profit attached to it.

In February, 1990, Tinner provided quotations to the Iraqis on several thousand tubes of magnesium alloy piping. The order came from "Dr. Ridha" of the Department of Engineering in Baghdad, part of the Bader group. Ridha's name had also turned up in Germany's investigation of its H&H Metalform Company. Bader was Iraq's prime purchaser of Iraqi centrifuge and vacuum equipment. Two scientists—Professor Marvin Miller of the nuclear engineering department at the Massachussetts Institute of Technology and David Albright of Friends of the Earth—examined the technical specifications as written on the quotation. They both said the pipes were of sufficient strength to handle uranium hexafluoride, and consistent with what would be required for the "cascade," the essential inner structure of a centrifuge system. In Albright's words, what was quoted "... was at least enough tubing for 650 centrifuges if not up to 1,000 or so." Those quantitites would provision an entire mid-sized plant.

Tinner spoke with me several times by telephone, but refused to meet me face-to-face. He first denied that he had ever been in contact with Iraq or offered the Iraqis any equipment at all. Later, when confronted with the details of the quotation on piping for the centrifuge plant, he reversed himself and confirmed he had quoted the Iraqis on the order but asserted that he had never actually delivered the goods. He told me during one conversation that he was about to take a walk in the pure air of the Swiss mountains and had no time for my nonsense. I learned that letters of credit were issued on the purchase of pipes. Yet U.N. investigators failed to come up with hard evidence that the pipes, which were visually indistinguishable from tubing for any petroleum plant, were in Iraq. Though I suspected the goods had been delivered, notwithstanding Tinner's denial, this could not be proved.

Other documents, discovered by investigators with whom I have spoken, showed that Tinner played a central role in offering technology for a uranium hexafluoride plant, one of the keys to successful centrifuge production.

Later, U.N. investigators found V.A.T. equipment in an Iraqi nuclear plant. Schoertler indicated that V.A.T.'s vacuum technology had somehow evaded Switzerland's less-than-stringent regulators. He had sold vacuum items to the George Fischer Company, one of Switzerland's largest heavy metal and high-tech companies, located in Schaffhausen to the north of Zürich, which then—without Schoertler's knowledge, he said— trans-shipped the goods to Baghdad. The Fischer concern had additionally acted as a sub-contractor for German firms that wanted to route their business with Iraq through Switzerland: in particular, as a conduit for shipments by the giant German steel firm, Thyssen. While Thyssen later faced prosecution by West German authorities, the George Fischer company went off scot-free. A Swiss Ministry of Economics official, Othmar Wyss, said Swiss firms were sometimes used—though invariably unknowingly, he asserted—as trading posts by sophisticated German companies used to shady dealings and evading their own country's increasingly tough laws.

Swiss authorities in the export regulation office of the Economics Ministry and in the Swiss Federal Office of Energy, responsible for nuclear matters, initially told me they knew nothing of Tinner or C.E.T.E.C. In fact, they said, they didn't even know who Tinner was. These officials had no reason to lie and I believed their professions of ignorance. Nonetheless, I learned later that one Swiss official in the Economics Ministry did speak to Tinner during late 1991, after some publicity about Tinner finally emerged. He advised Tinner to desist from his questionable trade pursuits.

•   •   •

The three German-speaking European countries—Switzerland, Austria and Germany—became manufacturing bases, depots and shipping points for dual-use technology items. Switzerland, in particular, proved to be a test case in an area of proliferation that was at the core of any Third World country's thrust to gain industrial and military independence: machine tools. Of 24 European companies targeted by the Iraqis for machine tools purchases, twelve were Swiss. This was according to an Iraqi list I obtained, which came to light during the investigation of the Banca Nazionale del Lavoro, known as B.N.L., the Italian-owned bank that organized sizable loans for Iraq, many of them guaranteed by the U.S. government as agricultural credits, through its branch in Atlanta, Georgia.

The Iraqis not only bought from Swiss machine tool companies, but even invested in one of them. That was Schmiedemeccanica, nestled in the small Alpine city of Biasca, near Locarno in the Italian-speaking section of the country. The firm's president was Dr. Gianluigi Martinelli, who had been named Swiss "Businessman of the Year" just a few years before. Acting through a London-based Iraqi procurement firm, the Trade and Development Group, or T.D.G., the Iraqis attempted to secure their long-term supply of machine tools and nuclear goods by buying a substantial interest in Schmiedemeccanica in 1989 and 1990.

Schmiedemeccanica sold the Iraqis a series of parts that nuclear experts identified as integral to the centrifuge process. About half a year after the BBC film "Saddam's Secret Arms Ring" initially exposed Martinelli's financial dealings, I called him to find out what precisely the firm had supplied to Iraq. Martinelli asked if I were working for the BBC. No, I answered truthfully, the film I was doing at the time was for Britain's Channel 4. He sounded relieved. "BBC is controlled by the Jews," he boldly informed me.

He shrugged off stories on what his company had supplied as false: "All this scandal for 50,000 Swiss francs of supply. It's ridiculous."

What documentation could he come up with? He provided one diagram which, he claimed, showed that what he had supplied the Iraqis were "harmless materials," part of a gear grinding machine. I obtained some additional Schmiedemeccanica diagrams from a second journalist. When I showed the drawings to a nuclear engineer, the engineer said it was equipment for a nuclear centrifuge program.

Among other items, the Swiss company was slated to produce for Iraq an extremely important part of centrifuge technology, "the mandrel." That is the interior tube within a centrifuge through which the all-important uranium hexafluoride flows. As the tube and the gas inside it spins at incredibly high speeds, the heavier particles are pushed away and fall out, while the lighter materials flow to the next centifuge. The six-inch tube is subject to extreme stress. A nuclear analyst studying the case—he is an official in one of those four or five governments paying careful attention to Iraq—said to me that Schmiedemeccannica's mandrel "fit" the German company H&H Metalform's flow-form machine and could fabricate the centrifuge rotor. In his view, there had to have been production coordination between the German and Swiss companies.

Martinelli pleaded ignorance on every important technical point.[4] Schmiedemeccanica works almost exclusively in the casting of exotic metals. In order to cast, the engineers in charge have to know the precise characteristics of the metals. The company got two tons of maraging steel, appropriate for nuclear manufacture, provided by the Iraqis, plus the design specifications for the work they had to do. But, according to Martinelli, "we didn't know the specifications on the metals. We just got it from the client and were ready to do what he told us."

•   •   •

The Schaublin Company, located in a mountain town called Bevilard in the French part of Switzerland, in the Jura mountain region, has a reputation of being one of Switzerland's very best machine tool manufacturers. Bevilard has one main street. Other than the cafés, gas station, and a few stores, Schaublin is the town's only industry and primary source of jobs.

In 1988, buyers from Iraq's Industrial Projects Company, or I.P.C., visited Schaublin and signed a contract with the firm. Schaublin agreed to provide the Iraqis with fifteen CNC (computer numerically controlled) lathes. The second part of the contract called for the provision of 40 prototypes, including production data and programs, some of them to be made from maraging steel, a type of metal resistant to extraordinary stress and, at its highest levels, suitable for nuclear production. Schaublin's contract had a value of eight million Swiss Francs, or about $5.5 million dollars. I.P.C. was later identified as a procurer for Bader, the nuclear purchasing arm of the Iraqi Ministry of Military Industries under Hussein Kamal and the buyer at Germany's H&H Metalform and

Switzerland's C.E.T.E.C. The parts Schaublin had to produce for the Iraqis included the bottom and top covers of the centrifuge, the baffles (the fins on the spinning rotor on the inside of the centrifuge) and the bottom rotor base.

Schaublin contacted a company in nearby La-Chaux-de-Fonds to sub-contract the small cup that fits into the base, though the two companies could not agree on commercial terms. A third company in the area, Henri Hauser, one of those firms providing critical equipment to the Sa'ad-16 missile project at Mosul, was contacted by the Iraqis to make the all- important "jig-grinder," a machine tool capable of molding hard metals with extraordinary precision.

Ulrich Spiess, Schaublin's general manager, said the whole Iraqi deal was "absolutely standard" and there was nothing special about it. "We don't know if they had the intention to make parts for nuclear projects," he told me. "Machine tools can be used to make any part. If a man sells a pistol and later someone commits a murder with that pistol, is the seller responsible? It's all nonsense. These are machine tools, they can make any part. This doesn't make us the person who squeezes the trigger. We just provide machines. It's the people who buy them who determine their use."

Spiess got angry when I persisted. His company, too, often used maraging steel, and he was familiar with its applications. But he claimed that, in the case of the Iraqi order, he didn't even know what kind of steel materials his machines had shaped. "The customer shipped us the metals, that wasn't our doing," he contended. "It came from Iraq. It was not the kind of maraging steel that is on any restricted list. This wasn't nuclear materials. It was of a lesser gauge."

Formally speaking, Spiess was correct, in that the maraging steel at 250 tensile strength hadn't reached the extremely hard 350 dimensions where export regulations began to apply. Maraging steel 250 could be used in missile and jet aircraft production, and could be made harder with processing. Maraging steel 350 was at a nuclear level.[5]

Spiess contended that Schaublin personnel had been responsible only for machine tools manufacture and not for handling the software that would run it. This software was provided to the Iraqis by a German company—which Swiss governmental officials separately said was

Siemens—and not Schaublin. Schaublin's culpability, or lack of it, and the extent of their knowledge about the equipment they were providing, lay at least partially in relation to its software: did company officials know what software would run their machine? That software would indicate the final uses of the equipment and whether and where it would be used in Baghdad's secret nuclear program.

One document obtained during my research provided a good indication of the extent of Schaublin's knowledge. It was a work order from the customer, Bader in Iraq, to Schaublin. The document listed two computer programmers in the company—named on the document as Haussman and Werder—involved in the Iraqi order. Dated the 6th of July, 1989, the letter dealt with the "contract for supply of 15 C.N.C. machines prototype parts and extension." It referred to "the previous exchange of telexes regarding the holding of the manufacturing of prototype parts due to modifications in design." The document specified which parts "remain as required originally and not charged or modified," and which not. This document, while not fully conclusive, indicated that company should have had knowledge of the software required for the Iraqis.

Meanwhile, according to information from U.N. inspectors who were in Iraq during 1991, the Iraqis used their purchases from the Swiss company to reverse-engineer Schaublin machinery. Having bought the sophisticated machines and its software, the Iraqis now wanted to avoid buying more and build their own.

•   •   •

More adventurous and experimental than the Pakistanis in some ways, Saddam Hussein and his scientists were ready to explore not only one or two routes to a bomb, as the Pakistanis had done, but four or five. Iraqi scientists and engineers pored through the open literature about how to make a bomb and develop the fuel options for it. They came up with the ingenious idea of using a 40 year old, long-since discarded method of separating uranium. This was through large-scale electro-magnetic isotope separation, E.M.I.S. for short. The process was nicknamed "the Calutron method" after its origin at the University of California in the 1940s during the Manhattan project, when American scientists were exploring different ways to manufacture heavily enriched uranium. American scientists had originally looked into it, then rejected it as unwieldy and too expensive.

The process had a number of advantages for a Third World bomb-maker. It used low-level technology, was labor- and energy-intensive, and had been extensively documented in early literature that was most-ly not classified and easily accessible. The Calutron also required no processes or equipment that would blatantly violate Iraq's own obliga-tions as a signatory of the Non-Proliferation Treaty and a member in good standing of the I.A.E.A., and thus no components that could be found on any of the Western-inspired "trigger lists" for nuclear weaponry. In effect, the Calutrons could be ordered and installed, far from the watchful eyes of nuclear inspectors, without setting off the alarm bells of the intelligence agencies or even formally violating Iraqi obligations to the I.A.E.A.—at least, until the first highly enriched ura-nium was actually produced.

From what is known, no one in the West, including the few special-ists trained to sniff out deviant methods for illegally procuring technol-ogy, picked up the Iraqi scent. When an Iraqi defector revealed to U.S. intelligence authorities after the Desert Storm war that Iraq had a Calutron program (at least, that is the story the authorities put out to explain how they found out), some bureaucrats had to run to their books to discover exactly what it was. Few modern professionals had heard of Calutrons—or, if they had, remembered much about them. Even the Mossad, legendary intelligence organization that it is, was caught sleeping. (Or, at least, that's the story Israeli governmental authorities leaked to me when I inquired.)

The vice-chairman of the Iraqi Atomic Energy Commission, Dr. Jaffar Dhia Jaffar, a member of a prominent Shi'a family whose father had been a governmental minister in monarchial Iraq, supervised the Iraqi Calutron program. British-educated, he specialized in high-energy accelerators and ranked on a par with top Western scientists. The Iraqis began to build their principal Calutron plant at Tarmiya, some 25 miles north of Baghdad, in the late 1980s. Plans seized by U.N. inspectors and on-site visits after the Gulf War revealed the project's dimensions. One of the U.N. inspection teams estimated that the main building at

Tarmiya would hold some 70 large "alpha" Calutrons that would start operating sometime after the summer of 1991 or by mid-1992. A second, smaller building at Tarmiya would hold 20 "beta" separators, expected to begin functioning in the first half of 1992.

The Iraqis made considerable progress with their Calutrons before Desert Shield and Desert Storm. Technicians were busy installing 17 Calutrons at the alpha facility when the Allied bombers struck in January, 1991. At the time of the first post-war U.N. inspection later that spring, eight alpha Calutrons had already been test-operated. Iraqi engineers succeeded in producing enrichment levels of uranium up to ten percent, with the average level at four percent. Over a pound of enriched uranium had been manufactured.

The Iraqi machines were fifty percent more efficient than the earlier American machines, U.N. inspectors estimated, representing a considerable technological advance. This led some inspectors to conclude that foreign experts would almost certainly have been needed to get them running. (This kind of conclusion was typical of Western attitudes—some would term it arrogance—about the abilities of Third World scientists in general and Iraqi scientists in particular.) The Iraqi plan was to use the "alpha" facilities to enrich the uranium to a low level of approximately ten percent. Then the "beta" plant would upgrade the already slightly enriched uranium to bomb-level ninety-three percent. No "beta" equipment had yet been installed when the bombs fell in early 1991.

In addition to the secret facility at Tarmiya, the Iraqis initiated construction of a second E.M.I.S. facility at Al Sharqat on the banks of the Tigris River. U.N. inspectors, based on their talks with the Iraqis, concluded that the Iraqis thought Tarmiya was vulnerable to Iranian bombing and wanted a back-up. But after the 1988 ceasefire with the Iranians, the Iraqis stopped work at the Al Sharqat facility. Additional plants scattered throughout Iraq could produce some of the components needed for the E.M.I.S. factories: for example, a facility near Mosul could manufacture uranium tetrachloride. Another facility for components was found at Zaafarniyah, some 200 miles southeast of Baghdad.

An initial tipoff on Iraq's nuclear intentions came in 1989. U.S. customs authorities sniffed out an Iraqi approach to buy capacitors from C.S.I. Technologies, a company based in San Marcos in southern California. These critical components in nuclear bomb technology are made to generate and transmit a 5,000 volt electrical charge inside the dense center of a nuclear device, where the high explosives encase a uranium sphere, within a fraction of a microsecond. The charge sparks a nuclear chain reaction that leads to an atomic explosion. Such capacitors are among the last items bought in a military nuclear program and an indication that the assembly of an atomic bomb is close.

Alarmed U.S. Customs officials devised a sting. As described by John Kelley of the U.S. Customs strategic investigations unit, "We put an agent under cover. He worked right alongside individuals from the American company, and established his bona fides with the representatives from Iraq." The agent, known as "Dan Saunders," executed a complex trap. Telexes flitted back and across the Atlantic from C.S.I. to the Al Qaqa installation in Iraq. Company officials received invitations to visit Baghdad. When negotiations got tough, the Iraqis approached a second U.S. firm, E.G.&G., based in Massachussetts. Customs discouraged the contact. When the Iraqis sought delivery of the capacitors in Europe rather than the States, Saunders told them that he sought a way of protecting himself "from any undue exposure to problems... I would ask that you meet me half way by providing a safe and acceptable method of delivering these items to you via a U.S. delivery point."

The Iraqis said they "understood" C.S.I. concerns. But they didn't want to receive the goods in the United States, because that could be dangerous. Saunders agreed to meet the Iraqis in London to work out the details, which he did, and both sides designated London as the transfer point. U.S. Customs didn't object because of its close working relationship with the British police.

The company that the Iraqis chose for the exchange was called "Euromac." Based first in Monza, Italy, and then incorporated in London, Euromac was typical of Iraqi fronts. The key entrepreneur in setting up the operation was Kassim Abbas Al Kafugi, a jovial and expansive type. Abbas, born in 1956 in Baghdad, also held interests in at least two other companies: one was S.M.I. Sewing Machines Italy S.P.A., part of Singer, also a Monza-based firm; and the second was Iraqi Systems GmbH, the cargo sales representative for Iraqi Airways at Frankfurt Airport.

Abbas chose an Iraqi engineer, Ali Ashour Daghir, to head up Euromac London. At the same time U.S. authorities worked hand in glove with British police officials to snag the capacitor shipment. The operation came to its climax in March, 1990. The Iraqis telexed C.S.I. on March 15th to ship forty of the C.S.I. capacitors to their representatives in London. The law required that the suspects be caught with the real goods in their hands. But, to be on the safe side, customs officers had fake capacitors on hand as spares, in case the sting didn't work and the shipment to Baghdad had to be made. When the capacitors arrived in London, an employee of Iraqi Airways in London, later identified as an Iraqi intelligence agent, came to pick them up and transport them to Baghdad. Police seized both the shipment and the agent. Shortly after, they arrested a French woman working at Euromac, Jeanine Speckman; her boss, Euromac London's managing director, Ashour Daghir, and others.

Within a day, U.S. authorities filed charges in a San Diego court. The indictment accused the Euromac executives and three Iraqi personnel of a conspiracy to smuggle "nuclear warhead detonation capacitors" out of the United States and into Iraq. The order corresponded to American military specifications and, in the words of Bryan Siebert, a senior official in the U.S. Department of Energy, showed that the Iraqis had "detailed knowledge of designs for weapons assembly." Only a few firms in a few countries make the capacitors, with companies in the United States the world leaders. The exposure gave a warning to Western businessmen who might be selling to Iraqis or their front companies, and made the Iraqis' purchasing job more difficult. Along with the Supergun affair—the Supergun story hit the headlines in the following months—the affair spurred press interest in Iraqi purchases.

Saddam Hussein and the Iraqis reacted with their own personalized brand of one-upsmanship. Immediately after the London seizure, Hussein proudly displayed a capacitor at a press conference in Baghdad.

He asserted that the triggers had more ordinary functions, not just for nuclear bombs, and in any case, his own engineers were able to manufacture them. Annoyed and insulted by the blatant U.S.-British interference in his "peaceful nuclear endeavor," he claimed he no longer needed the unreliable West to amass an Iraqi supply!

U.S. and U.N. investigators later identified the Al Qaqa center, at Al Atheer, as the Iraqi concern that had handled the capacitor order and the more general front for handling weaponization sub-systems. According to U.N. inspectors, the Al Atheer facility, which formally opened in May, 1990, "provided a missing link in Iraqi industry and technology." The site included laboratories for high explosive test firing, an internal explosion test laboratory and similar facilities. It was designed to meet "the needs of a weapons program," the U.N. team head, David Kay, summed up in one statement.

Following Desert Storm, the U.S. Treasury's Office for Strategic Assets officially labelled the entire Euromac group of companies, Abbas personally and his key Euromac employees as Iraqi agents and fronts. The capacitor case was the first alert, the first success since the bombing of Osirak, against Iraqi nuclear purchases.

At the very time that the U.S. was tracking the capacitor sales, American authorities permitted three engineers from Baghdad to attend a 1989 conference in Portland, Oregon, sponsored by three laboratories specializing in nuclear weapons. The conference was titled "The Physics of Detonation."

•   •   •

For all their nuclear ups and downs, the Iraqis made startling progress through the summer of 1990. They got close—within a couple of years—to manufacturing bomb-grade fuel through at least two separate processes. They initiated design drawings on weapon-making. They were well on their way to the bomb. Then Saddam Hussein, under considerable financial pressure, worried about oil prices, taunted by the supercilious Kuwaitis—but ultimately for obscure reasons that seem almost irrational—chose to invade Kuwait. That changed everything.

CHAPTER SEVENTEEN

Choosing Targets

"**The world was close, just very close, to a catastrophe.**"

David Kay, Uranium Institute, 1993

RICHARD sat in a small cubicle in a huge building with reinforced concrete that had nuclear-proof bunkers underneath.[1] His desk was scattered with small slips of paper. During a war crisis some analysts ponder stock prices and the effects of crude oil spills. A few count tanks. Others speculate on artillery pieces and airplanes. In Richard's case, his job was to explore whether Saddam Hussein could get his hands on a nuclear bomb or two—not a theoretical one or one good for some distant future but one for the short term, for possible use in the Gulf crisis?

This was late summer, 1990, the period during Desert Shield but before Desert Storm. Richard was tasked with the kind of intelligence analysis that a few other government officials and committees in Washington, and allied capitals, similarly undertook.[2] His job was to cross-reference materials and then come to his own conclusions. Western intelligence agencies had a problem. Confidential reports on Iraqi nuclear capability varied not by months, but by years and even a decade. For example, in the U.S., the Joint Atomic Energy Intelligence Committee, an interagency group, concluded that the Iraqis could build a bomb in a half year to a year. Assessments from the Department of Energy and the C.I.A. ranged wildly from one up to seven or eight years. A group of scientists from U.S. government-run weapons research laboratories insisted the Iraqis were still ten years away.

Basically, no one knew just how far along the nuclear path the Iraqis really were. Not only were the sources of information about what the Iraqis were up to limited. No one had yet made a thorough analysis a top priority. "The recent flurry of seemingly conflicting statements... is partly owing to a shortage of solid intelligence and definitive assessments on the issue," a *New York Times* reporter wrote.

The problem in getting precise information lay not only in the capabilities of Western intelligence agencies, but in the personality of Saddam Hussein. The Iraqi president wove labyrinthine webs to disguise his true intentions. Behind his studied mannerisms and deliberate use of language, he displayed a pattern of unpredictable behavior. More than once—in fact, at least three times, including the Kuwaiti invasion—he moved too fast, even impulsively, and lacked a fall-back position. He ultimately lacked patience, especially at crucial times.

The period from March until August, 1990, saw a splurge of Iraqi buying. Even though the war with Iran was over, the Iraqis frenetically chased the tools that would enable them to assemble weapons of mass destruction. The financial cost was high. They expended not only their current oil revenues but dug into future reserves. To stay financially sound, they needed to significantly increase their revenues, and they sought to push oil prices higher through O.P.E.C. This was a policy that was adamantly resisted by the neighboring Kuwaitis, who wanted to sell their own abundant oil at a profit, and didn't want to limit supply.

Annoyed and then angered by the Kuwaitis' intransigence, Hussein blustered and threatened, and then decided to back up his demands with a military move. In a surprise overnight attack, he sent his army marching into Kuwait. From the Iraqis' traditional viewpoint, Kuwait was no independent entity but a small contiguous province that was part of the larger motherland. The move was a tactical success but a major strategic mistake, resulting from bizarre political errors and misjudgments. By conquering Kuwait, Saddam Hussein put a finger on the Western oil lifeline. Hussein's precipitous actions goaded the West into a military confrontation with Iraq at least several years before the Iraqi bomb program was ready.

Not only would the West fight to preserve its strategically vital oil lifeline. Powerful Arab states such as Saudi Arabia and Egypt, and even Syria, otherwise afraid to tackle the Iraqis, joined the wide-ranging international coalition forged by President Bush. Hussein had not only misread the political landscape but broken an unwritten rule among Arab states: he had infringed upon the concept of the inviolability of borders, without which the Arab world would be exposed to volatile and violent change. The Arab parties sought to protect the sanctity of the Middle East region's illogically-drawn, and sometimes gerrymandered frontiers. To do otherwise was to invite the prospect of chaos in the already fractured Arab world.

As the crisis mounted, the nuclear alarm sounded. American and other Western officials feared that Saddam Hussein might get his hands on a weapon of mass destruction. American generals wanted to eliminate the possibility of major loss of American life in the upcoming conflict. They also wanted to undercut any credible threat to use the weapon, both because that would change the entire strategic picture and because it might also rouse domestic U.S. political opposition.

The U.S.' sometimes creaky apparatus geared up to do the kind of superior job that it sometimes does uniquely well. Agents pored over customs records and the sales lists of major companies throughout the West, trying to backtrack and figure precisely what the Iraqis had in their arsenal. Western officials authorized an all-out effort to block any further sales of potentially dangerous equipment to Iraq or deliveries of what had already been purchased. The German authorities got their act together. During the summer of 1990, German officials seized a large centrifuge order that was to be shipped from Schiedemeccanica via Frankfurt to Iraq. Shortly thereafter, Swiss federal agents raided the Schaublin firm's premises in Brevilard to confiscate equipment that, they believed, could form the basis of a rapidly advancing centrifuge program.

The suddenly transparent pattern of Iraqi buying raised a tangible fear: that Iraqi engineers would find ways to combine noxious chemical substances or even a dirty nuclear bomb with Saddam Hussein's already evident missile power.

With war pending, a decision-maker is obliged to be ready for a worst case scenario. George Bush personally got into the act at Thanksgiving time. This was nearly four months after Iraq's invasion of Kuwait. Speaking to American forces in Saudi Arabia, he said that the soldiers' mission had "a real sense of urgency" because Iraq might be able to get the bomb in a matter of a year or two. "Every day that passes brings Saddam one step closer to realizing his goal of a nuclear weapons arsenal."

Saddam Hussein had been talking about a "surprise" weapons package for a few years. The longer the Gulf crisis lasted, senior American officials feared, the more Saddam would be tempted to assemble an atomic bomb for possible use in the crisis—if he hadn't already begun. Was President Bush deliberately and provocatively raising war fever, as some critics accused him of doing?

Fuelled by Washington's non-official proliferation community, a select few experts outside the government, a debate ensued. Skeptics of the moment, including Gary Milhollin of the University of Wisconsin law school project on nuclear proliferation, openly questioned the accuracy of President Bush's comments. Milhollin, arguing from the perspective of America's disastrous Vietnam experience, charged that the President dredging up the specter of an Iraqi bomb was an attempt to lay the groundwork for a shoot-out with Saddam. David Albright, the resident expert on nuclear matters for Friends of the Earth and the American Federation of Scientists and a capable scientist himself, along with writing partner Mark Hibbs of Nucleonics Week, chimed in with a piece in *The Bulletin of Atomic Scientists* that Iraq was many years away from a weapon and there was no proof of any imminent nuclear threat. The Iraqi program was merely a long range concern: to use it as a factor in current policy was demagogic. Political and economic considerations, not the specter of an Iraqi atomic bomb, were the motivating factors pushing Washington into conflict with Baghdad.

A few U.S. officials with some, though limited, access to inside knowledge added anonymous voices to the gathering dissent, one of them telling a British *New Scientist* writer that while the official intelligence estimate was that Iraq could "deploy nuclear weapons in five to ten years," he personally believed this number to be a gross exaggeration. "I've been in this business long enough to know that you should always double whatever numbers they tell you."

If this official were right, Saddam Hussein would get his atomic bomb not before the end of the century and maybe only by 2010.

It was amazing to Richard that some experts—seeking to assert their expertise—would jump into the fray without having a solid sense of Iraqi undercover activity and clandestine buying. This seemed self-serving. Analysis had to be based on facts, and then probabilities, not only about what the Iraqis could definitely do but also what they might be able to do. The acerbic public controversy, much of it motivated by animosity to the conservative U.S. administration and intense personal dislike of Bush, recalled a conversation that took place a full decade before in early 1981. It also concerned Iraq. A French expert, working for one of the companies supplying equipment to Iraq's nuclear program, said the Iraqis were fully capable of undertaking certain aspects of a nuclear program, but only so long as they had foreign instruction. That expert's basic responsibility was to offer technical advice about the cooling systems within the reactor and thus justify his pay check. He proposed a course on light bulb insertion for Iraq's scientists and engineers, for whom he had a less than high regard.

Now, as the Iraqi crisis heated up, those same kinds of European and American businessmen—the ones selling all the nuclear-related and military equipment to Iraq and making fat profits for their companies—were saying that they wanted to get those goods shipped to Iraq immediately, and installed promptly. They demanded cash on the table. One of the more politically astute among them, a German, told me: "I want to be paid and out of here before the Israelis or Americans bomb the place out."

Then the whole process could begin once more. The West was preparing to fight a war in the Iraqi desert not only to protect its oil supplies and restore some sheikhs to power, but to counter the effects of its own exports. Sale, destruction, re-sale. So long as Iraqi incompetence could be relied upon, the cycle constituted the basis of a spectacularly profitable, and possibly not too dangerous, business.

• • •

The Iraqi dictator promised "a big surprise" in the mother of all battles. Whatever else he was, Saddam Hussein was not seen as the kind of braggart whose every threat was discountable rhetoric. There was usually some basis to his bluster. Precise meanings had to be checked.

One of the possibilities was an F.A.E., or fuel-air explosive, warhead. The spread of the F.A.E. to a Third World country like Iraq represented a significant proliferation of what the U.N. had called "a weapon of mass destruction." Because of the "aerosol" effect of its initial disperal, noxious chemical substances could be spread over wide areas. This could cost great numbers of American lives. Intelligence couldn't be sure how and if Iraq had combined MBB's F.A.E. technology with that obtained from Chile's Cardoen's Industries, the firm that supplied Iraq with cluster bombs. Though a number of American analysts closest to the ins and outs of the technology doubted that Iraq could really make an F.A.E. work, the American experts got more wary with passing months.

While the F.A.E. was one candidate for Hussein's "surprise" weapons package, the real worry was nuclear. What counted were numbers and precise scientific estimates. What was the exact state of Iraq's program? How much nuclear fuel did Hussein really have on hand, and what could the Iraqis conceivably produce?

The clues to Saddam's here-and-now possibilities lay in looking at Iraq's existing nuclear fuels. In the jargon of the nuclear game players, could the Iraqis, using what was currently in their possession, play out a "diversion scenario?" Could they take fuels designed for experimental use, or whatever they had on hand, and divert them to a bomb?

•　　　•　　　•

The more sophisticated a country is in its atomic weaponry, the less fissionable material it needs. As the bomb-makers progressed, the bomb itself kept getting smaller and more practical. The military people began to think of atomic bombs as tactical weapons for battlefield use. A highly sophisticated American tactical bomb required only eight kilograms [19 pounds] of enriched uranium. A Hiroshima-scale weapon might require 25 pounds. A real dirty and primitive bomb would take over 50 pounds of fissionable materials. Assuming a low level of sophistication in weapon-making capability, how much fissionable fuel could the Iraqis get their hands on immediately?

Iraqi nuclear fuels came from two sources. The French supplied the Iraqis with 27.5 pounds of 93 percent heavily enriched uranium (that is, bomb-grade fuel) in 1980 to power their now-destroyed Osirak reactor, called "Tammuz I" by the Iraqis after the date of their Ba'athist revolution. It had been manufactured at the French Pierrelatte facility. That 27.5 pounds of French fuel remained in Iraq. With it, Iraq probably had half to three quarters enough enriched uranium, or U-235, for a single bomb. The second source was Iraq's old ally and patron, the Soviet Union. The Soviets provided enriched uranium during the 1970s and '80s to fuel the Russian I.R.T. 5000 research reactor, nicknamed Tammuz 14 by the Iraqis. The reactor ran at two megawatts power in the late 1960s and was boosted to five megawatts in 1978. The Soviet fuel was enriched to eighty percent, and so was only marginally bomb-grade. The Soviet reactor had served as the training school for Iraq's surprisingly capable new generation of nuclear scientists. Until Desert Shield, the reactor's eighty percent enriched fuel had been considered relatively safe, its relevance discounted by the experts. They thought the Iraqis didn't have enough of it for bomb-making purposes. Thus, it was generally ignored when calculating Iraqi nuclear numbers. The question was, how much Soviet fuel did the Iraqis really have?

Publicly, the Vienna-based I.A.E.A. was cagey, not officially offering specific numbers to either journalists or member countries. The prestigious *New Scientist* magazine used the number "ten kilograms" in an article evaluating Iraq's nuclear bomb possibilities. An agency spokesman, Hans Friedrich Meyer, referred a number of journalists (including myself) to that number, which he indicated was approximately reliable.

At least one person outside the intelligence community noticed a discrepancy. That was David Albright. An astute scientist, he examined the technical numbers on fuel runs through the reactors and noticed inconsistencies. They could be explained only by the Iraqis having far more than ten kilograms, or twenty two pounds, of fuel. Because the Agency told him the "ten" number was accurate, he didn't pursue the point and considered the technical report mistaken. It was, after all, at that point in time inconceivable that representatives of the U.N. agency would be purposefully deceptive. Shortly, Albright and Hibbs rushed off to write their article, published in *The Bulletin of Atomic*

Scientists, effectively accusing President Bush and his administration of exaggerating the Iraqi nuclear danger for crass political purposes.

A government has the ability to check out information in a way that a private individual or journalist cannot. Richard, as a professional, decided to double-check every number he could—at the source. As he studied the figures, he put his finger on the French-Soviet fuel numbers and scribbled with a pencil. How much Soviet fuel did the Iraqis really have?

The reports that Richard got back surprised him and were potentially alarming. In fact, some 30 kilos (66 pounds) had been delivered to Iraq by the Soviet Union. Richard learned that, of this, a few kilos had been "irradiated," meaning that it was used, spent-out fuel that would not be possible to divert. What was left was 25 kilos (55 pounds) of Soviet- supplied 80 percent enriched uranium. Taking some variables into account, but working from the basis of verifiable information, the Iraqis could combine the Soviet with the French 93 percent enriched fuel. That would give them 37 or a bit more kilograms of enriched fuel, some 81.4 pounds. If the two fuel batches were mixed together, they would combine into an enrichment level of approximately 85 percent.

Richard's bottom line was disturbing. The Iraqis had enough fuel, he concluded—indeed, more than enough—for a single, quick and dirty bomb. It could conceivably make either two or three dirty bombs. This could well be "Saddam's surprise."

Questions, once of the theoretical type but urgent ones that now affected American and other allies soldiers' lives, followed: How fast could the Iraqis mix the fuel, then oxydize it, bringing it to metal form, and then make it part of a bomb, and what would Saddam do with it if he had it? A lot depended on the sophistication of Iraqi weapons design: if it were slightly more advanced than previously believed, a three-bomb scenario was a card-player.

Richard's analysis was restricted to an assessment of fuel actually known to be in Iraqi hands. It excluded a consideration of clandestine purchases, of which none were known, but of which some were always possible. His analysis had implications for the military planners: An Iraqi bomb now, though not likely, is not out of the question, and must become part of the strategic calculation.

Fissionable material was Iraq's biggest problem, but not the only one. Judging by the pattern of their nuclear purchases, the level of Iraqi engineering and chemistry was high. One purchase had been particularly surprising. That was the order of tiny, finger-size capacitors, a kind of nuclear triggering mechanism, ordered in the United States and then seized at London's Heathrow Airport in the spring. These had been made according to precise military specifications—the kind of measurements that indicated that Iraq was at the end of the nuclear process and not the beginning, as so many had assumed. These had been Iraqi-provided specs—meaning that the Iraqis were probably already designing the transportation vehicle for the bomb, either as a warhead for a missile or as an aerial bomb. (Within a few days after the "sting" at London's Heathrow Airport, Saddam Hussein appeared on Iraqi TV to announce the Iraqis were able to produce the capacitors on their own. He held what he said was an Iraqi-built one in his hands, and proudly displayed it to the camera.)

Richard continued his analysis. Intelligence personnel, now with growing resources and manpower at their disposal, re-traced Iraqi purchases and made another quick discovery: the Iraqis had bought adequate materials to turn their fissionable nuclear fuel into weapons. The Iraqis had H.M.X., the high melting-point explosive, and R.D.X., the rapid detonation explosive, to trigger the device. The Iraqis would not need to test the bomb itself with fissionable material and had "probable capability" to assemble an entire implosion mechanism and the various sub-assemblies. Putting together a device was trivial compared to the problems involved in producing working centrifuges, which the Iraqis had also apparently managed to do.

The Iraqis clearly had the ability and basic technical knowledge. With a war coming up, a nuclear bomb—not a proper tactical one but an explodable device, which could be looked on as "a dirty bomb"— now had to be assumed as being in place.

Going to war with a single bomb in your basement is like facing the U.S. Sixth Fleet with a single bullet. It's madness. In the words of a nuclear bureaucrat, "It's an invitation to become a former member of the nuclear club." Such an act could serve to guarantee Iraq's full destruction. But the Iraqis might have enough fuel not for one but two or even three dirty bombs. Having these down in the basement packaged and ready for a surprise would give Iraq a place at the table of the world nuclear club. It could make Iraq a genuine threat.

Richard thought that uranium was, in any case, "safeguarded," and was subject to regular inspections from the International Atomic Energy Agency. The I.A.E.A.'s last visit to Iraq had been in November. There had been a lot of hemming and hawing between the Agency and the Iraqis in trying to fix a date for the semi-annual visit. Finally, the agency inspectors came to Baghdad to find "all in order," as an I.A.E.A. spokesman described it.

Richard passed on the information. The decision to put Iraq's nuclear facilities at the top of the Coalition's target list would be made by American generals at least partially on the basis of this assessment.

•   •   •

Behind each story is another story, another layer of truth. Why did the I.A.E.A. knowingly or unknowingly deceive the public about how much enriched fuel the Iraqis really had?

The answer lies in two seemingly insignificant letters: what the nuclear experts, in their inimitable jargon, call an "SQ," or "Significant Quantity" of nuclear fuel. An "SQ" means having enough to make a bomb. How much fuel makes an SQ? Science, particularly when it is influenced by politics, sometimes lacks clarity. The I.A.E.A. position, the official line, as delineated by the Agency's spokesman and by guidelines, is that no less than 25 kilograms, or 55 pounds, of heavily enriched uranium—or eight kilos, 17.6 pounds of plutonium—can make an atomic bomb.

As the years passed, the SQ for an enriched uranium bomb had, on a practical weapons-making basis, been significantly reduced. Nuclear weapons states such as the Soviet Union and the United States halved the previously accepted minimum amount. Enriched uranium bombs could work with only ten or twelve kilograms, from 22 to 25 pounds, of fuel. Nonetheless, the relatively high 25 figure stayed enshrined in U.N. doctrine and regulations.

Now, not only politics, but its silent accomplice, money, enters into the nuclear equation. For the I.A.E.A., these numbers had not only scientific and political significance, but also budgetary importance. Twenty-five kilograms—and no less—of enriched nuclear fuel requires a resident inspector in the country that has it, according to the Agency guidelines. Resident inspectors cost money. Though the Agency kept such inspectors in Canada and Japan, these countries had hundreds of kilograms, and more, of plutonium. Iraq was believed to have only twenty five, a marginal amount for bomb-making. Most important of all, even if they wanted to, I.A.E.A. directors didn't have the budget authorized to put a resident inspector in Baghdad. One Agency official estimated informally that a "station" in a country like Iraq could cost as much as half a million to a million dollars a year—or even more.

The Agency never admitted or declared that Iraq had an SQ. That would implicate the U.N. in a violation of its own commitments. Mark Hibbs, the *Nucleonics Week* man in Bonn who was the first on top of the story, got furious when he realized he had been lied to by U.N. officials. But such an admission could also raise fundamental questions about the way the I.A.E.A. functioned. It could also spotlight the political bargain that underlay the Non-Proliferation Treaty. The numbers, if acknowledged, would lead to an expensive bit of administrative bother with Iraq. And, after all, Iraq as a member nation had been a solid citizen, fully trustworthy, in the past.

•   •   •

January,1991: U.S. Tomahawk missiles and other smart bombs whizzed through the air to hit Iraqi nuclear installations—before Saddam could get a chance to divert his fissionable fuel. The Americans and their allies left whatever could be seen by the human eye, or the satellite camera, in smoldering ruins. The more obvious sites—the nuclear research center at Tuwaitah where the reactors were, the military industries factory at Taji—experienced great damage. But the American smart bombs were handicapped by the limits, not of technology, but of human intelligence. Some of Iraq's most important sites were left untouched because little or nothing was known about them.

The surprise was not that Saddam Hussein had tried to hide his atomic bomb program and its military intentions. Given his situation, who wouldn't? Rather, when the revelations began to come out after the Coalition war against Iraq, Hussein and his scientists astounded the West by their high-quality research, their massive purchasing program, their competence in execution, and by having chosen not one route, but at least three, to get the bomb. The Iraqis pursued them all at the same time, all with considerable investment both of money and manpower, and all with the single-minded intention of making Iraq an autonomous military atomic power.

The Iraqis turned out to have hidden facilites dispersed throughout the country. Much of their equipment was stored away in hidden underground caverns. The West knew nothing of Iraq's Calutron program and the bombers missed many of Iraq's crucial nuclear installations. With just somewhat more effort, if pushed to the corner, Saddam could have pulled off a genuine surprise. He could have plucked a real nuclear rabbit our of his beret and shocked the Coalition in what the Iraqi president had designated as "the mother of all batles."

As it turned out, the Coalition got lucky. Iraq never used its F.A.E. technology because it was too complex to master, nor did it actually have an atomic bomb ready. The Iraqi Air Force was either bunkered up, destroyed, or fleeing to Iran. In the long run, only the United States, not Iraq, used F.A.E. bombs in the Coalition war, and ony the Allies had atomic bombs.

"It's too easy to forget that Iraq almost went wrong," nuclear inspector David Kay pointed out. "If Saddam Hussein had not attacked Kuwait in 1990, but had waited until 1993, he would have had a nuclear weapon. Many of the Western military forces that came to the defense of Saudi Arabia and the liberation of Kuwait would not have been there. Those forces were in Western Europe because of the threat of the Soviet Union. The Soviet Union doesn't exist today. In 1993 those forces would not have been there. It was a very, very close thing...."

He summed up: "The world was close, just very close, to a catastrophe."

Fortunately, that catastrophe scenario didn't happen. Richard hung up his pencil.

CHAPTER EIGHTEEN

After the Storm

"The Iraqis have gone—and are still going—to great
lengths to prevent the discovery of procurement data.
Most procurement-related information has been
removed and presumably destroyed."

The eighth I.A.E.A. inspection report of Iraq, published
December 11th, 1991.

"It was a technicality, that is correct, but you have
to understand... that was also the law. They did
nothing legally wrong. The steel, when worked on in
Switzerland, had not yet reached its ultimate strength....
It is the law that governs and must be obeyed."

Paul Laug, Federal Office of Energy,
Switzerland, 1991

DESERT STORM'S AFTERMATH turned a war over real estate, oil and aggres-
sion into one over the remains of some expensive hardware and some
ignored software. The U.N. Coalition demanded that Iraq abandon,
destroy or return to its source everything associated with weapons of
mass destruction—nuclear, biological, chemical, and missiles. The U.N.

231

created teams designed to deal with their dismantlement.[1] Mostly, the Iraqis resisted U.N. efforts at every step, responding positively only after severe pressure had been applied or renewed military action threatened. Chemical stocks had to be destroyed without environmental damage. Both the chemical and missile teams achieved success, as Iraq's stockpile was gradually dismantled and its ability to wage war reduced.

U.N. inspectors fought a running battle with Iraq's nuclear and missile authorities. When the I.A.E.A. tried to set up dates for its semi-annual inspection visit to Iraq in April, 1991, the Iraqis would have no part of it. Then, after considerable pressure, the Iraqis gave in.[2] The cat and mouse game lasted months. The more the inspection team cracked down on the Iraqis, the greater the resistance. A few times, the conflict led to high drama that unfolded step-by-step in front of the TV cameras. David Kay, an American, led the team that found itself surrounded and blocked in the Baghdad carpark during a September, 1991 visit, after they had found and seized reams of documents that the Iraqis had not wanted them to have. "The one thing we learned in Iraq was that if you ask the Iraqis to take you some place, they would certainly take you some place," he recalled. "But it wouldn't be the place you asked to go to."[3]

Therefore, he explained, his team added a measure of safety. They relied on a hand-held, satellite-based global positioning system to tell them where they were. "On a number of occasions the Iraqis tried to take us some place else and it was only those little G.P.S. systems that in fact saved us from being deluded as to where we were."

I spoke with an analyst who had inspected Iraq's plans for bomb design and the reports that Iraqi engineers passed on to the political hierarchy. "There was a tendancy to overstate their accomplishments in weapons design," he stated, "whether from fear, from desire for more budget, or for whatever other reasons."

The Iraqi engineers were reluctant to report technical difficulties, he noted, adding that weapons design was, so far as is known, the one area where the Iraqis had no foreign help in their program. This lack of foreign experts hurt them badly. "It was the biggest single block in preventing them from getting further. This wasn't a sufficient block but it hurt them. The actual bomb design was primitive, more so than could be expected from the kinds of purchases they made. It did not solve certain elementary problems. The yield, that is, the kilotons, was very diminished.

But, he concluded ominously, "it would have worked."

The Americans made the return of the enriched uranium to its original owners and the destruction of Iraq's other facilities of mass destruction a condition of the continuing ceasefire. The Russians sent a special cargo plane to Baghdad to collect that eighty percent enriched uranium still in Iraqi hands. Between November 17th and 19th, 1991, the fuel returned to its original owners. "They could have done anything with that fuel—moved it anywhere to protect it, or put it in a secret underground location to weaponize it. No one knows for sure," a Pentagon official told me.

The French-supplied heavily enriched uranium was a more complicated story. The Russians had a contract to reprocess it. But shipping the 27 pounds to Russia was a dangerous process that required careful packaging and extraordinary safety measures, to avoid an accident. By the time the wrapping was completed, the shipment weighed several tons. The I.A.E.A., in charge of the shipment, urged caution until inspectors could be satisfied that the hazardous cargo had been neutralized. It had not yet been shipped by August, 1993.

The most sensitive point for both the Iraqis and inspectors was pinpointing the specific sources of foreign aid to the Baghdad regime, in terms of materials and also men. "The Iraqis have gone—and are still going—to great lengths to prevent the discovery of procurement data. Most procurement related information has been removed and presumably destroyed," the eighth I.A.E.A. inspection report, published December 11th, 1991, noted, adding that "the manufacturers of most equipment used or intended for use in Iraqi efforts to establish a centrifuge production and operation capability have been firmly identified." The U.N. investigators cautioned that "identification of a manufacturer does not necessarily mean identification of the supplier... orders were often placed with manufacturers through intermediaries."

Some of the West's most advanced technology remained in Iraq, not only machines but, far more important, a lot of design plans and especially the software on diskettes, the kind that can run a computer, and in particular a computer numerically-controlled machine tool. The

Iraqis had the opportunity to copy everything. Not a single diskette got discovered or returned. This mass of assiduously acquired and highly prized technological information was, presumably, locked carefully away by Iraqi scientists and politicians for future use.

Most companies supplying Iraq's nuclear program broke no laws. All they did was provide dual-use technology that could be used for a military nuclear program as well as a civilian one. But even those few that did cross the line into blatantly illegal supply often got off without punishment.

Not only materials, but also men, were at the root of the aid. Sometimes, a good word from an expert could save weeks, months, even years of effort. U.N. inspectors, on their own, never discovered a single foreign individual who had helped the Iraqis.

•   •   •

U.N. inspectors saw one flagrant violation after Desert Storm that should have been discovered earlier. The Iraqis secretly separated plutonium, producing six grams, without notifying the I.A.E.A. This experimental action was against the nuclear agreements. The fact that the Iraqis did it resulted from inadequate surveillance. Investigating officials learned that the uranium used as the basis for the clandestine operation came from Al Qa'im in the country's north. The equipment used to separate the bomb-grade fuel was bought from the Italian nuclear agency C.N.E.N. in the late 1970s.

Curiously, a former Italian government official responsible for selling the Iraqis their "hot cells" and "glovebox," the equipment that was actually used to separate the plutonium and make it usable, became in late 1992 the I.A.E.A. official in charge of Iraq. He was Maurice Zeffararo,[4] who was personally friendly with numerous nuclear officials in his former client country, including Iraq's ambassador to the I.A.E.A. While he was considered a competent and even honest civil servant, critics suspected that he was part of an "old boy" network with Iraqi officials, and would be less than zealous in his attitude towards Iraqi nuclear infractions and deceptions. They feared that he might fail to carry out the dismantling of the Iraqi program as demanded by the Security Council.

Though Iraq's nuclear infrastructure had suffered a blow, like a phoenix it had at least some capability to be resurrected and to once again see the light of a Middle Eastern dawn.

Up to Desert Storm, spokesmen for the International Atomic Energy Agency had aggressively affirmed that no state signatory to the Non-Proliferation Treaty had ever broken its agreement and secretly developed the bomb. Iraq became the first provable exception. The revelations threw a giant spotlight on the nuclear arrangement that was the N.P.T., which Iraq had ratified in 1975. The basic bargain—nuclear technology in exchange for nuclear controls—came into question. How far could a Third World state go to get itself a bomb, playing inside as well as outside the rules, and what, if anything, could be done to stop that from happening?

Iraq become a test case, in which an errant Arab nation was pitted against the nuclear cartel headed by the United States, and the American desire to keep a tight rein on proliferation. For the first time, world attention was focussed on the "right" of a country such as Iraq, one headed by a megalomaniacal but still canny dictator with his own design for regional order, to hold on to its technologies of mass destruction.

The international system of control wobbled in the wind of politics and war.

CHAPTER NINETEEN

Iran: Going for It

*"The Iranians have pursued reactors that are opti-
mised for the production of plutonium rather than
nuclear power."*

**Robert Gates, director of the
Central Intelligence Agency, 1991-93**

REZA AMROLLAHI took over the directorship of the Iranian Atomic
Energy Organization in 1982. The Iranians do not easily release facts
about his personal life or his curriculum vitae, and his background
remains somewhat of a mystery. A dark, swarthy-complexioned man,
lacking confidence in his English and preferring to converse in Persian,
he is noted (if for anything) more for his lack of scientific training and
managerial record than any positive qualities. He was a puzzling
choice. Though apparently undistinguished, he had a meteoric rise,
paralleling the rise in importance of the ambitious Iranian nuclear program. His main qualification, according to Iranians who know him,
comes from the fortunes of birth: according to them, he is a relative of
the former speaker of parliament, and later president, Hashemi
Rafsanjani.

Reza Amrollahi's short-term, publicly-stated aims for the Iranian nuclear program are not much different from those of Akbar Etamad, the head of the Iranian A.E.O. from 1974 to 1979. They are limited to a civilian power program that would generate up to twenty percent of Iran's energy needs, and give the country an alternative source of energy to oil and gas. Whatever the economic merits of that argument, Amrollahi has publicly sought nuclear independence for his country. Iran should establish a well-rounded nuclear program, he and his underlings have argued, and thereby open up economic and political choices for the future. Neither Amrollahi nor any other Iranian official explicitly outline what these are. By pursuing energy autonomy—the Iranians are circumspect in delineating the precise means—Iran would generally gain expertise in all aspects of the nuclear fuel cycle. More precisely, the Iranians would gather the ability to manufacture enriched uranium, reprocess plutonium, experiment with lasers, engage in electro-magnetic isotope separation, and—concerning a prospect about which the Iranians are absolutely mum—they would even have the ability to produce the fissionable fuel for an atomic bomb.

Iranians acquaintances say that Amrollahi did not gain his job just because of his family connection to Rafsanjani—though that didn't hurt, of course—but because he aggressively sold himself to the two men who counted, who really ran Iran, as the right person to deliver the atomic bomb weapons option for Iran. According to these sources, Amrollahi spent many hours and numerous meetings in the early 1980s trying to persuade both his relative, Rafsanjani, and the Ayatollah Khomeini that a bomb program—and also an extensive nuclear infra-structure to back it up—was a practical proposition. He finally succeeded. Iran's leadership provided him with moral, logistical, and, most important of all, budgetary support. Officials within the U.S. intelligence apparatus have pinpointed Amrollahi as the man behind the Iranian bomb.

Amrollahi became one of Iran's four vice presidents in the 1980s, showing that he had developed a firm base within the Iranian power structure. He could independently push for an ample budget for his burgeoning nuclear project.

•   •   •

As early as 1985, Iran under Amrollahi's leadership energetically sought a series of far-reaching agreements with foreign countries that ranged, geographically, over five continents and, technically, over the entire nuclear fuel cycle.[1] The Iranians also built a plan dispersing their facilities throughout the country, so Iran would be less vulnerable to attack. Training and research would be augmented at a high level for a staff probably surpassing the 5,000 who had worked for the Iranian A.E.C. when Etamad was its chief. Old projects—such as the Bushehr power reactor—would be examined to see what could be salvaged, and gigantic investments that went back to the Shah's time, such as the partnership in the French-led consortium, Eurodif, would be sorted out, injected with new life, and made to serve Iranian interests.

In 1985, Iran was still in the midst of its war with Iraq. The country had been stripped of much of its expertise. Many of the top scientists remained in what the Ayatollah considered the fleshpots of the West. Still, the expatriates had their ears, eyes, hearts and hands out for invitations to return to their homeland, if their safety could be guaranteed, and if they received adequate salaries. Iran's physical nuclear infrastructure, still fragmentary, was itself in a deteriorating condition.

To start, Amrollahi focussed on existing assets. The Iranians' U.S.-supplied five megawatt research reactor of the Triga type worked with uranium enriched to a bomb-grade ninety percent level. As the Iranians got active again in the mid-1980s, they required fresh fuel. The Americans decided against supplying it themselves. Nor did they particularly want others to supply it. But, since Iran had signed the Non-Proliferation Treaty, the Americans had limited leverage in blocking a purchase elsewhere. The I.A.E.A. recommended Argentina as a supplier. In effect, the agency brokered a deal between the two countries: Argentina would modify the Iranian reactor to use a less volatile type of fuel, and then provide the Iranians with uranium enriched to twenty percent—far less than bomb-grade. The company handling the deal for the Argentinians was I.N.V.A.P., a publicly owned firm belonging to the Argentinian Atomic Energy Commission.

Though the contract with Argentina was suggested by the I.A.E.A., and the fuel supply was not illegal by any known I.A.E.A. guidelines, U.S. officials got cold feet as soon as the deal was signed. The problem was not just fuel for the Triga reactor, but the supplementary facilities that the Iranians requested from Argentina. These facilities included a medium-size research reactor that could provide enough plutonium for a bomb a year or thereabouts, a uranium oxide production plant, and a deuterium factory to produce what is known as heavy water—water composed of oxygen and the isotope of atomic-weight hydrogen—an ingredient that would help power a large-scale research reactor as sought by the Iranians both from the Indians and Chinese. Combined with natural uranium, heavy water could enable the Iranians to operate a reactor and produce spent fuel that could, in turn, become bomb-grade plutonium. These were all clues to a far-reaching program aiming for nuclear autonomy with little or no dependence on outside suppliers. If successful, it could provide Iran with a bomb anytime it wanted one.

The Argentinians' nuclear negotiations with Iran ran more or less concurrently with the Condor missile venture. The Argentinians, with a chronic deficit in their balance of payments, urgently needed hard currency. I.N.V.A.P., the state-owned company, was at the beginning of a "privatization" process demanded by the authorities, but still urgently seeking out profitable activity. While Argentina produced the fuel elements for Triga, according to I.A.E.A. officials, other areas of the negotiations were left unconcluded. I.N.V.A.P. was suspected of finding sub rosa means to attempt to continue its Iranian connection.

The U.S. could not halt the supply of twenty percent enriched uranium to Iran, but did get Argentina to abandon the idea of supplying additional facilities. By 1991, the sharp U.S. pressure exercised on Argentina caused it to pull away from its understandings with Iran, and finally desist from Iranian nuclear dealing altogether. Argentina's Foreign Minister, Guido Di Tella, announced in April, 1992, that it was "necessary" to stop I.N.V.A.P.'s contracts with Iran. What he failed to mention was that American pressure, backed by an implicit economic threat, had made it a costly enterprise, worthwhile in its own terms but not worth the price Argentina might have to pay in terms of its U.S. relations if it continued.

Eurodif was another problem. In the mid-1970s, the Shah had loaned one billion dollars to the French-inspired and run program for the enrichment of uranium, the competitor to the British-Dutch-French consortium, Urenco. Interest on the loan had accumulated. The negotiations to straighten out the ensuing financial mess took years, with the Iranians aggressively trying both to get their money back and the basis of their deal with France, including the original partnership conditions, restored. Reza Amrollahi personally oversaw the Iranian side of the negotiations. The French side had François Scheer of the French Foreign Office as its head, with an outside lawyer, Albert J.M. Tomasi, as, practically, chief negotiator on the legal and commercial aspects of the contract.

In a settlement finally signed in December, 1991, the French and Iranians agreed that France would pay all interest and principal due the Iranians from the seizure of their assets in Eurodif—a sum coming into well over a billion dollars—in three installments, and Iran would continue as a ten percent partner in Eurodif.

Part of the French-Iran agreement was officially labelled "secret" by the French, a categorization that aroused some concern from other governments and interest from a few journalists. The big question was whether Iran would still have first call on the enriched uranium produced by Eurodif, and also access to its industrial processes. In the original agreement, Iran had obligated itself to buy ten percent of the plant's product, equivalent to its investment share. A senior official in France's Ministry of Defense told me there were no special proliferation problems stemming from the settlement, and that Iran would have no special or preferential access to the product. Though this particular official was a man of his word, given France's history on proliferation and the secrecy clause, his was not a totally reassuring stance. The executive vice president of the French firm Cogema, Christian Gobert, in charge of Eurodif, repeated the same argument when I met him in Cogema's Paris offices, adding that the new agreement was "just an industrial arrangement" and that Iran "only has an investment position, nothing more." There were no special clauses assuring Iran a supply of enriched uranium above and beyond what anyone else in the market could buy, he contended.[2]

Another Iranian initiative touched a raw nerve in the West. That was the attempt to rehabilitate the project at Bushehr. Iran had already spent some 5.5 billion Deutschmarks, well over three billion dollars, on the power plants, without a single kilowatt of energy ever having been produced there. In 1979, directly after the Islamic revolution, the new leadership suspended construction in the belief that the project was a prime example of the Shah's profligacy, and left the project in limbo. The German government at the time saw this Iranian action as convenient, considering that Germany had already been paid for all the goods. It provided Germany with an excuse to embargo the sensitive nuclear goods already sold to Iran but not yet delivered, including steam generators, reactor pressure vessels, pressurizers, and nuclear fuel elements.[3] The Germans kept some of these goods in a bonded customs warehouse in Hamburg. The rest lay gathering rust and dust in Genoa, where they had been sent for further delivery to Iran. The Iranians set up a small company in Hamburg, West Sun Trading, to oversee the storage of the materials, and provide inspection and maintenance.

Iran renewed its requests to complete Bushehr. What would it take to make the power plants operational? Technical assessments differed. Though the Bushehr plant was designed in the 1970s, one knowledgable engineer contended that the nuclear materials previously purchased could still be used. He asserted that the Iraqi attacks on the Bushehr installation in 1985 and 1986 had not been as damaging as previously believed. "That plant was built solid like a rock. It was built to withstand earthquakes, not just Iraqi bombs." Other U.N., Iranian and German personnel disagreed, saying that the German equipment for the half-built plant had itself become outdated, and that totally new facilities would have to be acquired.

Germany found itself, once again, in the middle. On the one hand, diplomats and nuclear officials wanted to mollify the Iranians, on the other to keep in Washington's good graces. From 1985 to 1988, finding the excuse that would straddle the line was easy enough: the nuclear goods should not be shipped into a war zone, Germany contended officially. Among the reasons Germany offered was that bombing attacks could conceivably release radioactive elements and cause far-reaching environmental damage. That excuse held good until the end of the Iran-Iraq war.

From then on, not only the excuses, but also the legal situation, got muddy. On the one hand, the unhappy client, the Iran Atomic Energy Organization, pressed for delivery and argued, often stridently and with some justice, that the war with Iraq was over. Iran had paid fully for the goods, and now the embargoed nuclear items should be delivered— forthwith. The other, and more important, power for the Germans was the United States. U.S. intelligence officials, already well into their assessment that the Iranians were after the bomb, applied pressure on the German government to deny any and all nuclear export to Iran. This, in the American view, included everything except some laboratory-scale facilities. Germany split. Its government said one thing, the reactor company, Kraftwerk Union (K.W.U.), by now a division of the giant Siemens Corporation with other major projects under way or pending in Iran, another. K.W.U., with an extraodinarily profitable opportunity lurking, welcomed Iran's renewed interest in restoring the Bushehr project.

The German government, trapped between two contending parties, hesitated only briefly. Then, acting in accordance with American advice, German officials came up with a clever, but legalistic, solution. The Germans pointed out that, though the goods had been paid for, the original export licenses expired in 1984, when a different situation had applied. The German government simply denied the Siemens company a renewal of its export licenses. A Foreign Office official involved in the decision-making process, Dr. Johannes Preisinger, told me by telephone, "The Americans believe the Iranian nuclear program is going in a military direction and that's good enough for us."

An official from the Economics Ministry added: "There's no way that equipment is going to Iran. No way."

Germany also included Iran on what officials referred to as an "H-list" of countries, where licenses had to be reviewed and approved on an itemized basis. This grouping comprised 35 countries that were suspected of having programs for weapons of mass destruction. The list provided a basis for an unofficial, but potentially effective, embargo on nuclear technology. The requirement for German license approvals affected not only the Bushehr project, but all nuclear goods for Iran, according to Wolfgang Danner, head of the licensing bureau at Eschborn.

Foreign Minister Mohammad Ali Velayati, during a visit to Germany in July, 1992, called for the Germans to restore full, normal commercial relations with Iran. By this, he meant more specifically that the nuclear supplies, bought and paid for by Iran for the Bushehr installation, should be released, restored as necessary, and delivered. In the Iranian view, it was basically highway robbery, plain and simple, for the Germans to arbitrarily hold what rightly belonged to Iran. Iran had paid for this equipment, part of an astronomical three billion dollar investment. No one disputed it was theirs. The Iranian Atomic Energy Organization continued the offensive in early August, 1992, calling a press conference in Teheran to protest Germany's refusal to authorize Siemens to provide the balance of the plant. The Iranians intimated they would have to go to court, or take the case through the International Chamber of Commerce, to enforce what they viewed as a valid contract for supply.[4]

Iran, though pressing its case, did not want to go too far and risk harming relations with Germany, its best Western partner. By 1992, trade between the two countries amounted to eight billion DM annually, about five billion dollars. The Iranians enormously admired German engineering talent and industrial skill. During the Shah's time, the Iranian government bought twenty five percent of the giant Krupp industrial firm through the national Iranian steel company, an investment reflecting the affinity between the two nations. This closeness continued under the Khomeini regime. Iran's ownership of Krupp stayed at the same high level, even after a Krupp merger with another giant firm, Hoesch. Krupp profited by winning numerous contracts in Iran. The Iranians were on good terms with a number of German firms, including Siemens and its K.W.U. division, which maintained a full-time office in Teheran and initiated a number of major projects there, including at least one non-nuclear electrical power plant.

Could Iran get the equipment anyway, even if Germany clamped down on delivery? Another deal lurking around the corner—one in which Iran was not directly engaged—aroused concern in knowledgable nuclear circles in the West. This was a seemingly benign agreement whereby Germany would modernize Russia's antiquated power reactor equipment. The Germans, through Siemens, agreed to provide the Russians with state-of-the-art equipment, including electronic control systems and other advanced hardware and software, to run their civilian nuclear power installations. In 1986, one of the world's most terrible nuclear disasters had occurred at Chernobyl in the Ukraine, as a power reactor misfunctioned, exploded, and spewed off radioactive materials. Not only had hundreds and eventually thousands died, but nuclear waste had been carried by wind currents over central and northern Europe. No one wanted a second Chernobyl tragedy. Siemens set up a consortium together with Russia's Kurchatov Institute, an organization that under the Communists had handled much of the Soviet Union's nuclear research.

The problem did not lie in the German-Russian deal, a humanitarian as well as profit-making enterprise. Rather, attention focussed on a second, seemingly separate operation. Russia wanted to sell its nuclear facilities, just like everybody else, and during 1991 and '92 explored a sale to Iran. In August, 1992, the Russians and Iranians announced their agreement in principle to further "co-operation in peaceful nuclear fields." Within the framework of that agreement, the two states announced, "the parties have initiated co-operation for the construction and operation of two nuclear power plant units in Iran of the type VVER-440-2123 based on observing all safety rules and regulations and the codes and standards of the I.A.E.A.."

As negotiations on this contract proceeded, the obvious suspicions churned: that Iran had found a back-door way to get Siemens' state-of-the-art control equipment. Russia was then, and still is, nearly broke and in urgent need of foreign currency. How could such equipment be denied if the Iranians were really going ahead? The cost of these 500 megawatt reactors could amount to a hefty two billion dollars apiece. The very process of agreement with Russia could also be seen as subtle pressure by Iran on the German government to renovate Bushehr.

Writing in a September, 1992 issue of *Nucleonics Week*, Mark Hibbs quoted a "Western official" that the Russian-Iranian deal, if it went ahead, "would undermine the credibility of America's effort to obtain an international embargo on export of nuclear technology to Iran." The anonymous source said that if Russia made the sale, "it will be difficult to keep other suppliers in the U.S. camp."

•   •   •

A number of companies in Germany were or had been steady suppliers of the Iran Atomic Energy Organization. Not all, but some of them, were foreign firms operating in Germany. A firm in Darmstadt, Spectra Physics, supplied the Iranians with various lasers, which the company said were for industrial uses only, and could not be nuclear-related. Peter Brett, the company head appointed to his post in 1992 after a management shake-up, said he was compliant with American as well as German export regulations and got approvals from licensing authorities in both countries for all sales.

The Munich office of E.G.&G., a large publicly-traded American company with corporate headquarters in the Boston area, was another steady supplier of the Iranian Atomic Energy Organization. E.G.&G. had been part of the U.S. nuclear weapons program since its beginning as the principal developer of firing circuits. The company's late chairman, Bernard O'Keefe, was one of the most respected men in the American nuclear industry. "This is a company that has a lot of classified stuff on its desk," a wary Pentagon official told me. "We've spoken to them more than once here in Washington about our concern about their sales activities in Munich." Dr. Bernd Heck, the company's Munich-based sales chief for nuclear physics instruments, responsible for exports to Iran, said by telephone that he sold Iran what he described as university-type nuclear items, such as detectors for alpha particles, beta particles, and gamma radiation, and corresponding electronics for the alpha and beta. Additionally, he sold gamma and electronics analyses of software. Customers included the Iranian Atomic Energy Organization and, more indirectly, universities in Teheran, Isfahan, Meshad and elsewhere. He said the Iranians were interested in neutron physics and had applied for a neutron detector. "This one we refused," Heck noted. "You have to be very careful in this business."

In checking U.S. export license applications for sales to Iran, I discovered the company's bid to sell Iran its neutron detector was listed. U.S. authorities, not the firm, rejected that particular application. Generally, Heck recounted, "we are forced to fulfill the export regulations of the U.S. government. And we do that. If we don't get U.S. license approval on a sale, and would still ship it, well, frankly that's a cause for dismissal, for getting fired." Heck insisted that, like other German-American companies, whatever was sold to Iran by E.G.&G. in the nuclear field had licensing approval from both governments.

Company officials would only discuss their Iranian business up to a point. In Washington, officials said that since 1988, E.G.&G. had developed extensive business with China, and was even marketing elements of Chinese nuclear-related technology in the United States. A worry among some U.S. officials was that the technology being shared with China, an officially-recognized nuclear power, would also get somehow to Iran, as part of their broad nuclear cooperation.

The Iranians sought out other firms, in Germany and elsewhere, for chemical raw materials, experimental centrifuge technology, and ultramodern metals processing. One of the more interesting projects was a large industrial campus for high-tech companies to be established in Teheran. This was a technology-sharing venture. Called E.T.E.C., the Essen Technology center combined the efforts of various high-tech German companies, Krupp firms among them, in a common development and marketing enterprise. With its base in the heart of the Ruhr Valley, a hop and a jump from downtown Essen, a number of firms had developed advanced metal processes that could be helpful in nuclear development. E.T.E.C. was similarly engaged in a far-reaching effort with Kazakhstan.

The Iranians encountered problems. Numerous license applications were pending in the United States: for high-tech items such as computers, for major aircraft and engine sales amounting to several hundred million dollars, and for chemical installations. The Iranians made hundreds of applications for export licenses and had dozens of requests rejected. The vital center for high-tech computers and similar purchases was in Los Angeles. There, in the Newport Beach area, the Ray Amiri Company, owned by several Iranians, ordered literally millions of dollars of high-tech equipment from U.S. firms. When they began to receive rejections or suspensions of their requests, they tried to smuggle out what was needed in Teheran. Among the items was a high-powered oscilloscope, which was on the nuclear trigger list. Both Ray Amiri and his associate, Mohammad Danesh, were arrested. Amiri skipped bail bond and wound up back in Teheran. A year later, in January, 1993, U.S. Commerce Department agents arrested two other Los Angeles-based men, Reza Zandian, an Iranian, and Charles Reger, an American, for attempting to ship out a highly sophisticated computer via Los Angeles Airport. Commerce Department officials believed the case demonstrated only the visible tip of Iran's worldwide clandestine procurement network.

The Iranians claimed to be the victims of discrimination and an unfair process of technological denial. The head of the Majlis, or parliamentary committee on foreign affairs, Mohammad Larijani, in an interview with BBC "Panorama," spoke perceptively about the West, and the United States in particular, attempting to deny the Iranians access to the practical benefits of the modern science: "I think it is, in some sense, barbarous to put the new ideas in science and advanced technology into a black box—and then to lock the box, as if this never happened in history. Science is science, technology is technology. We [Iran] are a huge nation with a huge human resource. It is very impossible and impractical, I think, in the modern world, to keep a nation from advancement. I think it is very naive if they think it is possible. It is very unfair, also, to deprive a nation from access to science and knowledge because they may be, in the future, a dangerous man."

•   •   •

As Iran ran into problems in dealing with the West, Amrollahi and his associates in the nuclear program increasingly turned elsewhere.

For mining expertise, they approached their partners in missile technology, the North Koreans. The Iranians have considerable uranium mining deposits in Yazd Province on their eastern border. The North Koreans were expert miners and were themselves actively pursuing an atomic bomb project. Western intelligence agencies suspected that the North Koreans may have included the Iranians in on some of their own nuclear secrets, such as permitting the Iranians to examine the operation of their own 30 megawatt gas-cooled graphite reactor.

In India, the Iranians negotiated from as early as the mid-1980s for a number of facilities, including a mid-size research reactor and fuel facilities. The Iranians pressed for a reactor of at least ten megawatts, but would have preferred one of 25 megawatts. Reginald Bartholomew, U.S. undersecretary of state for international security affairs, traveled to New Delhi in November, 1991, to dissuade the Indians from making nuclear deals with Iran. Analyses he presented confidentially to Indian nuclear officials convinced them that Iranian aims were suspicious and that it would be prudent not to sell. The Iranians scaled down their demands from a ten to five megawatt reactor. They still could not make a deal.

Perhaps out of bitterness at his country's inability to obtain even a five megawatt reactor, an Iranian engineer said that the Indian nuclear program was a model to be avoided because it was "full of patchwork" and "broke and going nowhere." On their side, with or without nuclear agreements, the Indians sought to maintain correct if not friendly relations with Islamic Iran while keeping a tight grip on Moslem dissidents in Bombay and striking a firm but non-confrontational stance with their country's traditional foe, Moslem Pakistan. Rumors flew fast and thick in circles within the nuclear community about Iranian-Pakistani cooperation. The man who would be accused a year later as a spy by Iraq and eventually hanged, the (London-based) *Observer's* Farzd Bazoft, headlined a June, 1988, article: "Iran signs secret atom deal." He wrote that a pact between Iran and Pakistan was agreed at a secret meeting in 1987 between Reza Amrollahi, the head of the Iranian A.E.C., and Dr. Munir Ahmed Khan of Pakistan. Six Iranian experts went to Pakistan to receive training: including Saeed Reza, a senior engineer, Hadi Rambshahr, and four others. Bazoft wrote that the famous Dr. Abdel Qader Khan, the father of the Pakistani centrifuge-based enrichment program, had secretly visited Iran's Bushehr plant in 1986 or '87 and provided advice.

Though Khan apparently did visit Bushehr, reports of easy cooperation between the nations had to be treated with skepticism. Iran and Pakistan are Islamically-oriented neighbors, but they are wary rivals as well, the kind of countries inclined to maintain a "correct" relationship while remaining suspicious of the other's motives. General Ali Shahbazi, the Pakistani armed forces chief, visited Iran in March, 1990, to discuss joint military issues. At the time, Moscow radio issued a stern warning about the possibility of a military relationship between the two Islamic states. In November, 1991, Pakistan concluded a huge five billion dollar trade and aid deal with the Iranians, which was not known to have included a nuclear component. A Western European official responsible for aspects of nuclear intelligence indicated that the Pakistanis might have provided the Iranians with a partial shopping list for Western centrifuge technology, principally as a way of placating the Iranians with something less than full nuclear cooperation.

Surprisingly, South Africa also played a role in the Iranian program, though the white-run regime acted from commercial and not ideological motives. South Africa supplied Iran with the type of uranium concentrate known as "yellowcake" in 1988 and 1989. Iran paid hard cash for it. Rumors circulated in the nuclear community that the Iranians had then shipped the yellowcake to Pakistan for enrichment to a higher level—a spectacular but highly speculative story that could not be confirmed.

•   •   •

The most important Iranian nuclear supplier was a country that was part of the international cartel of atomic weapons states, but outside the Western orbit. That was China. Just a decade before, Chinese nuclear officials had asked the Shah's nuclear chief, Akbar Etamad, if they could read his contracts with Western nuclear suppliers, presumably in order to gain a window on how the West operated. China was a country hungry for hard currency and eager for sales. China became Iran's billion-dollar plus nuclear source.

The Chinese and Iranians signed agreements for nuclear cooperation both in 1989 and 1991. Chinese Prime Minister Li Peng, visiting Teheran in July, 1991, expressed his belief in "a new order, based on reciprocal respect, non-interference in the internal affairs of other countries, peaceful coexistence and respect for the territorial integrity of other countries. " Amrollahi, in a statement issued in early November, 1991, stressed that the aim of nuclear cooperation between China and Iran was "for peaceful purposes only." Numerous Iranian engineers travelled to China to study Chinese nuclear techniques. Similarly, Chinese engineers flew to China and were especially prominent in activities at the Isfahan research installation and at Kharaj. At the top of the agenda was a large research reactor and several power reactors. These sales in and of themselves—when and if realized—could result in some five billion dollars' worth of business for the Chinese traders.

The Chinese supplied Iran with a lot of their modern infrastructure. Among the goods: an isotope production reactor known as the Miniature Neutron Source Reactor. In addition, the Iranians got two subcritical facilities, small reactor-type installations that were ideal for training Iranian scientists and engineers in a variety of nuclear techniques. One was, according to a United Nations report, "an open tank type light water moderated uranium fuelled vertical assembly." The other was a "graphite moderated horizontally configured assembly." A U.N. team sent to Iran in February, 1992, declared that these facilities "...are no proliferation risk since they are suitable only for certain elementary physics experiments such as buckling measurements and lattice experiments."

Less well-known, but acting through a number of affiliates of C.N.E.I.C., the Chinese overseas nuclear corporation, the Chinese also sold a number of items linked to laser equipment and research. The Chinese had been among those countries investing resources and energy in lasers (other countries active and believed to be advanced in this field include the U.S., Britain, Israel and, at a lower level, South Africa). With two separate teams of scientists in the Shanghai area pursuing two opposing methods of laser enrichment, the Chinese had made some dramatic breakthroughs. Enriching uranium through the use of lasers is an extraordinarily difficult process to master, and up to now it has been scientifically feasible, but not industrially or commercially viable. The system has some enormous advantages for the proliferator: it takes place in small areas, even medium-sized rooms, and is extraordinarily difficult to identify or prevent.

As an indication of their interest in the subject—which started with their purchase from American scientist Jeff Eerkens of a set of lasers and related technology in 1977—the Iranians officially announced the opening of their own laser research center in December, 1992. Additionally, the Chinese provided the Iranians with a tiny electromagnetic separator for producing isotopes. Not a proliferation danger in and of itself, the unit could provide essential training for Iranian experts if they should ever decide to pursue the "Calutron" method of producing nuclear fuel, as the Iraqis had. U.S. sources told me that there were signs that the Iranian authorities had engaged in a bit of "reverse-engineering" in Calutrons, and there were indications that the Chinese might be helping the Iranians develop along this path.

Whereas in the 1970s the Chinese sought out Iranian knowledge for their nuclear program, by the early 1990s, the Chinese were the ones with nuclear experience and worldwide legitimacy. The Iranians, parrying about for nuclear items and expertise, found the Chinese useful partners. The two countries' cooperation extended throughout the fuel cycle.

One of the most potentially dangerous agreements allowed the Iranians to purchase from the Chinese a large nuclear research reactor that operates on a combination of natural uranium and heavy water. Similar to the one provided to Algeria by China, the basic principles of this reactor are the same as for the Canadian-made CANDU reactor in Pakistan and elsewhere, or the Dimona reactor in Israel. As noted by Robert Gates, head of the Central Intelligence Agency from 1991 to 1993, Iranian attempts to buy a research reactor have been characterized by one common factor: "The Iranians have pursued reactors that are optimised for the production of plutonium rather than nuclear power." That included the one that the Chinese consented to sell to Iran: "...the reactor that the Chinese have agreed to sell is optimized for the production of plutonium. So this is a matter of concern...."[5]

This is the kind of reactor that produces plutonium in amounts adequate for making atomic bombs—according to informed sources, in the case of the possible Iranian sale, at least six kilograms yearly. U.S. officials expressed concern not only about the sale itself but about possibly secret elements in the agreement. As expressed by Gates: "We are also concerned that there may be some secret codicil to whatever arrangement has been established between the Chinese and the Iranians.... The Chinese have not paid as much attention in the past to safeguards as we would like."

The issue would become a decisive consideration in the decision as to whether to extend China most favored trading status with the U.S., as avidly sought by the Chinese. In the spring of 1993, the research reactor deal was put in obeyance, partly because of pressure from the American administration. At the same time the Clinton administration, notwithstanding both Chinese human rights violation and the broad range of nuclear and other sales, in one of its first major foreign policy decisions decided to extend "m.f.n." status to China for a period of at least one year. Later, because of suspicion about a chemical shipment to Iran that could be used for poison gas, the Americans reconsidered their decision.

A major 300 megawatt reactor deal, for either one or two reactors, was still under active consideration. Chinese and Iranian engineers were actively engaged in site selection through the summer of 1993, and seemed to prefer placing either one or two reactors on the southern rim of the Caspian Sea. While the seismic risks were greater, political and security considerations were more important. The Iranians believed it more prudent to place the reactors there than near the border with Iraq or near the Gulf. Though such reactors could also be a proliferation risk, monetary factors held up the deal. The Chinese, like the Russians, wanted cash on the line. For the moment, though still a high priority, the Iranians didn't have the kind of billion dollar cash required to get the project off the ground.

•   •   •

The Iranians had laid out for themselves a program of acquisition that, if fulfilled, could provide them with the bomb before the end of the decade. The signs on the ground were alarming enough as early as 1989 for Admiral Thomas E. Brooks, the head of U.S. Naval Intelligence, to tell Congress that Iran was "actively pursuing" a nuclear bomb capability. The U.S. Undersecretary of Defense for Policy, Paul Wolfowitz, added in congressional testimony three years later, in January, 1992, that "there are disturbing signs they're pursuing weapons of mass destruction, including possibly nuclear weapons."

Both attempting to ascertain Iranian intentions, and the actual difficulty of establishing facts, made Iran and its atomic bomb a hot issue. "Right now the Iranians are at the stage of laying the foundations for a nuclear program," David Kay, formerly the U.N. inspector in Iraq and later the head of the Uranium Institute in London, told BBC in early 1993.

He drew a parallel: "Iran, in many ways, is like Iraq at the early stage of the Iraqi program. That is, it's a shop until you drop strategy, essentially.... The Iraqis, in the early stage, had a very broad-fronted shopping program—for training skills, for manufacturing capability, for design and technological information. The Iranian program is similar. They're not narrowing their options. They're trying to acquire technical skills, training technology and manufacturing capability on as broad a front as possible."

Kay went on that "there are just too many signs that it [the nuclear program] is moving in a weapons direction." In fact, he added, there are so many signs "that you really don't know what the full scope of that program is."

Iran—well before public attention had focussed on its nuclear program—became the next test case for Western proliferation policy in the Middle East with the future well-being of the region—and perhaps the world—at stake. The Iranian effort focussed attention on the Non-Proliferation Treaty, the role of the U.N.'s International Atomic Energy Agency, and the degree to which states would be able, practically, to exercise an option to gain atomic bomb expertise, technology, and the bomb itself.

CHAPTER TWENTY

Checking Iran

I'm not at all reassured by what the I.A.E.A. found in
Iran and I'm particularly not reassured by their assurance about it."

David Kay, former nuclear inspector, I.A.E.A.

THE INTERNATIONAL ATOMIC ENERGY AGENCY'S BOSS, Hans Blix, is very
much the patrician, though sometimes aggrieved international civil
servant, ready to do his job and eager to create a positive image both for
himself personally and his organization. He has a reputation for bland,
non-descript assessments of potentially alarming situations. While he
has been blamed as the man who over-trusted Iraq and thereby permitted Iraq's violations of the Non-Proliferation Treaty, Blix feels himself
unfairly accused. The I.A.E.A. is not an intelligence organization, he has
pointed out. It is an international body with limited powers, no independent powers of investigation, and is essentially dependent on the
goodwill of its member nations.

One of his agency's jobs is to measure and verify a country's nuclear
fuel balances, to make sure that what is there is what that country says
should be there: that is, to be certain there has been no diversion of fuel
for military uses. That is what "safeguards" are about. It is what the

I.A.E.A. does in Japan, Canada—and also what it is supposed to do in North Korea, Iraq and Iran. Though many proliferation experts, and concerned governments, have pinned responsibility for Iraqi violations on complacent I.A.E.A. procedures, the agency has a good excuse: the I.A.E.A. was left out of the Western intelligence loop, and had no access to spy satellites, export lists, or similar tools of intelligence.

Throughout 1991, the United States and other countries communicated their concerns about Iran to the I.A.E.A. Hans Blix, as outwardly reassuring as he is occasionally arrogant, made his customary defense of a member nation. He emphasized that Iran had signed the N.P.T., agreed to safeguards and inspections, and the agency had no evidence that Iran was anything but a law-abiding member state. Nonetheless, as the stories swirled, the U.N. agency was prodded to take action.[1]

In February, 1992, with the consent of the Iranians, the I.A.E.A. sent a high-level fact-finding mission to Iran. This was not an actual inspection—Iran did not yet have nuclear fuels in bomb quantities, nor reactors churning out radioactive materials. Instead, the U.N. emissaries came as invited guests. The team included Pierre Villaros, special assistant to the director general, who had formerly been with the French firm, Framatone, and had also been a part of the French atomic bomb program; Jon Jennekens, the Canadian who headed up safeguards for the U.N. agency; Mohammed Ridwan of the technical cooperation projects division; and Gustavo Nowotny, who worked under Jennekens in the safeguards unit.

The visit turned into a whirlwind tour of Iran's nuclear facilities. The Iranians wanted to dispel any notion that their nuclear program was a military one. Reza Amrollahi registered a complaint to his guests about Western countries having increasingly closed their doors to Iranian purchasing. The only places the Iranian Atomic Energy Organization could buy nuclear goods, he said, were China, the former Soviet Union, India and Pakistan. Amrollahi stressed that his government intended to resume construction of the Bushehr nuclear power project and pushed the Iranian position: that some 5.7 billion DM, over three billion dollars, had already been spent in the 1970s. A further five billion DM— around three billion dollars—was estimated as what would most likely be needed to get Bushehr operational.

The first afternoon the U.N. group flew down to Bushehr in a chartered twin engine passenger jet. The flight, which took just a bit more than an hour, was followed by a brief tour. The overall initial impression, team members later reported, was "one of a sudden cessation of construction activities with a virtually complete absence of subsequent 'house-keeping' activities to tidy the site." However, once the team had a chance to look around, "it became apparent... that the A.E.O.I. had taken extensive measures to preserve all critical components of the two reactor sites in order to maintain them in a first-class state for eventual installation."

From Bushehr, back to Teheran, and then a quick visit to the province of Yazd in eastern Iran to look at uranium exploration activities. These were at an early stage, the group concluded, with at least two to four years of development necessary just to reach a decision whether to commence full-scale mining work there, since the economic viability was "far from proven."

During a seven hour visit to the Isfahan nuclear center, the team found little physical equipment actually installed, but a lot in common with the center's Western-educated head, Dr. M.K. Rassouly, about 38 years old, a principal architect of the program. He turned out to be a capable spokesman who explained how Iranian plans linked together. Rassouly explored the all-important nuclear fuel question with his U.N. guests. He told them that Iran's ten percent ownership share in Eurodif, and the recently concluded agreement with France, was intended to secure a low enriched uranium supply for fuelling the Bushehr plant. He asserted that there was no intention on the part of Iran to obtain highly enriched uranium, since the Teheran Research Reactor and its Triga reactor would be fuelled with the low enriched uranium assemblies from Argentina. The only exception was the Chinese-supplied Mini Neutron Source Reactor, which took highly enriched uranium. That fuel, Rassouly said, would be purchased directly from China.

After Isfahan came Teheran, headquarters for Iran's nuclear program. The main facility at the Teheran Nuclear Research Center was the five megawatt pool type research reactor supplied by the American Machine and Foundry Co. (later, General Atomics) under a bilateral cooperation agreement between Iran and the United States. The Iranians had been able to run the reactor only intermittently because of the lack of fuel. The low enriched uranium to be supplied by Argentina was due to be available only after the U.N. team had completed its visit.

The team also visited the Karaj Agricultural and Medical Research Center. This is where the Chinese-made electromagnetic separator, or mini-calutron, was to be installed, in a gymnasium-sized building of conventional construction. Building was under way. Since no facilities for handling radioactive materials were to be installed at Karaj, the process of irradiation would be carried out in Teheran.

Finally, the U.N. investigators took an Iranian Air Force helicopter up to a mountain camp to the northwest of Teheran. This site, Moallem Khalliya, was already a subject of controversy, believed by more than one Western intelligence agency to be a suspicious site. Depending on which government you believed, it was either a center for bomb design, or an experimental center for enriching uranium. As the unit left Teheran it was a gray, cold day and by the time the group arrived in the mountains it was snowing and even colder. The helicopter couldn't find the site. After some false starts, the chilly U.N. officials finally did find what the Iranian officials accompanying them said was Moallem Khalliye—in a deserted, mountainous area, far away from civilization, with few signs of human life or activity. The area, noted the later U.N. report, had "two small streams of fresh water from the mountain snow and a nearby spring that will provide sufficient water for up to 400 persons." A number of buildings were under construction but the site seemed anything but nuclear. "The only buildings currently in operation are a small bunk house which was the first building constructed (in 1989) and which houses the maintenance staff, a relatively large kitchen building and a nearly completed dining hall. There are six temporary buildings currently used for storage of construction equipment, tools and vehicles and the first of four dormitory buildings."

•   •   •

Considerable controversy arose over whether the Iranians had taken the U.N. team to the correct site. Had the U.N. been fooled? Jon Jennekens, the Canadian heading up I.A.E.A. safeguards operations, said in Vienna that he didn't think so. But former nuclear inspector

David Kay criticized his ex-colleagues for not taking instrumentation that would enable them to precisely verify their geographic position: "...the I.A.E.A. chose not to take global positioning satellites because it would not indicate trust in the Iranians. I think, in fact, that inspectors have to go with independent means of verification, and certainly knowing where you are is the fundamental basis of any inspection.... It's exactly, in fact, the way you should not conduct a hostile inspection. So right now there is considerable doubt as to where the Iranians took them."[2]

Kay was especially critical of what he termed "the diplomatic dance" of inspections. "The bulk of I.A.E.A. inspections are with friendly states that have no intent—nor ever will have an intent—to acquire an illegal nuclear weapons program.... So when you come up against a tough possible proliferator, a clandestine proliferation program like in Iraq, the rules of the game you normally play be are not applicable. This is really the problem of learning when to be tough and how to be tough in those cases where you have to be.... I'm not at all reassured by what the I.A.E.A. found in Iran and I'm particularly not reassured by their assurance about it."

While the U.N. team was still in Iran, the Iranians offered them a forum to state its conclusions. The U.N. members participated in a press briefing in the capital. The straight-talking Jennekens pronounced his impression that what they had seen of Iran's nuclear program was peaceful, failing to emphasize to the Iranian press the usual qualifier that his comments were restricted to what the I.A.E.A. team had itself visited. Iranian radio and television happily broadcast and re-broadcast the statement. The U.N. visit became a minor propaganda triumph for Iran.

Blix later cautioned Jennekins about speaking too openly and an Agency official told me, "by the way," that his superiors at the Agency thought Jennekens had a case of "foot in the mouth." When I visited Vienna, the officials in charge didn't want me spending too much time with Jennekens lest he put his foot in his mouth again. Jennekens looked to me like a straight type of fellow, honest about what he saw, much more of an engineer and technician than politician.

The more official conclusion of the U.N. team was more cautiously phrased, and stuck rigidly to what had been personally observed by the visitors: namely, all six Iranian nuclear sites which the team visited "were presently used to conduct activities which are consistent with the peaceful use of nuclear energy and ionizing radiation." However, the team was only reporting on what members had personally seen, and "...is therefore not in a position to draw any conclusions regarding any additional facilities of the Atomic Energy Organization of Iran." They affirmed, though, that the Iranians had promised them an open ticket to visit anywhere they wanted to go in Iran.

An official in Washington—the kind that doesn't like his name in books or newspapers—offered me an inside assessment of Blix and the I.A.E.A. "The man's difficult to work with, we don't know what to do with him," the official lamented. "We provide him with information, let's say, about a particular place or activity in Iran. That's a huge country. Instead of going to that place, he'll first turn back to us to ask us, how do we know that?"

The official shrugged. That kind of response was, for him, not only naive but absurd and possibly dangerous. "It's difficult to deal with him," the U.S. official repeated.

When asked by the BBC's Jane Corbin his assessment of Iran and whether it was ultimately trying to get a bomb, Blix answered with typical caution: "You are always in a dilemma that you cannot go to every nook and corner of a huge country—in basements, attics, in factories, what have you.... Therefore, one has to be cautious about giving any general clean bill of health.... It would be wrong for me to pronounce any opinion.... We are reporting on what we are seeing rather than speculating. We are like a radar that scans the horizon...."[3]

Not surprisingly, the international team found no evidence of an Iranian bomb program. Both Villaros and Jennekens—both of whom I met at the U.N. agency in Vienna—struck me as cautiously aware of Iranian ambition, but convinced that the nuclear program, or as much of it as they had seen, had not yet turned the corner.

Behind the scenes, the Iranians were going all-out to gain mastery of the fuel cycle and the ability to manufacture nuclear fuel. With nuclear cooperation coming from South America, North Korea, and China, it became a severe intelligence problem to identify, much less limit, Iran's nuclear advances.

The Iranians actively sought raw materials and equipment from the German chemical industry. They were particularly interested in fluorine gases, which are a part of the process of making uranium hexafluoride and are thus a key indicator of centrifuge production. Fluorine gases have other uses as well. Among the companies contacted in Germany was the Darmstadt-based division of E. Merck and W.E.C.O in Siegburg. Other companies contacted by the Iranians for chemical raw materials were scattered throughout Europe. These included Interchim in Paris; Janssen Chimica in Geel, Belgium; the Fluka Chemie A.G., located in Buchs, Switzerland, and the Medical Export Company, or MEDEX, of Leicester, England.

One stop for the Iranians had been visited by the Iraqis previously. That was Schaublin Industries in Bevilard, Switzerland. Iranian buyers wanted the same kinds of equipment to produce centrifuge technology that the Iraqis had bought. With the government court case against them squashed, Schaublin personnel hosted Iranian buyers, hoping to find a balance between what they had sold Iraq and what others might find to be nuclear centrifuge technology.

I spoke with managing director Ulrich Spiess, who contended the company's Iranian sales were not recent, and they were at a considerably lower level of technology than the orders placed by the Iraqis. "Iran was one of our customers, sure, but not in the last year or two. They're regularly coming back. But they don't have to visit us. Anyway, we've got a representative there," he said.

There had been Swiss government pressure against selling sophisticated materials to Iran. "What we sold Iran are normal machine tools, nothing more, and it's much less than what we sold Iraq," Spiess said. It could not be ascertained through Spiess where the Schaublin machines were to be placed in Iran, though I learned that there was some suspicion they were to be used not in the nuclear program but for missile construction.

An additional Swiss-based company where the Iranians placed orders was Varian, based on the outskirts of Zug, that beautiful lakeside city where the Condor conspiracy had been headquartered. The company was known for its "very good corporate culture," according to a former employee with whom I spoke, and was thought by some insiders to be "thoroughly compliant" in the matter of export regulations. Gary Simpson, the company's spokesman in Palo Alto, recounted that the Iranians required spare parts for its once U.S.-supplied armed forces. Iran, along with some other customers, tried for years to gain possession of a Varian tube used in the Hawk missile system, seeking to make the diversion through third and fourth parties. The company had cooperated with U.S. Customs to head that off. "Our policy is straightforward—we export what the U.S. government allows, and we don't sell what it forbids," Simpson said.

At least until late 1992, Varian selling agents courted the Iranians, hoping that the U.S. government would eventually ease up on specific guidelines on what they could sell and what not. Varian applications to U.S. authorities for sales to Iran mounted to millions of dollars. Varian had sold gas chromometers to the Iranian Atomic Energy Organization, and other Iranian organizations, during the time of the Shah. Simpson said that the company had once had an active Iranian business, but currently "does relatively little business.... Sales to Iran have amounted to one percent or less of total company sales for the past several years." Barring a change in the world situation, Simpson said, "we don't expect that will change much."

In October, 1992, Simpson pointed out, the U.S. government determined that all future applications for shipment of products to Iran that required a license would be denied." In 1993, he said, "the issue of licenses for Iran is now moot.

One Swiss engineer who knew about Varian's European operations, and the practices of the trade, cautioned: "What you have to worry about is packaging. That is, someone will buy a group of items from a number of different places and consolidate them into one shipment. That shipment goes, let's say, to an address in Italy, so all is legal. But in fact there's a trans-shipment that's going to be made in Italy, and the goods will still get to Iran. That's common practice. There's a problem on how to stop it."

High on the Iranian agenda was electrical discharge machinery, or E.D.M., technology to cut heavy metals. Hans Egli, formerly head of sales for A.G.I.E., the industry leader, got involved in a separate new venture based in Germany by 1992. Egli pinpointed Iran as a market worth developing. He was soon invited there for detailed discussions and orders. "These people may be Islamic in name but, I can assure you, they are very shrewd in all business, not just Islamic business," Egli commented about a trip he took to Teheran in early 1992.

The Iranian negotiators were suave, according to Egli, not only polished and cosmopolitan in their manners, but fully in command of business affairs. Egli was not allowed to pick up a check and was the constant guest of his hosts. He lamented the fact that he also could not find an alcoholic drink—even a nice wine—in all of Teheran.

• • •

To look at just how Iran acquired the building blocks of its nuclear program, you have to look at specific sales: in the case of centrifuges, the Shariff University of Technology. Western services began to see evidence in 1991 that identified Shariff as actively engaged in nuclear research, particularly in an experimental centrifuge program.

In spring, 1991, the Iranian institute approached a British subsidiary of the American company, Air Products, which manufactures specialized gases. They requested 45 cylinders of fluorine. Fluorine is a gas with a number of industrial uses, but it is also an ingredient in the process of making uranium hexafluoride, part of the necessary process in the centrifuge process. Air Products, though it was told the gas was to be used "in research laboratories for academic purposes," knew the product was a sensitive one. A small order got shipped. Then the company checked out the larger order with the British Department of Trade and Industry. The D.T.I. told the company not to ship. The company politely declined the order.

Shariff tried to order large computers from the United States: among them, according to the application to U.S. authorities, a system to be installed at the university's computer engineering department for educational and training services for engineering students. The order was worth $1.5 million for the Digital Equipment Corportation. U.S. governmental authorities split on their recommendations. Both Defense and S.N.E.C. recommended rejection, while State and the Department of Energy recommended approval. D.E.C. decided to withdraw the application. A D.E.C. spokesman, Martin Frederickson, said the kind of computer to be sent was totally legal by 1993, much the same as shipping a pencil. He said U.S. refusals to grant licenses simply meant that the Japanese or Europeans would fill the order, and Americans would lose the business.

Most, but not all, of the Iranian university's hardware and technology search concentrated in Germany. Shariff approached a division of Germany's giant Thyssen firm in 1991, Thyssen Edelstadewek, trying to buy ring magnets of the samarian cobalt type, the kind that would be ideal for centrifuge production. Thyssen had fulfilled orders for suspect nuclear buyers previously. Now Thyssen was more careful. Thyssen asked Shariff what the magnets would be used for, a company spokesman said. When the company didn't receive a reply, officials decided not to take the order.

Shariff then approached a firm in Bonn, Magnetfabrik, for another type of industrial magnet. Magnetfabrik specializes in a slightly less sophisticated type, called "alnico" magnets, a combination of aluminum and nickel. Such magnets would also be appropriate for centrifuge production. They are also used in car loudspeakers. Dr. Martin Gronefeld, one of the heads of the company, said that the firm had indeed received a substantive order from Iran, and it was a major one for the company, but he would not go into any details. He said that the order was the business of the firm and its clients, not journalists, and releasing details would only help his competitors.

Over the next months, despite my repeated attempts, Gronefeld refused to supply additional information on his company's trade. In the meantime, I discovered that U.S. officials filed an official demarche to the Germans about the company. The Americans did not receive an answer very quickly. This usually meant, according to one of the officials involved, that German officials were investigating the case in depth. As we have seen in the instance of Karl Kolb/Pilot Plant, investigations in Germany can take a long time.

Another stop on Shariff's shopping expedition was the Carl Schenck company of Darmstadt. The firm specializes in balancing machines, an essential part of a centrifuge process. One or two machines could be applied to an experimental program. Schenck had previously supplied these same kinds of machines to the Iraqis and other nuclear-ambitious nations. A Schenck representative said his company asked Shariff to provide a letter about the uses of the equipment. Shariff did so, assuring the German firm in writing that the equipment "would not be used for military, technical purposes." The company delivered at least one such balancing machine to the university. A Schenck spokesman said that the supply of balancing machines was totally legal at the time it was done. The German licensing bureau at Eshborn confirmed this was so, adding that the policy had since changed, and the supply of balancing machines required actual licenses beginning March 1, 1993.

A university in Teheran bought a vacuum pump from Leybold, one of the German firms that had supplied Iraq, also in the 1990-91 period. Leybold later stopped all similar sales of vacuum pumps to countries like Iraq or Iran. In fact, Leybold instituted an aggressive internal policing policy headed by a former Foreign Office official and newly-appointed company director, Dr. Michael Jansen, to halt sales to sensitive locations. Jansen pointed out to me that his job was more complex than it would initially appear. He said that German law now required a board member to be personally responsible for export sales and violations, and thus subject to prosecution if illegal sales were made, and that the president of the company had chosen himself for this post to serve as an example to others.

The overall pattern of supply fit that of an experimental centrifuge program. As David Kay, the former U.N. inspector, pointed out about such equipment, "In and of themselves, those are certainly the components that one would expect to find around a gas centrifuge program designed to enrich uranium to weapons grade levels. You can't be sure just from the specifications but certainly it's a key list that, if anyone knew about a centrifuge program and was concerned about proliferation, if he heard that someone was getting [these things], their eyes would light up and the hair would literally stand on the back of your neck."

The German licensing authorities at Eschborn said they put Shariff on a list of especially sensitive destinations in the spring of 1992. Iran was itself on the German "H-List," meaning it was a destination to which all nuclear sales were blocked or required special approval. The agency's head, Dr. Wolfgang Danner, told me that any and all nuclear production equipment for Iran was now effectively embargoed, ranging from major items for Bushehr to the smallest vacuum pump. He expressed particular surprise about the Schenck sale to Iran, since that company had never made an export application. On the other hand, he conceded, the company was not obligated to do so at the time of the sale, which was in 1991.

Joachim Jahnke, head of export regulations in Ministry of Economics, said the German government learned numerous lessons from the export scandals that began in 1989, one of them not to trust all German companies. Speaking specifically about Bushehr and Iran, and nuclear supplies to Iran more generally, Janke declared categorically: "The Iranians won't get nuclear goods. Obviously, in the past, the international framework wasn't good enough. We have to recall there's always a risk. It's not only our government that has learned this. Industry also learned it."

•   •   •

Then there was Kazakhstan.

An Iranian opposition group, the People's Mujahadeen, based in Washington, announced in October, 1992, that Kazakhstan, exploiting loose regulations in the former Soviet Union, had sold Iran four nuclear warheads. Though the story was picked up by some newspapers, and pushed by a staff member of a U.S. House of Representatives sub-committee on terrorism, there was no way to verify it, and knowledgable persons in at least four different governments with whom I spoke denounced it as "rubbish."

Yet Kazakhstan was an active player in Iranian purchasing and a natural source for materials. Kazakhstan was one of the principal locations in the U.S.S.R. both for the fabrication of certain types of fuel and the maintenance of their bomb and missile force. Kazakhstan's nuclear assets after the demise of communism included 104 missiles and forty strategic bombers. Factories in Kazakhstan still manufactured nuclear fuel for Russia's reactors. There were fears that, as BBC-TV's Jane Corbin put it, "the new republic must trade its natural resources to survive and that has raised the specter that Kazakhstan is bartering its unique Cold War inheritance."4

The vast majority of Kazakh citizens shared cultural roots with Iran and considered themselves Moslems, though most were secular in their beliefs and remote from fundamentalist orthodoxy. As expressed by Iranian Foreign Minister Velayati, "We have the same religion, the same tradition, the same history, the same culture. That's quite understandable if we have good relations with them. And if they want to have free access to the open sea, Iran is the best way for them [to do it]."

A danger existed that the Kazakhs would provide foreign states, especially those with common cultural roots, with access to their nuclear stocks, an allegation fiercely denounced by the Kazakhs. Intelligence sources monitoring the situation said that the Iranians sought and purchased C.O.C.O.M.-listed equipment, and built trading relationships that could serve their nuclear program. When the Iranians didn't get a uranium oxide plant from the Argentinians, they made inquiries in the deepest reaches of central Asia to try to obtain this facility that would help them to become self-sufficient in the production of enriched uranium.

In the snowy steppes some 700 miles north of Alma Ata lies a massive Kazakh factory for manufacturing nuclear fuels. In particular, the plant produces beryllium, a rare silver-white hard metal inserted at the heart of an atomic weapon, and thus classified as strategic. The factory also manufactures uranium dioxide pellets, enriched to five to seven percent, which is the stage of enrichment that is the most difficult to obtain. From that level it's an easier (though by no means simple) process to attain bomb-grade levels of heavily enriched uranium. The plant has 16,000 workers.

Security loosened both with independence and the uncertain future faced by factory workers. Kazakh military conscripts tried to smuggle nuclear material out of the plant and sell it sometime in early 1992, according to local stories. In August, 1992, an Iranian delegation visited the plant. The question was, did they succeed in buying any of the factory's product? At least one Western intelligence service believed that the Iranians did obtain what they needed. The Iranians, it said, succeeded in obtaining low quantities of beryllium, and one hundred tons of uranium.

The Kazakh Ministry of Foreign Trade had just instituted a sort of export control system a few months before. Adilbeck Aimonov, an official, said that governmental controls were in effect and, henceforth, licenses would be required for export of any nuclear goods, and only the government could provide them. However: "Perhaps some of the old, unofficial channels are still available. But I don't know anything about them."

In fact, BBC "Panorama" colleagues did learn considerably more about "those old unofficial channels," which consisted of a select few trading companies in the Kazakhstan capital, Alma Ata. A meeting with one of these trading firms, though, failed to elicit admissions that it had been involved in sub rosa trade in nuclear materials.

•   •   •

For all their technological innovation and energy in pursuit of equipment, the Iranians' best chance for a bomb lay not in uranium enrichment but plutonium. There were numerous indications that they wanted to thoroughly explore the plutonium route. They searched intensively for a research reactor that could serve both as a research base and as a plutonium producer. They spoke to the Argentinians, Indians, Russians, and finally landed a deal with the Chinese. This was for a reactor in the 25 megawatt range, similar in design to what the Chinese had already supplied Algeria. It could produce plutonium waste in sufficient quantities for over one bomb each year. Furthermore, I learned, the Iranians were seeking not one such research reactor but up to three from the Chinese.

What was disturbing was not only the reactors—whether one or more, and whether they were to be used for research as well as plutonium production—but the entire pattern of Iranian activity. One of the Iranians' most longed-for purchases—though one not known to be consummated—was a fabrication plant for the production of deuterium, or heavy water. The Iranians experienced problems acquiring it from the Argentinians and Indians.

However, even without their own plant, the Iranians did get heavy water elsewhere: namely, from their favored nuclear partner, China. A

U.S. official confirmed a suspicion I had. He said heavy water was originally supplied by China to Iran as part of the contract for the zero power reactor, one of Iran's sub-critical assemblies. This was for several tons of heavy water. Another official added that Iran possessed heavy water "in militarily significant quantities," which he refused to spell out. As I pieced the story together, the Chinese shipped heavy water to Iran, in quantities amounting to as much as twenty tons, by cargo plane from an airfield in a restricted part of China. The I.A.E.A.'s spokesman, David Kyd, told me that Iran had not reported any transaction concerning heavy water and would be obligated to do so only if the amount was 20 tons or more, which is what the agency officially views as a militarily significant quantity.

Do the Iranians have supplies of heavy water in these quantities? Two Western officials in a position to know believe so. This is one of the key indicators that has made them distrust Iran's professions of peaceful intent, as expressed by the Iranian nuclear chief, Reza Amrollahi, or Dr. Mohammad Ayatollahi in Vienna. The bottom line is that if the Iranians can obtain a 25 or 30 megawatt research reactor, they could use natural uranium to power it. Combined with the use of heavy water already in their possession, that would very quickly provide the basis of an Iranian atomic bomb, at the rate of at least a bomb a year. If they could get three reactors they would have enough heavy water for at least three bombs a year. They could also use a 300 megawatt reactor to produce plutonium and find the ways to hide its production.

•   •   •

Iranians felt continually victimized: just as they had suffered from Iraqi poison gas attacks, now they were the victims of an embargo of Western technology. Ayatollahi, Iran's ambassador to the U.N.'s International Atomic Energy Agency in Vienna, is a graduate of the University of California at Berkeley with a Ph.D. in chemical engineering. During a lunch I had with him at I.A.E.A. headquarters in Vienna, Ayatollahi said Iran wanted nuclear technology in order to gain an independent and non-oil base for electrical power. Iran's aim was to get twenty percent of its energy from nuclear power. Told that many in the

West believed that Iran was actively seeking a military nuclear program, he repeatedly said the notion was "absurd."

Later, in an interview with the BBC's Jane Corbin, he contended that the political pressure directed at Iran emanated from "sinister quarters."

"Where in particular?"

"The Western Superpowers," he answered.

"The United States?"

"Yes. Definitely," Ayatollahi answered, arguing rhetorically that the West had been hostile towards Iran's Islamic Republic from its beginning.

He recalled the example of the Shah's atomic program, which he (mistakenly) argued got full cooperation from the West. He accused the West of trying to halt Iranian development in general. He blamed rumors about an Iranian bomb program on political pressures, reminding me that an atomic bomb is only one "non-peaceful corner" in the whole cycle of nuclear fuel. He argued that all Iran's nuclear acquisitions were, and would be, under safeguards, as proscribed by the I.A.E.A. In the filmed interview with BBC, he added: "There's nothing to hide. There's full transparency."

I asked the same questions about Iran's ambitious nuclear plans to other concerned Iranians. One, a senior Iranian engineer, confided, "What the present government is doing is no different from what the Shah did in his program or any Iranian nuclear program would do—that is, to get full capability."

This Iranian didn't agree with the hypothesis that a bomb was the only logical outcome of Iran's nuclear quest. He confided that his compatriots were only going for "mastery of the fuel cycle." The capability to make nuclear fuel was one essential ingredient of nuclear and industrial independence. That was not the same as going for a bomb, he argued. Both Germany and Japan, the two defeated powers of World War II, could independently manufacture nuclear fuels and possessed literally tons of plutonium. Either of these powers could produce an atomic bomb within weeks of deciding to do so. Just as Germany or Japan could make nuclear fuels, but had never made the political decision to go for a bomb—so, too, Iran.

"But why would such a country need this kind of program," I countered, "especially when it has as much oil as it might want—and also natural gas?"

"It's a question of energy independence," he replied, "a matter of what will happen to Iran when the oil runs out."

In 1993, the Iranians were negotiating nuclear deals amounting to over $15 billion, ranging from power plants to come from China and Russia, to research reactors and fuel fabrication facilities. The country was using all its oil reserves, and then some, to finance the effort. Yet, according to the best estimates, based on known reserves and current use rates, Iran had the world's most bountiful gas reserves, enough for decades if not a century. Iran's heavy expenditures during 1992 and '93 brought them significant financial problems, resulting in enormous cutbacks in their administrative and development budgets. To attain nuclear independence and a bomb option, Iran was ready to go into significant debt, at a time when pressing economic problems were causing social unrest at home.

But, as one Iran-watcher commented, "You can bet that the last thing they're going to cut back on is their nuclear, and their other defense and weapons programs."

Chapter Twenty-one

Towards 2001

"It's a painful debate. You can't refuse that kind of
equipment to developing countries. But, on the other
hand, you've got to refuse its delivery to some. But can
you know for sure if it's got a military use? And some
of the goodies today can be baddies tomorrow."

Dr. Joachim Jahnke,
German Economics Ministry official

"The agency (I.A.E.A.) was not designed to police
nuclear weapons research and does not possess the
political or technical capability to do so."

Peter Zimmerman, C.S.I.S., nuclear physics professor

"Look, if you're sitting and looking at a beautiful girl,
and you're beginning to talk to her, do you tell her
right off you're married?"

Hans Egli, Swiss businessman

ONE THEME dominating futuristic disaster movies is that of a madman,
always a demogogue, usually a dictator, lurking with his bombs of mass
destruction, eventually destroying life on earth as we know it. This
specter—that of an unstable personality, with his finger on some
nuclear or biological trigger—haunts the public imagination.

By 2001, some new nations, possibly even a group of them, will have weapons of mass destruction. These countries may not necessarily be more inclined to use their arms of mass destruction than the larger powers that got similar weapons before them. But they may be. They will study what those who have had the arms before them have done. They will examine for themselves the circumstances in which they would consider the uses of new weaponry at their command.

Proliferation has its zones, and its ripple effects. In South America, Argentina plays off against Brazil. Either country getting the bomb would impel the other to get it. North Korea obtaining the atomic bomb would echo into Japan, which would be forced to react, probably bringing ripples throughout Southeast Asia, where other countries would have to examine their options. The Arabs and the Israelis balance each other: the Arabs do not have atomic parity with Israel but, with their vast numbers and wealth dwarfing Israel's, still have essential weapons parity.

Of all the proliferation zones, the most potentially dangerous one for world peace and order is the Persian Gulf. With Saddam Hussein having proven himself a world-class survivor—he is perceived in the Middle East as a victor because he emerged essentially unscathed and still in power after Desert Storm—the occasional presence of U.N. inspectors is still slowing down the prospects of a new and potentially terrifying arms race. Yet Hussein retains a firm technological base. Now, Iran is moving ahead with intelligence, care and caution in its drive to reach superpower status. The effects of either Iran or Iraq getting even greater weapons of mass destruction than they now have, and especially the atomic bomb, would rebound not only on each other, but through a wide arc of countries. Among those most directly affected: Kuwait, Saudi Arabia and the other Gulf states, all of which are opposed to Iran's fundamentalists and Iraq's hegemonistic ambitions. To the North, the situation is no less ominous: Turkey and the southern ex-Soviet republics, all with advanced technological infrastructures, could not allow either state to become a nuclear power, or a major military power, without becoming one themselves. Turkey has NATO's largest standing army in Europe and a proud military tradition, while the southern republics are among the direct inheritors of the Soviets' nuclear legacy.

To the East, Iranian weapon advances would impact on Pakistan, which would suddenly find itself hedged in by both nuclear-capable India and nuclear Iran. Though Iran and Pakistan are Moslem countries, Pakistan's capable generals would be induced to further their own already-advanced bomb program, possibly stirring an Indian response. To the South, a new strategic situation would impact on countries like Ethiopia, the Sudan, Tanzania, Chad, and Mauritania, which would have to assess which side would be the winning one, look at their own weapons program, and decide how much aid to request, and from whom, to improve their own position. The ripple might even be felt in the Western part of Africa, in an oil-rich country like Nigeria.

Lastly, there is the Arab-Israeli conflict, now at a turning point for peace. Either Iran or Iraq getting and deploying weapons of mass destruction like an atomic bomb would turn the strategic cards in the Middle East upside down, and cause the always-aware and nervous Israeli's to reassess their own strategic needs and concerns. Both Iran and Iraq are among the region's most radical and both are still ideologically, if not practically, committed to Israel's destruction.

•   •   •

The world is now at the watershed. A few more steps and there will be no turning back on massive proliferation of weapons of mass destruction. Looking back some decades, the politics of deterrence—as opposed to export regulation—dominated the politics of nuclear controls. It led to a massive race to build and perfect nuclear bombs and the refinement of strategies, finally ending in the demise of one of the two Superpowers that couldn't keep up economically. The decade offered hope and opportunity as much as it did despair and ill fortune. The politics of deterrence between East and West worked, in that the two Superpowers did not engage in combat between themselves directly, did not idly threaten each other with atomic bombs, and even at times of crisis worked mainly through surrogates in places like Vietnam, Afghanistan, Cuba or Pakistan.

When it came to proliferation, the 1980s showed that danger points loomed ahead. Though the most powerful weapons—those in the nuclear family, such as atomic, hydrogen and neutron bombs—never got used, and their spread was restricted to a few nations, access to the underlying technologies became easier. The lesser tools of non-conventional warfare, such as poison gas, nerve agent, biological weapons, and missiles, mercilessly proliferated.

The information explosion threatened to lead to other, lethal explosions. Although the finished form of technologies—that is, weapons and their immediate sub-systems—could be regulated and banned, it would be far more difficult to control and regulate knowledge. More and more Ph.D.s came from disparate parts of the world, could use computers, and could gain access to the component technologies of weapons of mass destruction—whether these weapons were nuclear, missiles, chemical or biological. The same technologies could be used for microwave ovens, radar and Calutrons. The cobalt samarian, or aluminium nickel alloys in modern industrial magnets can be obtained in their raw forms, and then used in either car radio speakers or centrifuge programs.

Although it is impossible to outlaw knowledge, it is still possible to severely restrict access to it. Iraq and Iran both needed foreign experts in chosen specialties to help them get a military program going. And though the two countries could succeed in one or two areas, they could not succeed in all—not without significant foreign help.

The decade demonstrated that more widespread ownership of the tools of mass murder, while not totally controllable, may not be as swift as feared. Political pressure could be mounted on a proliferator to desist. But, in an era when dual-use technologies often held many of the keys to mass destruction weapons, it would be harder, not easier, for the international community to create choke points that could block technological progress.

·   ·   ·

I sat with Hans Egli in the small but elegant dining room of the Schwyzerhof Hotel across from the main station in Zürich. He ate a salad and steak tartare, ordered a glass of white wine, and encouraged me to order the specialty of the house, a particularly delicate fish tartare. Suave, middle-aged and rich, Hans Egli is a successful businessman. With his white-flecked hair and receding hairline, he looked older than his 46 years. He relishes not only what money can bring but the game of making it. "What's surprised me most is the power of money. It shouldn't be as powerful as it is. It is a drug, a disease, and its attraction cannot be underestimated," he said.

He sipped his wine before continuing. "I pursue it like anybody else, of course," he added.

Egli made a small fortune as chief salesman for the Swiss firm A.G.I.E. selling electrical discharge machines, or "E.D.M." units, mainly to the Soviet Union. E.D.M. machines are the kind of technology and equipment that is essential to an understanding of future issues of export control. The technology was originally a spin-off from America's N.A.S.A. Swiss manufacturers learned to master E.D.M. technology and apply it to industrial use more easily than did American industry. A.G.I.E., Switzerland's industry leader, was able to patent key processes. Guided by numerically controlled computers, E.D.M. machines cut heavy metals with the kind of micron accuracy that can be used for jet airplane production, missile manufacture, or nuclear tooling. As Third World countries seek to establish sophisticated military industries as well as domestic manufacturing, sales of E.D.M. machines and other equipment incorporating advanced computer technologies will become increasingly controversial.

Among A.G.I.E.'s clients was Iraq. Engineers from Baghdad trained in company headquarters in Losone. A Pentagon official responsible for export supervision told me that Iraq ordered the A.G.I.E. E.D.M.s for the all-important nozzle work on Iraq's Project 1728 SCUD-B modification program. Some 21 machines were purchased in 1989 by Iraq, though by 1990 sales dropped to zero. Today, Iran continues as a prominent E.D.M. customer both for A.G.I.E. and its Swiss rival, Charmilles Technologies, part of the giant George Fischer Company. "The Iranians are big in the market," Egli told me. "They're the ones with money to spend and ready to build up their industries. The end use is their business, not mine."

The Swiss originally applied export controls in vintage manner—one that affirmed the traditional Swiss view of the proper relationship between corporation and government. The Swiss machine tool industry association, known as V.S.M., oversaw license applications for machine tools on behalf of the government. V.S.M. acted like a semi-governmental body because, supposedly, the government didn't have the expertise to do it. Making the Swiss machine tool industry the guardian of its own exports is much like making a thirsty cat the guardian of the milk. In the mid-1980s, U.S. pressure forced a tightening of controls and the way they were applied. Until then, according to Bryen, "there wasn't a whole lot for Swiss officials to do."

Right at the beginning of its sensitive sales to the Soviets and other clients, Egli remembers, his firm offered the machine tool association its design plans for approval. How precise were A.G.I.E.'s plans as submitted, and did the company point out the danger spots to V.S.M.?

Egli's rhetorical but honest answer: "Look, if you're sitting and looking at a beautiful girl, and you're beginning to talk to her, do you tell her right off you're married?"

E.D.M. machines typify the problems of regulating high-technology in the future. From a strictly legal viewpoint, strategic sales to Iran and Iraq were totally legal while those to the Soviets were restricted. Unless there is a climate of moral exactitude, regulating trade is complex and harrowing. Should sales of machines like E.D.M.s be stopped? Also to the point, can they be stopped? The only step that can ultimately stop questionable export is the threat of an embargo against those countries which might make such sales or purchases. And, regretfully, the only country today that can make such a threat and make it stick is the United States of America.

Egli's argument is that goods will somehow find their way to clients. Big European companies are served by "packagers" who buy machines and ship them. In order to avoid cumbersome regulations meant to control movements of sensitive technologies these packagers often divert shipments through one or two additional countries before delivering them to their final destinations. "Your offer is going to Italy—or France or even Brazil. That's where you make your applications. But you have to be packed for sea freight. You can ask about this or not ask.

You can see by both the packing and the spare parts specs that it's going to go somewhere else.

"Who's doing this? Let me throw you back a better question: who's not doing this? We were shipping 1,000 machines a year. How can anyone control this? Or want to...."

Then he adds an old saw: "You know, if we don't deliver, it will be delivered from somewhere else. If technology is asked...and is ready to be sold...technology will be delivered."

Put another way, what was once thought will not be unthought.

•   •   •

Some of the main leakage of Western technology and components to Third World countries had come from Germany. During the late 1980s, Germany's leadership went a long way to cleaning up its act. A modest amount of soul-searching in the Federal Republic produced new legislation. The Bundestag, the German Parliament, authorized extra budget for the governmental licensing organizations that enabled them to buy Nixdorf computers for the first time and hire additional staff. From only 80 responsible officers working at the licensing agency in Eschborn in 1989, by 1990 there were 100, by 1992 in excess of 250, and the Bundestag provided authorization and funds to build towards a staff of 400 people.

Theoretically, each of the 250 supervisory clerks at the licensing bureau in Eschborn, a suburb of Frankfurt, had responsibility for 72,000 approvals every year (or nearly 300 approvals for every clerk each working day)—a tall order. To narrow the job, Germany additionally tried to focus its regulatory resources on countries of danger. The government published a warning list of 53 countries that were "countries of concern." Officials later cut this list to 35. Still, it was painful for Germany's diplomatic relations.

The Germans reduced their dependence on foreign intelligence services by augmenting the government's right to check into the activities of domestic firms. As part of the reforms, the Germans gave the Customs Authority and its investigative unit extraordinary powers to investigate illegal export, including wiretapping telephone calls, so long as a judge approved the interception on a case-by-case basis. These were the kinds of draconian measures, enabling governmental intrusions into a person's private life, that hadn't been seen in Germany, except in national security cases, since Hitler's time.

One innovation in the German legislative package had a particularly strong potential to curb illegal or questionable sales. This measure compelled companies to designate a board member to be personally in charge of the company's exports and make sure that the company acted in conformity with the law. Otherwise the company risked not only paying a fine: the director bore a degree of personal liability for the company's transgressions of the law. Germany even introduced tight supervision on the sales of machine tools. "Now all machine tools are fully controlled—that is, on all digitally controlled machines," Joachim Jahnke of the Economics Ministry explained.

Still, with Germany at the cutting edge of technology and with Third World countries keen to buy German goods, the proliferation battle continues to focus on Germany. "It's a painful debate," Jahnke elaborated. "You can't refuse that kind of equipment to developing countries...but on the other hand, you've got to refuse its delivery to some. But can you know for sure if it's got a military use? And some of the goodies today can be baddies tomorrow."

With the rising costs of the country's unification, there remain serious questions on how effectively the government will apply the law and the extent to which industrialists will comply. German officials fear that they are so far in front of their European colleagues in their legislation and export controls that their industrialists could be put at a commercial disadvantage. In view of the Germans' sorry record of the past, many experts have raised considerable doubts on the extent to which German firms would comply with regulations.

At best, restrictions on exports could significantly slow down the process of proliferation. It can not stop it altogether.

•   •   •

Back in 1981, the spokesman for the C.E.A., the French Atomic Energy Commission, told me that commercial nuclear contracts—such as Osirak—henceforth "would no longer be kept secret. This is the big lesson after the bombing of Osirak."

Nuclear contracts would and should be published, he said. Then the public could see there was nothing to fear. But honesty in relationships between governments, just like between lovers, is considered a positive virtue only up to a point. Some things don't change in the nuclear field. After the Ayatollah Khomeini and his Islamic revolutionaries seized power in 1979, the Iranians cancelled a multi-billion deal they had entered into with the French for the development of a gas centrifuge uranium enrichment project. It took years and new governments in both Paris and Teheran to unravel the strings. At the end of the discreet negotiations, which were finally concluded successfully in late 1991, the French reverted to old tricks. They put a "secrecy" stamp on parts of the agreement—meaning that anyone who would release it would bear liability for breaking France's espionage laws and and was subject to arrest and trial.

The French couldn't help themselves. The desire for confidentiality was not only "business as usual" but life as usual in the nuclear business. In one sense it is unfair to single out France. An old friend of mine who had become one of the top French officials in the field assured me about the French-Iranian agreement: "You have nothing to worry about."

Regretfully, I have heard that line before. That is the one phrase that invariably causes me to start worrying.

•   •   •

The U.S. position is itself occasionally contradictory and self-serving—and often hypocritical. On the one hand, the United States is the leading proponent of a slowdown in dangerous high-tech and weapons sales to developing nations. On the other, the Americans are themselves the chief purveyors of all kinds of military weaponry and the leaders in worldwide sales. Though they do not sell missiles outside the North Atlantic alliance, the United States has sold F-15 and F-16 warplanes and other advanced weapons to such countries as Saudi Arabia and Taiwan. The U.S. tried to cut back Chinese sales of M-9 missiles to Saudi Arabia and other Middle Eastern countries, using the threat and promise of "favored nations status" to extract concessions. The Chinese said they would halt their missile sales—that is, until the United States authorized sales of advanced American jets to Taiwan, which was in itself prompted by French and even Israeli competition.

The Americans had the effrontery to insist that these sales were both "moral" and right—when what was usually at stake was American jobs and profits. These often took precedence over stability and the reduction of the military threat between one nation and another.

Some thought the Americans should either soften their objections or at least play them down out of consideration for the feelings and perceptions of others when confronted with obvious hypocrisy. At the very least, the Americans should stop lecturing others and start examining themselves.

•   •   •

So long as the main industrial countries, especially the U.S., Britain, and France, backed by the two defeated powers of WWII, Japan and Germany, unite in a policy of denial, it will be a difficult job for a lone country to develop a full nuclear program. An isolated bomb or two remains a possibility—the breach that can create a precedent whereby proliferation becomes irresistable. The Western powers seek to increase coordination with the ex-Soviet Union, with its traditionally strict proliferation policies, to enforce a policy of denial. The cumulative effect could make it even more difficult for the potential warrior nation to emerge with weaponry.

The first key to stopping proliferation is to continue to discourage either Germany or Japan—and other nuclear-capable countries—from engaging in military nuclear programs that would result in atomic bombs. Paradoxically, the United States is encouraging the consideration of both these countries as permanent Security Council members. This membership would encourage recognition of Japan and Germany's de facto status as economic powers. But Security Council membership, up to now, has been reserved, whether coincidentally or not, only for nuclear weapons states. Their admission to membership could create countervailing pressures that would legitimize any latent weapons tendancies they might have.

The next step is to create political and legal structures to inhibit Third World countries from going after their own bomb. The 1980s saw great advances in this. It is up to the 1990s to close the loopholes.

The third step is to freeze any existing programs and to begin to apply arms control concepts in bilateral and multilateral negotiations to reduce the flood of arms into areas such as the Middle East. This would be done best by having the states in potential conflict negotiate their differences directly. In the case of Israel, a small country facing five or six key Arab confrontation states and a potential of 22 states with a total population 25 times its own, it would mean balancing reductions in advanced conventional arms against those in non-conventional arms.

The fourth step is to clamp even more rigid controls on technology transfers and sensitive dual use items than before—and to use agreements framed by the East-West conflict and apply them to the North-South split, to potential bomb-makers in the Third World. Sellers could take part of the responsibility as to where dual use technology gets sold and would not sell weapons of death and mass murder to areas of conflict and third world tyrants.

A fifth step is to provide the I.A.E.A. with what is required to do its job. As spokesman David Kyd laments, "our budget is on zero growth and has been for eight years. The powers that be"—meaning the states that provide the agency's funds, particularly the United States—"ask us to take on Iran, Iraq, North Korea, South Africa, Argentina, Brazil, the former republics of the Soviet Union, with inspections and familiarization visits, but those august bodies supporting us make no sign they want to support us with extra budget."

•   •   •

The Non-Proliferation Treaty has a 25 year term and is to come up for review in 1995. "For nearly 25 years, the world has depended on the Nuclear Non-Proliferation Treaty to stop the spread of weapons. But Iraq and North Korea have exposed its dirty secret: It legitimates, even facilitates, production of weapons materials—plutonium and bomb-grade uranium," Paul Leventhal of the Nuclear Control Institute in Washington wrote in *The New York Times*.

This is the main paradox of the treaty. Designed to prevent the spread of the bomb, its less-discussed aim is to provide a legitimate framework for the spread of what industry officials call "peaceful" nuclear technology. Major countries such as Japan or Germany, with advanced nuclear industries, spew off hundreds of kilograms of plutonium that can be diverted for military use if the leaders of those countries made the decision. Possibly, as I.A.E.A. officials have confidentially admitted, diversions of plutonium could go unnoticed in massive amounts: as many as 600 pounds a year, or enough for 40 nuclear weapons (if not more). The world-wide trade in plutonium could exceed 300 tons a year by 2000 and more by 2001, and Paul Leventhal calls for strong measures to toughen up the N.P.T. treaty when extending it, "conditioned on a ban on production of bomb-grade nuclear materials." This is the position adopted by President Bill Clinton.

Peter Zimmerman, a nuclear engineer pursuing an arms control and verification study at the Center for Strategic and International Studies in Washington, points out that many I.A.E.A. inspectors sent to Iraq hailed from non-weapons states. The agency has a commendable policy that "any international civil servant detailed to the Vienna-based agency is trustworthy." Still, argues Zimmerman, "the agency was not designed to police nuclear weapons research and does not possess the political or technical capability to do so." The inspectors had the opportunity to gain bomb-making knowledge because of their inspections. So did the Iraqis.

•   •   •

The lessons of the Iran-Iraq war and then Desert Storm provide powerful arguments for Third World generals to develop their own non-conventional forces. They can get a bigger bang with comparatively less buck. The missiles used in the Iran-Iraq war and by the Iraqis in Desert Storm had conventional high-explosives. But missiles, properly fitted, can carry different types of warheads: chemical, biological, even nuclear. The more murderous the warhead, the greater the threat to world peace and world order.

Condor was slowed and possibly stopped, but advances in SCUD technology developed in North Korea, designed to be shared with Iran, could revolutionize the battlefield both in the Far East and the Middle

East. Still, an Israeli military expert I interviewed after Desert Storm who had access to his country's analyses of Iraqi missile expertise and the SCUD-B was less than awed. "The SCUD-B may be an adequate rocket for Iraq, but it's still a case of Russian design, German improvements, and Arab plumbing," he said dismissively.

Like chemical weaponry, the spread of the science and art of missilery is, in varying aspects and degrees, judged illegal by leading powers in the world. But during the earlier Gulf war between Iran and Iraq only Iranians and Arabs got killed—so, at least for the world's press if not for Western officials responsible for policy, it didn't really matter.

Two and a half years later, Desert Storm showed that even a minor power could create havoc if it had effective missile forces. The use of SCUDs against Israel and against American forces in Saudi Arabia provided invaluable lessons for the would-be missile owner. It sent a signal to other nations acquiring a missile force. Missiles could work: if not militarily, then politically.

The Missile Technology Control Regime came into force in 1987. M.T.C.R. had little direct effect on the nations of the world that sought and got missile capability (or a fair percentage of that capability) during the 1980s: countries such as India, Pakistan, Iran, Israel, Saudi Arabia, Syria, or Brazil. M.T.C.R. showed why international agreements don't always work. Enforcement of the agreement was problematic. As Dr. Stephen Bryen remarked, "They never ran the M.T.C.R. provisions through C.O.C.O.M. because there was no way for C.O.C.O.M. to control licenses on it. The Europeans drove a truck through the agreement. Iraq, Brazil, Argentina, China... everything was being sold and being bought."

The treaty was effective only when backed by strong diplomacy. That pressure was invariably American. The threats of reward or punishment invoked by the Americans worked more readily with U.S. allies or those who shared Western values than against enemies. Argentina, for example—counted among the countries that shared Western values—disengaged from the Condor missile project only after the Americans engaged in some old-fashioned gunboat tactics. Potential enemies were more problematic.

The tensions between Iran and Iraq are rooted in the rivalries and history of the Persian Gulf. After Desert Storm, Iran, sustained by its fierce and spreading Islamic fundamentalism, had a rare opportunity. With much of Iraq's infrastructure destroyed, the Iranians could gain a strategic grip on the Persian Gulf, and establish a kind of hegemony in the area.

Though it has severe financial problems, there is no sign that Iran is letting up in its push for weaponry, including both conventional arms and weapons of mass destruction. At least five intelligence services—the U.S., Britain, Russia, Germany and Israel—have estimated that Iran's nuclear goals could be achieved around the turn of the century. (A sixth service, Iraq's, is suspected of issuing specific leaks concerning Iran's program.) Iran's buildup is financed in large part by foreign borrowing. In early 1993, Iran owed foreign creditors more than $30 billion and was about $5 billion in arrears in repaying outstanding loans. Michael Eisenstadt of the Washington Institute for Near East Policy, has predicted that as Iran's economic problems mount in coming years, "Iran will find it increasingly difficult to fund its conventional buildup. It is therefore likely to devote available resources to developing unconventional weapons and sponsoring subversion and terror as a means of deterring its enemies and achieving specific foreign policy objectives." He urges the U.S. to make a concerted effort to deny Iran foreign loans and credits.

Iran's push puts a spotlight on a related strategic situation: that of Israel and the Arabs. It is more than three decades too late to prevent Israel from having an atomic bomb. Contrary to the fears of some observers, the specter of an Israeli bomb has not been especially provocative to the Arabs, but has unofficially provided a measure of deterrence that convinced many of Israel's enemies in the region that it was better to deal with Israel rather than to try to destroy it. A few, like Iraq, sought parity. Still, Israel's bomb program will come under increasing scrutiny as peace talks progress. Egypt in particular has pursued a policy aimed at getting the Israelis to put their still-unadmitted bomb program on the negotiating table. The Israelis have called for a "nuclear-free zone" in the Middle East, and their underlying thrust is to play off reductions in, or the eventual abandonment of, their own nuclear arsenal against sharp reductions in the region's conventional forces, where the Arabs hold a vast quantitative edge.

•   •   •

A great challenge of the 1990s will be the creation of the economic and political conditions to inhibit the spread of weapons of mass destruction and put a stop to their sale. New and old nationalisms, ancient rivalries between ethnic groups, the forces of economics and the drive to sell dangerous, but profitable, dual-use technologies could all unite to force a fission-based explosion, with disastrous consequences for mankind.

World tranquillity in an interdependent age requires imposing real penalties on potential transgressors—both sellers and buyers. It means reinforcing the existing conventions and regimes against the spread of weaponry.

A window of opportunity exists, though it may already be closing: to soften old hatreds, to halt the spread of arms of mass destruction, to restrict new technologies, to deny technology to potentially dangerous countries, and where necessary to channel these dual-use technologies for the betterment of mankind. The fragmented forces seeking to sell or to buy weaponries of mass destruction must be brought under tighter control. Those engaged in the deadly business of selling technologies of mass murder must be more precisely identified, so their unconscionable activities can be controlled and then halted.

The planet has not become smaller but, rather, more vulnerable—and will become more so.

CHAPTER NOTES

Chapter One. A Nest of Vipers.

1. Early French and Monaco suspicion concerning the car bombing focussed, curiously, on Consen relationships with Iran, which so far as I could determine never existed in fact.

2. Research for this chapter is based on my own visits to the French Riviera and Monaco, extensive Monaco police records and French intelligence notes on the incident, and interviews with selected though anonymous officials.

Chapter Two. Nuclear Dawn.

1. The conversation with Yves Girard was first reported in my earlier co-written book, *The Islamic Bomb, The Nuclear Threat to Israel and the Middle East* (Times Books, 1982).

2. I initially interviewed Dr. Akbar Etamad in 1981.

3. Germany was extraordinarily successful during this mid-1970s period in procuring nuclear contracts. Along with Bushehr, Kraftwerk Union concluded a major deal with Brazil, potentially worth up to $14 billion. K.W.U.'s Brazilian contract included up to eight major power reactors in the first stage and a package that included enrichment, fuel fabrication and plutonium separation facilities. All facilities would be safeguarded by the I.A.E.A. The uranium enrichment plant was based on the jet nozzle system designed by a German engineer, Professor Erwin Willi Becker.

4. The groundbreaking Robert Gillette article on Jeff Eerkens was published in *The Los Angeles Times*, Aug. 22, 1979. I met and interviewed Jeff Eerkens in Pacific Palisades, California, office during the fall of 1992.

5. A strategic relationship between Iran and Israel existed during the Shah's regime. This relationship developed in 1976 and '77, culminating in a visit by an Iranian general to Israeli missile installations.

Although, following the Khomeini-led revolution, Israel became "the little Satan," (as opposed to the U.S. being the Great Satan) in official Iranian eyes, Iran still sought spare parts and other supplies from Israel for its U.S.-supplied equipment. Israel apparently coordinated most of its actions with figures in the U.S. administration. This led to the Iran-Contra scandals of 1985 and thereafter.

Chapter Three. Crisis!

1. Though the French are remarkably secretive about their own governmental affairs, this re-construction of French policy derives from French sources, including officials in the C.E.A. and other departments of government, scientists, and others working in the French nuclear establishment.

Chapter Four. Perfume: Samarra's Secrets.

1. Initial Iraqi experimentation in manufacturing mustard gas took place at the "Al Hazzan" institute located in the Baghdad suburb of Salman Pak. Other scientific experiments in the areas of biology and nuclear matters also took place at Salman Pak.

2. Selling empty shells is an unusual, but not unheard of, industrial/military practice. The only other likely explanation, besides poison gas, was that such weaponry would be used for smoke ammunition. Neither artillery shells nor bombs are themselves subject to international export regulations.

3. The "Spot Image" resolution was extraordinarily precise. The image was used time and again by various media as the 1990 Gulf crisis grew.

4. In addition to the interview I conducted, Bernd Meyer provided a signed statement to German customs police concerning his period in Iraq.

5. Much of the technical data for this chapter comes from material submitted into German court records by the public prosecutor in Darmstadt, Germany, U.N. reports and records, and talks with various governmental officials.

6. Schott is a world leader among optical firms and producer of Karl Zeiss lenses. Glass-based facilities are anti-corrosive and often used in sen-

sitive chemical production. Schott itself provided sensitive production lines to a second country, Syria, which officials in several Western governments believe were incorporated into Syria's own nerve gas facility.

Chapter Five. Saddam's Hunt Begins.

1. Sa'ad's undersecretary was Adnan Abdul Majid Al-A'ani Jassim, believed to be the same Dr. Al-Ani who oversaw the Iraqis' raw materials purchases in Europe. Attar, possibly also known as Raouf, was project organizer in charge of raw materials and equipment acquisitions.

2. Technical data on the nature of the orders placed in Holland derive not only from Bravenboer, but from the Dutch economics investigations unit and, in the Melchemie case, from the prosecutor's office in Arnhem.

3. Bernd Meyer, though he says he actually saw many of the chemical raw materials from Holland stored in Samarra and clearly labelled, told me that couldn't recall if POCL3 was specifically included.

Chapter Six. 1984.

1. The number of countries having chemical weapons programs rose dramatically during the 1980s. Thomas Welch of the Pentagon testified before Congress in 1988 that those states with chemical weaponry had swelled from seven to twenty in a single decade. Welch, who I interviewed in 1989, was far more concerned at the time with the potential Soviet threat to build up poison gas manufacture than with Third World use.

2. The director of the State Department's Arms Control and Disarmament Agency, General Eugene Thomas Burns, testified before the Senate Foreign Relations Committee on 24 January, 1989. He spoke about twenty nations other than the U.S.A. and the U.S.S.R. having "offensive CW capability." But of these, he said, "no more than a handful, five or six, actually possess a stockpile." He was not explicit about which countries had such stockpiles.

Chapter Seven. Men of the Pentagon.

1. The chapter is based on interviews with the principals and with other figures within the Washington diplomatic and proliferation community.

Chapter Eight. The Saga of Sa'ad-16.

1. Crucial help in researching this chapter came from I.G. Metall, the German trade union; official sources in Germany; and sources within MBB. Much of the historical material on MBB comes from the company's own published records.

2. Bowas InduPlan is a Salzberg-based concern owned by Bohlen Industries.

3. Among other elements in what MBB would later claim was a "peaceful" research center at Mosul were a testing station quoted at 1,204,880 DM; a pilot lab for caps and detonators at 1,280,902; an explosion bomb lab for 328,690 DM; a Crawford bomb lab at 265,495 DM; a pilot plant for homogeneous powders and propellants at 3,759,100 DM; a second pilot plant, this one for heterogeneous propellants, for 2,974,800 DM; a pyrotechnics pilot plant for 813,000 DM.

4. Training for Lab 0614, to be provided at MBB centers in Germany, in Iraq, and at the headquarters of some of the equipment sub-suppliers, involved twelve Iraqi technicians and engineers. According to the contract, MBB provided the training in explosives use for four of the labs, 0401, 0402 , 0514, and 0515, at the company's Schrobenhausen headquarters. This included instruction for a physics engineer, four chemical engineers, and six chemical technicians. The contract also called for MBB to train five Iraqis to work in seven propellant labs, those called 0501, 0502, 0503, 0504, 0510, 0511, and 0516 in the contract. The training was designated to take place in two venues: one, at MBB's daughter company, Bayern Chemie, based in Aschau about fifty kilometers from Munich, and a second at the R & D Center in Mossul, Iraq.

5. The equipment ordered from the United States included 37 linear microcircuits, a modulation analyzer, a system voltmeter, a 1250 MHz microwave section and 40GHz wave guide mixer, a 10MGz-40GHz scalar network analyzer, a 100 MHz universal counter and numerous microwave frequency counters, linear microcircuits, a 19.9 Mbit computer system, and various other instruments and computer-related control items.

Chapter Nine. The German Question.

1. In the first appeal, decided in 1986, the Kolb/Pilot Plant case got dismissed in what the Germans call "a financial court," with the court declaring itself the wrong address for the case. The government lost another time in a court in Darmstadt in 1988, the court supporting the lower court's 1984 decision that the government had acted illegally in promulgating regulations without a physical quorum among governmental ministers. Another governmental appeal resulted in a similar ruling in favor of Pilot Plant in 1990.

2. One of these plants was Neuberger Wood and Plastics Industry, a manufacturer of laboratory equipment. The second was Lenhardt Metal Construction and Roofing. Prosecutors got evidence that Klaus Franzel, Karl Kolb's man in Baghdad, was a 13 percent owner of Neuberger.

Chapter 10. Halabja.

1. The Halabja tragedy compares in every way to the Guernica incident during the Spanish Civil War. So far, there has been little interest among independent Western military historians in documenting the actual battles that took place in the Iran-Iraq war or in the Kurdish rebellions against various Middle East state authorities. Therefore, the reporting here is based largely on Kurdish sources and, though I have no reason to doubt the accuracy of the lists of villages attacked by chemical weaponry, the information has not been independently verified by independent witnesses.

2. One lesser known aspect of the Iran-Iraq war is the extent to which the Iranians relied on video cameramen to document it. In fact, many of these cameramen and still photographers risked their lives. Iranian military personnel told French journalist Gilles du Jonchay that over 250 Iranian cameramen were killed in action. TV producer Robert Ross independently received the same information.

3. The color of dead persons' lips is a key factor in determining what kind of poison gas or nerve agent was used. Some experts thought that cyanide had been used. Others analyzed the lip colors as indicting nerve agent.

4. Many Kurds fled to Turkey for refuge where they were grudgingly received. Ancient enmities between Turks and Kurds ran deep and the Kurds found they were unwelcome guests. Within a year, the running Turkish battle with Kurdish separatists would flare up again. No country neighboring Iraq wanted more Kurds in their country than they already had. The Turkish government did not want to offend their powerful Arab neighbors. They feared a revolt from Turkish-born Kurds in their own eastern provinces.

5. Even France, homeland of political refugees and depositary power of the Geneva Protocol of 1925 concerning chemical weaponry, published only a brief statement about Halabja. This statement was deferential to the Iraqis. It condemned "... the use of chemical arms wherever it occurs"—without bothering to specifically castigate Saddam Hussein, his regime and its continuing use of chemical warfare.

Chapter 11. The Flight of the Condor.

1. Zug is a story in itself. It is a sedate, lovely Swiss town on a lake with Switzerland's highest per capita income rate, well over $20,000 per person. Its private homes are both large and well-protected, and many have their own electronic alarm systems or privately installed video surveillance cameras to inspect visitors or deter thefts or peeping toms.

2. Otto Boese, G.P.A.'s managing partner, was also a financial adviser for the second Consen-linked company—Project Betreungs Gesellschaft, or P.B.G., situated a few miles to the north of Munich. P.B.G. officially served as a sub-contractor to I.F.A.T. in Switzerland but shipped many of its Condor products directly to the Egyptian Ministry of Defense in Cairo from Frankfurt Airport. Among key Consen personnel or contractors originally associated with Bowas Induplan was P.B.G.'s managing director, Werner Schoffel. Company papers listed him as a "prokuristen," or buyer, for Bowas.

3. Bowas AG Fuer Industrieplanung of Zug changed its name to Condor Projekt AG on January 7, 1986 and transferred its office address from Im Rotel 7 to a local accountant's office, Planzer and Lenzinger. Iso Lenzlinger, an accountant, was a Swiss national who served as a board member of six Consen-related companies, part of a lucrative sideline as a professional director of over 30 companies.

4. According to testimony presented in 1988 in a U.S. court, ten missiles were to be produced in Argentina and sent to Egypt and Iraq.

Chapter 12. Stopping Condor.

1. The chapter is based on my meetings with many of the principals, including German Economic and Foreign Ministry officials, MBB personnel, Dr. Brunner, a number of U.S. officials. U.S. court documents submitted by federal prosecutors in the Helmy case, tried in Sacramento, were particularly useful.

2. MBB personnel adamantly denied the suggestion that the firm had betrayed some of the West's most sensitive missile secrets. Though these accusations became the impetus of later semi-official American inquiries, there was never to my knowledge an official accusation. U.S. investigators, so far as I know, never obtained hard evidence that MBB betrayed the West and provided Condor's clients with the West's most advanced missile technology. Henry Sokolski, the deputy for proliferation at the Pentagon during the Bush years, told me his own investigations of MBB had not turned up damning evidence

3. A recent book by two Argentinian journalists on Condor includes an extraordinary perspective of the affair from the Argentinian point of view. Called *Carnal Relations: The True Story of the Construction and Destruction ofthe Condor-II Missile*, by Eduardo Barcelona and Julio Villalonga, published by Ediciones Planeta, Buenos Aires, 1992. The authors assert that Argentina currently has two ready-to-use Condor-II missiles, which have been secreted away by the Argentinian Air Force.

Chapter 13. Warhead.

1. A letter dated July 3rd, 1986, from P.B.G. to the I.F.A.T. Corporation in Zug revealed the tip of the iceberg. It concerned Project FK 120. "Gentlemen," the letter went, "As agreed with you, we have obtained an offer for Project FK 120 from the MBB company. The offer is in our possession.

"We are willing to place an order with MBB, as soon as we have your order and a binding cover agreement," the letter went. "We are enclosing a photocopy of the MBB offer. We propose to charge a handling fee of 2%. Please let us have your cover agreement at your earliest convenience." Werner Schoffel signed the letter.

I.F.A.T. paid P.B.G. 1.4 million DM on Aug. 8, 1986.

2. The name of the Bremen-based shipping company was Ruppel-Sohn. The man directly in charge of the business with Egypt was Udo Glinder. I spoke to the manager of the firm by telephone. He was eager to clear his company's name of any involvement in "illegal" shipping operations. So far as he knew, he told me, the shipments to Egypt were totally innocent. German investigators already had his records when I spoke with him.

Chapter 14. Raid in Munich.

1. Official investigative work in these high-tech areas is extraordinarily complex. The difference between legality and illegality is sometimes measured in micro-millimeters and nano-seconds, making it difficult to press charges against even those who are most suspect. Furthermore, in Germany as in the United States, minor procedural errors can invalidate an entire case.

Chapter 15. Turning the Tables.

1. A series of Iranian quotes, derived from public and Iranian sources, was compiled by Joseph Bermudez in his study of Iranian/North Korean missile capability entitled *Ballistic Missile Development in Iran*.

2. The American analysis that the Iranians had used hydrogen cyanide against the Iraqis during the Iran-Iraq war led to a decision by the Bush administration to forbid large-scale chemical sales to Tehran. In particular, in January, 1993, the Bush Administration ruled against providing an export license for a multi-million dollar chemical installation to be built by the American division of British Petroleum.

3. An early tipoff on Lampart came in the Italian publication, *Panorama*, January, 1992. A Hungarian official later suggested that the Italians' interest in the story stemmed from their companies' own commercial interest in Iran. My own investigation in Switzerland revealed that the Swiss, as well as possibly the Hungarians, lost several contracts to Italian firms: Krebs, a company in Zürich, bid seriously for a water

purification plant which had a possibility to be converted into a chemical weapons facility, but an Italian firm, De Nira, won the contract.

4. The interview with Dr. Kohalmi was broadcast by BBC-TV "Panorama," "Arming for Islam," March 8, 1993.

5. The third raid on Bio-Engineering was a seemingly isolated incident in Switzerland, but one that received considerable local publicity. By chance, I had called a Swiss federal official, Othmar Wyss, to verify the background of attempted Iranian purchases in his country. He thought I was calling to question him about the raid.

6. Peter Lehrmann was interviewed on "Arming for Islam," BBC-TV "Panorama," March 8, 1993.

Chapter 16. Of Superguns and A-Bombs.

1. British free-lancer Alan George, writing for a number of general and trade magazines, led the way on the Supergun story. Additional aspects of this story derive from Jane Corbin's excellent reporting for BBC "Panorama," the later U.N. reports, and my own reporting at the time. An early 1980s film by producer Bill Cran on Gerald Bull, broadcast on PBS and elsewhere, played a pioneering role in exposing Gerald Bull's multi-country arms dealings.

2. David Kay was interviewed by Jane Corbin, "Arming for Islam," BBC-TV "Panorama," broadcast March 8, 1993.

3. Research on Swiss aspects of the story derives from a film, "The Swiss Connection," for Channel 4's "Dispatches" program in Britain, broadcast in November, 1991. Ed Harriman was director, Leo St. Clair the researcher, and I was the producer.

4. Although Swiss authorities were convinced that Schmiedemeccanica's goods were destined for an Iraqi nuclear centrifuge, the government dropped charges against the firm because of what Paul Laug, the head of the nuclear section of the Federal Office of Energy, called a "technicality." I.A.E.A. document INFCIRC 254, restricting sales of nuclear items, was mis-translated into German and then adopted independently into Swiss regulation. In it, maraging steel 350, or any maraging steel "capable of an ultimate tensile strength" that would bring it to nuclear-applicable levels, was barred from export. The

words "capable of" were omitted in the translation. The goods, when seized, were not yet of nuclear strength.

5. Spiess thus used the same arguments as had Schmiedemeccanica in contesting Swiss federal authorities. The government's charges against Schaublin resulted in a court case against the firm. In April, 1992, a cantonal court in Moutier, officially the administrative center for the French part of the Bernese canton, declared Schaublin innocent of all charges. The judge not only exonerated Schaublin but ordered the federal government to pay Schaublin's court costs, which were considerably more than the fine would have been.

Chapter 17. Choosing Targets.

1. Richard is a pseudonym. Neither his family name nor his correct first name is used.

2. The time of Desert Shield, before Desert Storm, was a period of exceptionally fruitful cooperation between Western intelligence services. For the first time, considerable initiative was taken to identify and analyze Iraqi weapons capabilities.

Chapter 18. After the Storm.

1. The various I.A.E.A. reports undertaken under Security Council resolution 687 provide a wealth of background documentation on Iraqi activities. The consolidated report on the first two inspections, issued July 11, 1991, already noted that the team "had found the Iraqis had been pursuing an undeclared uranium enrichment programme using the elctromagnetic isotope separation technique (EMIS)," or the Calutron method. The fourth report noted that advances had been made by the Iraqis on Calutron techniques.

2. An article by David Albright and Mark Hibbs, "Iraq's Bomb: Blueprints and Artifacts," published in the January/February 1992 issue of The Bulletin of Atomic Scientists, provides an excellent summary of the information derived from U.N. investigations up to that point.

3. David Kay, interview for BBC-TV "Panorama," "Arming for Islam," and PBS, "A Bomb for Iran."

4. See Gary Milhollin's article, "The New Arms Race: The Iraqi Bomb," The New Yorker, February 1, 1992.

Chapter 19. Iran: Going for It.

1. This chapter is based on discussions with Iranian, Israeli, French, German and American nuclear officials, and American experts involved in the anti-proliferation struggle.

2. In the original contract, Iran committed itself to a purchase of the plant's enriched uranium product equivalent to its capital share (ten percent). Now, as Gobert explained it to me, Iran would be treated as any other customer.

3. German government officials informed me that as a result of the Iran experience, all nuclear materials were treated as licensable exports, even those for civilian power plants.

4. In view of the fact that the Iranians had already paid for the goods, some experts I consulted believed that Iran would be able to mount a valid claim in an international court of law--if not for delivery of the goods, then for repayment. Iran threatened during the summer of 1992 to mount such a claim, then seemed to back off.

5. Robert Gates was interviewed for BBC-TV "Panorama," "Arming for Islam," broadcast March 8, 1993.

Chapter 20. Checking Iran.

1. Much of the reporting on U.N. visits to Iran come from the U.N. team's document on the trip, and also my own discussions with two of the four officials who were there and other related U.N. personnel.

2. As interviewed for BBC-TV "Panorama," "Arming for Islam," March 8, 1993.

3. Ibid.

4. Ibid. The BBC team was headed by correspondent Jane Corbin, who conducted her interviews with Kazakh officials in January, 1993.

Chapter 21. 2001.

No footnotes.